Key issues in economics and business
International economics

Key Issues in Economics and Business
Series editors: Alan Griffiths, Keith Pye and Stuart Wall

International economics

Graham Donnelly

Longman
London and New York

Longman Group UK Limited
Longman House, Burnt Mill, Harlow
Essex CM20 2JE, England
and Associated companies throughout the world

Published in the United States of America
by Longman Inc., New York

© Longman Group UK Limited 1987

First published 1987

British Library Cataloguing in Publication Data
Donnelly, Graham
   International economics. – (Key issues
   in economics and business)
   1. International economic relations
   I. Title   II. Series
   337   HF1411
ISBN 0-582-29685-4

Library of Congress Cataloging-in-Publication Data
Donnelly, Graham.
   International economics.

   (Key issues in economics and business)
   Bibliography: p.
   Includes index.
   1. International economic relations.   I. Title.
II. Series.
HF1411.D625   1987   337   86-2853
ISBN 0-582-29685-4

Set in Linotron 202 10/11 pt Plantin
Produced by Longman Group (FE) Limited
Printed in Hong Kong

Contents

exchange rates – Fixed exchange rates – Fixed versus
floating rates – The gold standard

The International Monetary Fund (IMF) – The
evolution of the international monetary system –
Special drawing rights – The collapse of the Bretton
Woods system – The Smithsonian Agreement 1971 –
Post-1973 floating – Expansion of world liquidity

Types of capital movement and their importance –
The evolution of capital issues – Eurocurrencies –
The growth of the eurocurrency markets – The
eurocurrency markets and domestic monetary policy
– The eurocurrency markets and international
liquidity

The growth of international debt – The problem of
the debt – The rescheduling of debts

The institutions of the Community – The economy
of the Community – The budget – The European
Monetary System

Origins and growth – Structure and operations – The
economic impact of multinationals – The parent
country – The host country – The control of
multinationals

Editors' preface

Each title in this series takes a particular area of economics or business studies and subjects it to rather more scrutiny than is possible in most introductory textbooks. Part one of each book concentrates on the key issues which present themselves for investigation or enquiry. It is hoped that a careful analysis of principle and data will save the reader considerable 'search time'. The issues selected will be those which are frequently the subject of examination questions at 'A' level, on professional courses and at the start of an undergraduate programme. At the end of each chapter, or group of chapters, a range of past questions will be presented to indicate the type of question the student is often expected to answer. Part two of each book presents specimen answers/worked examples to the questions outlined in part one. Except where worked examples are essential, the main objective will be to help students identify that part of their acquired knowledge which could be used in answering particular questions. A guide to sources of current information and data will help those who wish themselves to keep abreast of current developments or who intend to undertake essays/projects or dissertations in that particular area of economics or business.

Alan Griffiths
Keith Pye
Stuart Wall

Syllabus Guide

The following table indicates whether particular chapters are relevant to the syllabuses of the examining bodies listed. In each case the syllabus under consideration is 'Economics' or a similar title, except where indicated in the table.

Table (1)

Examining board	Chapter								
	1	2	3	4	5	6	7	8	9
GCE 'A' Level	X	X	X	X	X		X	X	X
GCE 'A' Level (West African)	X	X	X	X	X		X		X
Institute of Bankers, Conversion	X	X	X	X	X			X	X
Institute of Bankers, 2A		X	X	X	X	X	X	X	
Institute of Bankers, 2B*						X		X	
Institute of Purchasing & Supply	X	X	X	X	X			X	X
Institute of Marketing, Certificate	X	X	X	X	X			X	X
Institute of Marketing, Diploma†		X					X	X	X
Foundation Course in Overseas Trade‡	X	X	X	X					X
ICSA	X	X	X	X	X			X	X
ACCA, Foundation	X	X	X	X	X		X	X	
ICMA, Foundation	X	X	X	X	X		X	X	

Table (1) cont'd

Examining board	Chapter								
	1	2	3	4	5	6	7	8	9
ICMA, Professional Stage 1	X	X	X	X	X	X		X	X
LCCI, Higher Stage	X	X	X	X	X				
RSA, Stage III (Advanced)	X	X	X	X	X			X	X
RSA, Diploma for Personal Assistants	X	X	X	X	X			X	X
Association of Accounting Technicians	X	X	X	X	X			X	

* Finance of International Trade
† International Aspects of Marketing
‡ International Trade and Payments
Note: Only the European monetary system section of Chapter 8 applies to Stages 2A and 2B of the Institute of Bankers

The list in the table is by no means exhaustive and students pursuing other courses should consult the appropriate syllabus for guidance as to the chapters relevant to their needs. In particular, those studying for Shipping, Freight Forwarding and Export courses, as well as for Banking courses in many parts of the world, will find several of the chapters useful.

Author's preface and Acknowledgements

It is intended that this book will serve two purposes. First, like all the books in the 'Key Issues in Economics and Business' series, it examines a number of related topics which together form an important area of most examination syllabuses in Economics. Each topic is considered both in theory and in practice and guidance is given as to how the main types of examination question should be answered. Second, the book could be used as a principal text for some of the specialist papers in Economics and related subjects which are biased towards International Trade, International Payments and the World Economy. These would include, for example, the Monetary Economics paper of the Institute of Bankers and the International Aspects of Marketing paper of the Diploma in Marketing.

My thanks are due to all those who offered advice and comments both as to the contents and the format of this book, notably to Stuart Wall and Alan Griffiths who read the manuscript in its entirety. Thanks also to Carolyn for all the work done in such areas as typing and proof-reading.

We are grateful to the following for permission to reproduce questions from past examination papers:

The Associated Examining Board; The Institute of Bankers; The Institute of Chartered Secretaries and Administrators; The Institute of Cost and Management Accountants; The Institute of Export; The Institute of Marketing; The London Chamber of Commerce and Industry; Oxford Colleges Admissions Office; The Royal Society of Arts Examinations Board; University of Cambridge Local Examinations Syndicate; University of London School Examinations Board; The West African Examinations Council.

Any answers or hints on answers are the sole responsibility of the author and have not been provided or approved by the Examination Boards. The Examination Boards accept no responsibility whatsoever for the accuracy or method of working in any of the given answers.

The Institute of Bankers: The questions on applied economics and monetary economics were taken from the Banking Diploma examinations and have been reproduced from the Examiners' Reports which are published annually by the Institute of Bankers.

Part one

Chapter One
The theory of international trade

As with some other areas of Economics, the construction of the various theories of international trade has taken place against a background of long-established practices and prejudices. The subject of international trade is further complicated by its close connections with national rivalries and the conduct of international relations. Nevertheless the attempts made to formulate a theory of international trade have been useful in that they have sought to identify rational economic criteria on which to base trade policy. However, the complex economic and political pressures surrounding international trade place limitations on the value of these theories so that they must be examined critically rather than taken at face value.

Early theories

Mercantilism

From the sixteenth century until the middle of the eighteenth century the theory of trade was dominated by Mercantilism. The Mercantilists believed that national power depended on national economic wealth, with wealth being seen as the holding of precious metals. Trade policy should therefore seek to maintain and increase the country's stocks of gold and silver. Since exports resulted in an inflow of gold and silver, a principal means by which bullion reserves could be increased was through a surplus of exports over imports. This in turn implied that the country should seek to achieve a favourable balance of trade. Mercantilism therefore supported both protectionism and the regulation of trade as means by which the holding of precious metals, i.e. national economic wealth, might be increased. As not all countries could simultaneously achieve a favourable balance of trade, such policies were inevitably a source of rivalry, hostility and conflict among the major trading nations.

Mercantilism was never universally accepted but survived in various modified forms until subjected to the incisive criticisms of the great political economists of the latter half of the eighteenth century. One of these, David Hume, argued that a mechanism similar to what we now term the quantity theory of money made the maintenance of a perpetually favourable balance impossible. For instance, a balance of trade surplus would lead to an inflow of gold which, according to an analysis similar to the later quantity theory, results in an expansion of the domestic money supply and a rise in the general level of prices. This inflationary effect reduces the competitiveness of the country's goods and leads to a fall in exports and a rise in imports. Similarly a deficit country would experience a fall in the price level following the outflow of gold and consequent contraction of the domestic money supply so that its exports became more attractive and imports less attractive. While Hume placed too much faith in this crude version of the quantity theory of money, his criticism contained an element of truth which the Mercantilists were unable to answer.

The theory of absolute cost advantage

If Hume attacked the assumptions of the Mercantilists, Adam Smith went further and questioned their whole philosophy by extolling the benefits of free trade rather than its regulation. He applied his familiar arguments in favour of specialisation and the division of labour to the international scene and advocated that countries should specialise in the production of goods in which they had an absolute (real) cost advantage *vis-à-vis* their competitors, and trade the surpluses for the imports they need. Only in the rare case of a country having no absolute cost advantage in any good, *vis-à-vis* another country, did Smith argue that trade would confer no benefits. Regulation of trade would only be valid in this exceptional circumstance.

Adam Smith argued that, in a two-country model, trade would be beneficial when each had an absolute cost advantage in one product. Thus in Table 1.1 the production of wheat and iron in two countries, X and Y, is related to the cost, measured in units of labour employed, of producing these commodities. Country X can produce wheat more cheaply than it can produce iron since ten units of labour can produce twice as much wheat as iron, i.e. the

Table 1.1 Units of production by 10 units of labour

	Country	Iron	Wheat
(a) Before	X	3	6
specialisation	Y	5	4
(b) After	X	—	12
specialisation	Y	10	—
(c) After specialisation	X	4	7
and trade – 4 units	Y	6	5
of iron trading for			
5 units of wheat			

labour cost of producing one unit of wheat is only half that of producing one unit of iron. Country Y can produce iron more cheaply than wheat as the same input of ten units of labour will produce five units of iron compared to only four of wheat. With the mobility of factors of production from one country to another being limited, labour and other costs are less likely to equalise *between* countries than they are within a country. Countries should therefore benefit by specialising in those products in which they have an absolute advantage. In this two-country model, (world) output is clearly larger in *both* products after specialisation than it was before. Of course, whether or not countries would benefit from specialisation and trade would depend on the rate at which iron and wheat are exchanged in the international market, i.e. the terms of trade. As can be seen in Table 1.1(c) an exchange of four units of iron for five of wheat will enable *both* countries to have more of iron *and* wheat after trade than before. This simple example takes no account of economies of scale. It is likely that specialisation will have the added benefit of enabling unit production costs to be reduced as resources are diverted away from the production of less suitable goods into those in which the country has an absolute cost advantage.

The theory of comparative advantage

The principle of **absolute advantage** is self-evident and countries clearly benefit from trade in these circumstances. Less obvious, though more important, is the principle of **comparative advantage** which was developed in the early nineteenth century by David Ricardo. This principle is based on the premise that it is comparative, rather than absolute, costs which should determine trade between countries. Thus even if one country, because of its efficiency, is able to produce *all* goods more cheaply than another, there will still be differences in the extent of the absolute advantage from product to product. The efficient country is said to have a comparative advantage in those products in which its *absolute advantage* is greatest, whereas the inefficient country has a comparative advantage in those products in which its *absolute disadvantage* is least. Countries should specialise in the production of those products in which they have a *comparative advantage*, and leave to others the production of those in which they have a *comparative disadvantage*.

To illustrate his case, Ricardo took the example of England and Portugal and the production of wine and cloth, as shown in Table 1.2. In Table 1.2(a) both England and Portugal produce wine and yarn. Portugal has an absolute advantage in both products since she need expend less labour than England to produce either 1X units of wine or 1Y units of yarn. However, England's absolute *disadvantage* is less in the case of yarn because only 11 per cent more labour (100 units instead of 90) are required to produce the same amount of yarn, whereas 50 per cent more labour (120 units instead of 80) are needed to produce the same amount of wine.

In Table 1.2(b), England's comparative advantage in the production of yarn is exploited with the labour previously employed in the production of wine diverted to cloth production. Portugal, meanwhile, concentrates on the production of wine in which she has a comparative advantage. As a consequence of this specialisation, total production of *both* wine and yarn is increased.

Ricardo did not consider the question of the *terms of trade* between the two countries but one possible outcome is shown in Table 1.2(c). Here a rate of exchange of 1X for 1Y leaves both countries better off after trade. Thus with the same expenditure of resources, England is able to consume more yarn, by specialising according to comparative advantages and trading the surpluses.

Ricardo based his theory on the gains to be made through more efficient use of resources. It is also possible to explain the benefits of comparative advantage in terms of **opportunity cost**. Thus a country has a comparative advantage in the production of a good when it has a lower opportunity cost in producing that good than has another country. This is illustrated in Table 1.3, where the information in Table 1.2 is used to show opportunity costs.

5

Table 1.2 Production of wine and yarn in Portugal and England

	Country	Units of labour used	Barrels of wine	Yarns of cloth
(a) Before specialisation	England	100		1Y
		120	1X	
	Portugal	80	1X	
		90		1Y
	Total		2X	2Y
(b) After specialisation	England	220		2.2Y
	Portugal	170	2.125X	
	Total		2.125X	2.2Y
		Consumption of wine and yarn		
(c) After specialisation and trade – 1 unit of wine trading for 1 unit of cloth	England		1X	1.2Y
	Portugal		1.125X	1Y
	Total		2.125X	2.2Y

In Table 1.3 the opportunity cost of producing one extra unit of yarn in England is 5/6 unit of wine, i.e. the foregone wine which could have been produced using the same resources. Since the opportunity cost of *cloth* is lower (5/6X wine) for England than for Portugal (9/8X wine) England has a comparative advantage in cloth production, and should specialise in cloth. Conversely, Portugal has a lower opportunity cost in *wine* production (8/9Y cloth) than has England (6/5Y cloth), and should specialise in wine. Both countries could potentially gain from such specialisation.

If we take a *marginal* change in either commodity in line with specialising according to comparative advantages, we have no change in one commodity and a net gain in the other. (Table 1.4).

Criticisms of comparative advantage theory
Ricardo and the later writers who refined comparative advantage

Table 1.3 Opportunity cost ratios

	Barrels of wine	Yarns of cloth	Opportunity cost of producing one extra unit of cloth	Opportunity cost of producing one extra unit of wine
England: alternative production using 100 units of labour	5/6X	1Y	5/6X barrels of wine	6/5Y yarns of cloth
Portugal: alternative production using 80 units of labour	1X	8/9Y	9/8X barrels of wine	8/9Y yarns of cloth

Table 1.4

(a) England produces 1Y extra cloth:	loss	5/6X wine
Portugal produces 1Y less cloth :	gain	9/8X wine
	Net gain	7/24X wine
(b) England produces 1X less wine :	gain	6/5Y cloth
Portugal produces 1X more wine :	loss	8/9Y cloth
	Net gain	14/45Y cloth

theory were attempting to show the advantage to be derived from free trade and to explain why trade patterns should vary between countries. Unfortunately the theory does not stand up well to close inspection because of its reliance on several conditions which are unlikely to be met in the real world.

1. Factor mobility. The theory assumes complete mobility of factors of production within countries and total immobility of factors between countries; neither assumption is valid. Firstly, within countries there is a limit to the process by which factors of production can be transferred from one use to another; eventually the opportunity cost of transferring a factor from its present use

7

to the use in which the country is specialising will be so great as to outweigh the benefit to be gained from specialisation and trade. Thus in Ricardo's own example, not all labour in Portugal will be equally efficiently used in the growing of vines for wine production, while some labour *will* be skilled in the production of yarn. To transfer these skilled cloth workers to wine production would be very costly in terms of foregone cloth production. Secondly, comparative advantages are even less likely to stay constant when factors of production such as capital and enterprise are mobile between countries.

2. Constant costs. The theory assumes that production takes place at constant costs per unit of output and takes no account of the possibility of economies or diseconomies of scale. In fact these are likely to occur; the former through specialisation, and the latter through over-specialisation. The southern states of the United States before the American Civil War and the one-crop economies of Africa and the West Indies are examples of the long-term economic harm experienced by countries which have over-specialised.

3. Free trade. In order for countries to enjoy fully the benefits deriving from the law of comparative advantage, they must have unfettered access to the markets of other countries. In practice, trade in commodities and manufactured goods is restricted by customs duties, tariffs and quotas. Many countries also have trading agreements which favour the parties to the agreement at the expense of other countries, e.g. the Common Market. In such circumstances, comparative advantages are distorted or even cancelled out.

4. Static economies. The decision to specialise in some industries to the exclusion of others requires confidence that present comparative advantages are likely to persist into the foreseeable future; this implies that the conditions making for these comparative advantages are permanent. No allowance is made for the changes in technology, in industrial structure or in the supply of factors which could alter existing comparative advantages. Britain, for example, could not have expected in the 1850s that she would lose her comparative advantage in the manufacture of steel a hundred years later.

5. Transport costs. These tend to be ignored despite their importance. High transport costs are quite likely to wipe out a theoretical comparative advantage. For instance, it is unlikely that India could exploit a comparative advantage in cheap bulk goods in her trade with Europe because of the shipment costs involved.

6. *Interdependence.* The pursuit of comparative advantage inevitably leads to a greater reliance on other countries. For strategic reasons, or to maintain some degree of self-sufficiency, countries will not abandon key industries entirely merely for the sake of comparative advantage, nor will they risk the dangers of over-specialisation. Interdependence of the kind envisaged by comparative advantage theory is likely to be achieved fully only by an imperial power and its colonies, where economic policy decisions can be imposed by the 'mother' country. The post-colonial period has in fact witnessed several examples of newly independent countries suffering economic difficulties because of their reliance on one or two primary products introduced during the colonial era.

7. *Demand factors.* These are largely ignored by comparative advantage theory. It is assumed that demand patterns are able to adjust to the increased volume of production resulting from greater specialisation. No attempt is therefore made to take account of different demand patterns between countries. If Britain had a comparative advantage in cricket bats, garden shears, umbrellas and bowler hats, it can hardly be assumed that world demand patterns for these goods would match this profile. Britain may *not* in fact be able easily to sell surpluses of these goods abroad.

8. *Terms of trade.* These can be such as to negate any advantages to be derived from specialisation and trade. In the previous example, England will only gain from specialising in cloth *if* it can trade 1Y cloth for *more than* 5/6X wine. Otherwise it might as well remain self-sufficient.

The Heckscher–Ohlin Theory

The most significant contribution to trade theory in modern times was the work of Bertil Ohlin. He based much of his work on the ideas of Eli Heckscher, so that the theory formulated by Ohlin bears both their names. Ohlin followed Ricardo in accepting a static economy with perfect mobility of factors within countries and immobility of factors internationally, constant returns to scale and an absence of both trade restrictions and transport costs. In addition, he made a number of assumptions markedly different from Ricardian analysis. Firstly, he recognised the need to consider *all* factors of production rather than just labour. Secondly, he considered money costs instead of real costs; in other words he recognised that there are differences between countries with regard to both factor *and* product prices. Thirdly, he recognised the importance of demand patterns in different countries as a major cause of price differences.

Central to Ohlin's theory is the view that trade exploits the differences which exist between countries in the *supply* of factors of production. Those countries, for example, which are well-endowed with natural resources, but suffer from a shortage of labour, will produce primary products such as grain or coal cheaply and export these in return for labour-intensive manufactures produced more cheaply elsewhere. Countries will tend to specialise in products which make *intensive* use of their abundant resources. The Heckscher–Ohlin theory is sometimes referred to as a factor endowment theory. The idea is that if the factor is abundant, its price will be low and products which make intensive use of this factor will tend to be cheap. The country will therefore tend to export such products.

Even where countries enjoy *identical supplies* of the various factors of production, trade will still be beneficial provided that they have different *demand patterns*. These differences in demand will affect the prices of factors of production and therefore product and export prices. Thus climatic differences between countries will affect the demand for different kinds of clothing so that wool prices will be higher in a cold country than in a warm country, providing scope for the export of wool from the warm country to the cold country. Differences in income levels or the distribution of income are likely to affect the demand for consumer durables; so electronic equipment produced in Taiwan is more likely to be made for the export market than for the low-income domestic population. An important contribution of this theory, then, is that it shows how important is demand in determining the price of a factor, on occasion outweighing the importance of supply.

The other key contribution of Heckscher–Ohlin is its recognition of the effect of specialisation on factor earnings. Suppose that Country A is well-endowed with land but has a shortage of labour, while the opposite is true in Country B. In Country A, agricultural products will be relatively cheap and manufactures relatively dear; in Country B the reverse will be true. Country A will tend to export agricultural products to Country B in exchange for manufactures. This additional demand for Country A's agricultural goods raises the return to land and pushes up rents, while the decline in demand for Country B's agricultural goods causes rents there to fall. Meanwhile the extra demand for Country B's manufactured goods leads to wage rates rising in Country B while in Country A the fall in demand for home-produced manufactures leads to a fall in the wages of industrial workers. There is therefore a tendency for free trade to raise rents and lower wages in Country A, but to lower rents and raise wages in Country B. Over time, rents, and wages in both countries will tend to equalise with landowners gaining at the expense of wage earners in Country A, and wage earners gaining at the expense of landowners in Country B. Heckscher–Ohlin theory predicts, therefore, that free trade in goods tends to *equalise* factor prices across national borders. As such, free trade is a substitute for the international movement of factors of production. Thus low wage rates in a particular country can be pushed up either by workers emigrating and forcing up the wages of those who remain, due to the reduced supply of labour, *or* by an increased demand for the goods produced by these workers. Ohlin was, however, aware of the limitations on the process of factor price equalisation because of the dynamic forces at work within the economy. He recognised that a rise in the price of a factor will alter its supply so that when wage rates of low paid workers begin to rise, new workers will be drawn into the industry.

Criticisms of Heckscher–Ohlin

The great contribution of Heckscher–Ohlin is that it attempts to broaden traditional theory to explain *why* different production possibilities, and therefore trading advantages, exist. Unfortunately, like earlier theories, it relies heavily on a number of assumptions which have proved unrealistic.

1. Inherited classical assumptions. Though he knew them to be unrealistic, Ohlin continued to use many of the assumptions of Ricardian analysis. Firstly, he assumed a worldwide similarity of tastes and ignored those cultural and economic factors which form demand patterns. Secondly, he assumed that tastes are constant; he therefore neglected the demonstration effect whereby countries experience changes in demand patterns as a *consequence* of witnessing the acquisition of new products by other countries. Thirdly, constant technology was assumed despite the overwhelming evidence that technological progress is a major contributory factor in the development of new products and thus of new trading opportunities. Fourthly, the assumption that production continues to take place under constant returns to scale neglects the very real importance of economies of scale to the development of international trade. Fifthly, the assumption that international trade takes place under conditions of perfect competition ignores the many monopolistic pressures which influence trading patterns, notably the control over world markets exerted by the great multinational corporations and state trading bodies. Finally, units of each factor of production are assumed to be homogeneous, when this is clearly not the case.

2. *Over-simplification of industrial production.* While Ohlin was correct to stress the diversity of forms of industrial production, his distinctions between capital-intensive and labour-intensive industries were rather simplistic. Many products can be produced by a variety of means for the same cost, so that a rise in wage rates might lead to a labour-intensive industry becoming capital-intensive. Furthermore a change in the demand for one factor will alter the demand for complementary factors and cause changes in relative factor prices. For instance, a rise in demand for sophisticated engineering equipment will also affect the demand for skilled engineers and for any other factors involved in the production and utilisation of the equipment. In this, as in other areas, trade theory relies heavily on a static situation and is severely strained by the dynamic inter-relationships of a complex economy.

3. *The stress on economic diversity as a basis for trade.* Ohlin claimed that different 'factor endowments', i.e. different balances in the supply of the various factors of production, was what made trade worthwhile for the trading nations. In fact most trade in manufactures takes place between countries with *similar*, rather than diverse, economic structures. The European Economic Community was formed by countries with close trading ties based on common interests, and it is countries like Britain and Greece, with their different economic structures, who have had most difficulty deriving benefits from membership. This observation would come as no surprise to a successful exporting company since international marketing operations are likely to be most successful in markets with similar demand structures to that of the exporting country. A Japanese car manufacturer, for example, is likely to be more optimistic about exporting to a country like Britain than to a developing African country. This is because Britain has proved itself capable of supporting a large car market, while the African country not only has no car industry but also has too low a per capita income to support a large car-buying market. Very often having a competitive edge is not enough in exporting; potential

markets must be receptive to the type of product made by the exporting country, so that similarity of demand conditions is an advantage.

Despite these failings, Heckscher–Ohlin has at least assisted in defining some of the main factors which are likely to influence the structure of world trade. Unfortunately, by attempting to provide a theory rather than to make some general observations, Ohlin has adopted many unrealistic assumptions which often make his theory untestable under real world conditions.

With all its weaknesses, the theory of comparative advantage illustrates beyond doubt that many countries can benefit from international trade because of the differences that exist in the *relative* efficiencies of different industries from one country to another. Countries can then gain by specialising in those industries and products in which they have a comparative advantage, exporting these to finance the import of goods in which other countries have a comparative advantage. Even in the extremely unlikely case of two countries having identical relative efficiencies in every industry, international trade would enable them to specialise and so attain greater economies of scale and more efficient production. The Heckscher–Ohlin refinement of Ricardian analysis predicts further that international trade will tend to equalise factor rewards across national boundaries, so supporting the view that international trade substitutes the movement of goods and services for the movement of factors of production.

The terms of trade

The principle of comparative advantage indicates the circumstances under which trade might advantageously take place but it cannot predict exactly how much of one good will exchange for another, i.e. the **terms of trade**. In Ricardo's original example shown in Table 1.2, a terms of trade involving a rate of exchange of $1X = 1Y$ enables both England and Portugal to benefit from trade. It would of course be possible for the terms of trade to favour one country more than the other and still leave the other country better off as a result of trade. The two limiting situations would be:

(a) $1X = 1.2Y$ (no gain to England)
(b) $1.125X = 1Y$ (no gain to Portugal)

At any terms of trade *between* these two extremes both England and Portugal would gain from trade. What actual terms of trade occurs depends on the demand and supply conditions in both countries for the products in question.

Firstly, there is the responsiveness of demand to price changes in a country's exports, i.e. the **price elasticity of demand** for exports. The terms of trade will tend to favour goods with inelastic demand in export markets. The oil-producing countries, for example, enjoy stronger terms of trade than do producers of other primary products.

Secondly, there is the ability of suppliers to respond to higher demand in overseas markets, i.e. **the elasticity of supply** of exports. Where supply is highly responsive to price changes, the exporting country will find little improvement in its terms of trade as the result of increased export demand.

Thirdly, there are **changes in demand or supply conditions.** Where changes in the patterns of world demand favour a particular country's exports, its terms of trade are likely to improve; while a glut in a country's staple commodity will inevitably weaken its terms of trade. The West Indian sugar cane producers have been adversely affected both by the decline in world demand for sugar and by the rise in the world production of sugar beet.

The measurement of the terms of trade

The principal method of measuring the terms of trade is the **barter terms of trade**, which is the ratio of the export price index to the import price index over the same time period. This ratio is expressed as an index number using the formula:-

$$\text{Index of terms of trade} = \frac{\text{Export price index}}{\text{Import price index}} \times 100$$

Starting from a base of 100, a rise in the index to, say, 105 signifies an 'improvement' in the terms of trade: fewer exports need be sold in order to pay for a given quantity of imports. The term 'improvement' is somewhat misleading since there is no guarantee that the country will enjoy a stronger position externally as a result. This is because it is the *prices* of exports relative to those of imports which have risen, rather than the volume of exports themselves. The effect of a rise in the terms of trade index depends on the cause of that rise:

1. If, for example, the relative rise in export prices is due to a rise in domestic costs of production, there may well be a fall in overseas demand for the country's goods and therefore in the volume of exports. If this fall in volume is large enough,

the value of goods actually sold abroad may fall. A similar situation could occur in the case of a country experiencing a rate of inflation considerably higher than that of its trading competitors. In both these examples the effect of an improvement in the terms of trade depends on the price elasticity of demand for the country's exports – only where demand is inelastic will higher export prices result in increased export revenue.

2. If the relative rise in export prices is the consequence of increased demand for the country's products, the rise in the terms of trade index will represent a real improvement in the country's external position. In this case the value of exports will rise.

Attempts have been made to allow for changes in productivity in the terms of trade by use of the **factoral terms of trade**. In this case, greater efficiency in a country's export industries may lower the price of exports and cause the *barter* terms of trade to deteriorate. However, the country's external position might actually improve, with the lower costs and prices making exports more attractive abroad. The factoral terms of trade may be expressed as the formula:

Index of terms of trade =

$$\text{Productivity index} \times \frac{\text{Export price index}}{\text{Import price index}}$$

Unfortunately the concept of the factoral terms of trade is difficult to apply since it is little used for statistical purposes. When changes in a country's terms of trade are discussed, it is normally the barter terms of trade to which reference is being made.

Limitations of the terms of trade index
Before examining the practical application of the terms of trade index, reference must be made to the limitations under which the index operates, quite apart from its inability to distinguish between the various causes of a movement in the index.

Firstly, it suffers, like all indices, from the fact that decisions have to be taken as to what should be included in it, e.g. what weighting should be given to the items included and what reference period should be used. The value of the index depends, therefore, on the appropriateness of the decisions taken with regard to these issues.

Secondly, a lack of data as to the prices of many services often leads to them being excluded from the terms of trade, despite the growing importance of the service industries to the external trade of most countries.

Thirdly, comparisons are difficult over long time periods. There is a lack of reliable statistical material from earlier periods, and over a time span of even fifty years the pattern of trade is likely to have changed so much as to make any comparison between the beginning and the end of the period almost irrelevant. It is also the case that major world economic events may well have a strong enough impact on the terms of trade to outweigh any discernible long-term trends.

The UK terms of trade

In the 1930s Britain experienced a strong movement of the terms of trade in her favour. This was due to a slump in the prices of most foodstuffs and raw materials during the Great Depression which benefited the industrial nations importing these items at the expense of those countries producing them.

After the Second World War, the post-war reconstruction period saw the terms of trade turn against Britain; in 1946 exports needed to be nearly 10 per cent higher than in 1938 to pay for the same volume of imports. The situation became even worse when the outbreak of the Korean War in 1950 led to a further rapid rise in commodity prices. Throughout the period 1946 to 1951 the average price of imports doubled while those of exports rose by only 60 per cent. In consequence, 40 per cent more exports were needed in 1951 than in 1938 to pay for the same volume of imports. After the Korean War and for the rest of the 1950s the UK terms of trade improved as commodity prices declined.

In the 1960s there was a further improvement in the UK terms of trade since between 1961 and 1967 UK export prices rose by 14 per cent while UK import prices rose by only 9 per cent. However, this 'improvement' was due to the comparatively high rate of inflation in the UK and was lost when the pound was devalued in 1967 and import prices rose sharply in consequence.

In the early 1970s inflation once again pushed the terms of trade index upwards but the very rapid rise in oil and associated commodity prices in 1973 caused a sharp deterioration in the terms of trade from 1973 onwards, a deterioration exacerbated by the decline in the value of sterling in 1975–76. The recovery of sterling in the late 1970s was reflected in the terms of trade, and Britain was confronted by the new problem that her oil-producer status kept the pound artificially strong and export prices generally higher

Table 1.5 The UK terms of trade (1980 = 100)

1981	102
1982	99
1983	98
1984	97
1985	99
1986	101

Source: CSO Economic Trends: 1986

than they might otherwise have been. In the early 1980s many British manufacturers found that the strong terms of trade position proved detrimental to their prospects of selling overseas.

International trade and the domestic economy

So far it has been established that international trade benefits countries in two ways. On the supply side, specialisation permits the attainment of economies of scale and a more efficient use of resources. On the demand side, the home population enjoys a greater variety of goods and services and, consequently, higher living standards. At the same time overseas demand enables the country to make use of its surplus production and over-abundant natural resources, so that foreign trade is a major contributory factor to economic development. However, the precise impact of foreign trade on a particular economy is not necessarily beneficial, and some understanding of the relationship between international trade and national income is helpful to an assessment of this impact.

The national income of a country can be measured as the total output of goods and services produced by the economy, or as the total incomes earned by its population, or as the total expenditure of its population. Each measurement should yield the same answer since they represent three ways of assessing the economic activity of the nation, whether as producers, as factors of production or as consumers.

In the *absence* of any external intervention, either by governments or through overseas trade, all national income will flow between producers and consumers. There will be no tendency for the national income to change unless there is a spontaneous decision by consumers to alter the pattern of consumption or by producers to change their production level. If, for example, consumers choose to withdraw part of their incomes from the circular flow of income, by saving in preference to consumption, then the earnings received by producers will fall. This will eventually result in the incomes received by consumers falling as national income returns to equilibrium at a lower level. On the other hand, an autonomous injection of new investment into industry by producers will stimulate production and ultimately raise the level of national income. Keynesian income analysis, on which the above outline is based, goes on to predict that when there is a change in the level of either savings or investment, national income will expand or contract until savings and investment are once again equal. National income is only in equilibrium when savings and investment are equal.

The effects of both government economic activity and international trade on national income are similar to those of savings and investment. Thus government expenditure and exports constitute injections into the circular flow of income, while taxation and imports result in withdrawals from the circular flow of income. The national income is only in equilibrium when total injections equal total withdrawals, i.e.

Investment + Government expenditure + Exports =
Savings + Taxation + Imports

If injections exceed withdrawals there will be a tendency for national income to rise as aggregate demand for domestically-produced goods and services exceeds current output. If withdrawals are greater than injections there will be a tendency for national income to contract as current output exceeds total demand. If it is now assumed that savings and investment are equal and that government economic activity is neutral with government expenditure being equal to taxation, the effect of changes in foreign trade on national income can be examined in Fig. 1.1.

In Fig. 1.1, exports (X) are held to be constant whatever the level of national income. This is because the decisions taken by overseas residents to buy our exports are made without reference to our national income. Imports (M), on the other hand, are assumed to rise with national income. This is likely to be the case as increased income results in higher consumption, and it is almost inevitable that some of this extra consumption will take the form of expenditure on imported goods or services or on holidays abroad. Initially the equilibrium level of national income is at Y, where exports and imports are equal. At points to the left of Y,

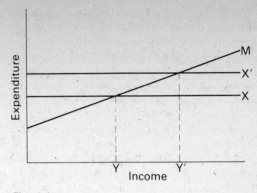

Fig. 1.1.

imports are below exports so that income withdrawn from the circular flow by consumers buying foreign goods is more than matched by the injection arising from export demand. The result is that current production levels are inadequate to meet total demand, so that output is stimulated and national income grows. National income will once again be in equilibrium when it has risen sufficiently for expenditure on imports to match export earnings, i.e. when withdrawals and injections are equal. Income levels greater than Y are not sustainable since, with expenditure on imports greater than export earnings, domestic production exceeds total demand and firms must contract output as stocks pile up. National income will go on contracting until falling earnings lead to consumers reducing expenditure sufficiently for imports to fall to the level of exports and thus for withdrawals to again equal injections.

An income level other than Y can only be achieved by a shift in either exports or imports. Exports are shown as increasing in Fig. 1.1 from X to X'. This increase in export demand leads to a rise in national income. National income will continue to rise until imports have risen to match the new and higher level of exports, at which point equilibrium is restored, i.e. at Y'. A similar rise in national income could result from a downward shift in import expenditure.

To summarise, therefore, national income analysis indicates that export earnings lead to growth in national income, while imports cause a decline in national income. Furthermore, the above analysis indicates that exports and imports are always brought into balance by changes in national income. This conclusion is clearly an over-simplification since it is rarely the case that a country's exports and imports even approximately balance. In Fig. 1.1 the situation is simplified by assuming that all other injections and withdrawals are neutral but, in practice, as long as *total* injections and *total* withdrawals are equal, exports and imports need not balance. Thus a rise in exports could lead, via a rise in national income, to an increase in savings rather than imports; a fall in exports could prompt increased government expenditure to prevent national income falling, rather than bring about a fall in imports. One important qualification must be made with regard to the expansionary effects of export earnings. This is that expansion will only be effective if there are unemployed factors of production within the economy which can be brought into use. At times of full employment, higher exports and/or lower imports will only enlarge the *money* national income and create inflationary pressures as incomes are raised without any addition to the domestic supply of goods. If inflation already exists, then a reduction in exports may not, in fact, result in a decline in real national income. Instead there may be a fall in the rate of inflation, with more goods now being available for the home market.

The foreign trade multiplier

From the preceding section it can be seen that, provided there are unused resources in the economy, an increase in exports will cause a rise in national income. The question remains as to how much national income will rise in response to a given injection of exports of, say, £10 m. The likelihood is that national income will rise by considerably more than £10 m. because of the dynamic nature of national income changes. Suppose that the £10 m. is an order with a British engineering company for machinery. As long as this order is in addition to the company's normal business there will be an immediate increase in national income of £10 m., though this is not the total impact on the economy. The company will have to take on extra workers or may pay overtime to the existing workforce and it will certainly have to buy more raw materials and perhaps install extra capital equipment. The various factors of production thus receive £10 m. and as long as part of this is spent in the UK there will follow another wave of income creation. This process will be repeated until an amount equivalent to the original injection has been withdrawn from the circular flow of national income in the form of savings, taxes and import expenditure, and total withdrawals once again equal total injections. This tendency for an injection to have a multiplied effect on national income applies whatever the nature of the injection and, in the case of exports, is known as the foreign trade multiplier.

The size of the foreign trade multiplier is governed by the rate at which the original injection is dissipated by withdrawals at each successive wave of income creation. In the example of an export injection of £10 m. quoted above, if the engineering firm were to subcontract the entire operation overseas there would be no multiplier at all. The greater the proportion of new income creation that is withdrawn from the circular flow, the smaller will be the multiplier effect, and vice versa. The multiplier may be given a numerical value by measuring the value of withdrawals at each stage of income creation, i.e. the **marginal propensity to make withdrawals (MPW)**. The MPW is itself made up of three components: the **marginal propensity to save (MPS)**, the **marginal propensity to pay taxes (MPT)** and the **marginal propensity to import (MPM)**.

Thus, MPW = MPS + MPT + MPM

If the MPW has a value of 0.5 this may comprise an MPS of 0.1, an MPT of 0.2 and an MPM of 0.2. Applying these figures to an injection of £10 m. there will be a second round of income creation of £5 m., a third round of income creation of £2.5 m. and so on, a half of income being sliced off at each round. The value of the multiplier is the reciprocal of the MPW, i.e.:

$$\frac{1}{MPW}$$

and in this case will be 2 (as the MPW is $\frac{1}{2}$), resulting in total new income creation of £20 m. When the process of income creation is complete, withdrawals will have risen by £10 m. to once again equal injections, and will consist of an extra £2 m. savings, £4 m. taxes and £4 m. imports.

There is not space here to consider all the various permutations which can influence the value of the multiplier, but even if the MPS and the MPT are held to be constant, the value of the foreign trade multiplier will be greatly affected by the MPM, which itself varies with the nature of the export injection. Accordingly the multiplier is likely to be smaller where exports are made from imported raw materials than where the entire exported item is made from indigenous factors of production. The foreign trade multiplier is therefore higher in the case of earnings from tourism than in the export of manufactured goods assembled in the UK but using components from overseas. Finally, it must be remembered that the multiplier works downwards too, both through a fall in export earnings and a rise in imports. A growing problem for British governments is that a high MPM reduces the value to the national income of domestic injections of government expenditure and investment. It may lead to an injection into the economy causing a boom in imports rather than providing a stimulus to demand for domestically-produced goods.

Examination questions

The following questions are taken from the examination papers of various examining bodies which include the areas covered by this chapter in their syllabuses. Those marked with an asterisk (★) are representative of the main types of question asked and specimen answers for these will be found in Part II.

1. In the present-day conduct of international trade, to what extent does the law of comparative costs apply? What are the circumstances which tend to prevent its application? (FCOT, May 1984)

2. Explain the benefits to be obtained from the application of the principle of comparative advantage. Show the application of the principle by means of a numerical example. (LCCI Higher, Spring 1985)

3.★ Discuss the assertion that it is not possible for two countries to gain from international trade if one of them is more efficient at producing all goods than the other. (ICSA Part I, December 1980)

4.★ Is the principle of comparative costs an adequate explanation of the pattern of international trade in manufactured goods? (London, June 1984)

5.★ What is meant by terms of trade? What causes changes in these terms and why may they be favourable or unfavourable to the economy? (ICMA Foundation, May 1982)

6. In what circumstances may an improvement in a country's terms of trade not be advantageous? (Cert. Marketing, June 1984)

7. What is meant by: (a) the terms of trade and (b) the balance of trade?

 How might changes in the terms of trade come about and what will be their effect on the balance of trade? (Cert. Marketing, June 1983)

8.★ 'A change in the level of export earnings will lead to a more than proportionate change in national income.' Discuss. (AEB, November 1983)

9. How might a significant rise in the price of your country's exports affect the economy of your country? (Cambridge, Caribbean Section, June 1980)

10. What factors determine the total value of imports? Is an increase in imports necessarily undesirable? (London, June 1984)

Chapter Two
International trade in practice

World trade patterns

The theory of international trade indicates the economy advantages which may be obtained by countries engaging in trade with each other. However, the patterns of world trade reflect the various historical and political pressures underlying relations between countries as much as the economic gains to be made from these trading patterns. Once established, these patterns change remarkably slowly and are, in the 1980s, little different from the patterns of the 1950s. In 1955 the developed market economies accounted for 64 and 66 per cent of world exports and imports respectively and in 1982 these percentages were unchanged. One significant change over this period was that among developing countries the oil price rises of the 1970s boosted the importance to world trade of the Organisation of Petroleum Exporting Countries (OPEC) at the expense of other developing countries. The OPEC members' share of world exports rose from 6 per cent in 1955 to 10 per cent in 1982 and their share of world imports rose from 4 to 8 per cent over the same period.

While there has been little change in the total shares of world trade of the main blocs over the past thirty years, there have been major changes in the trading importance of individual countries, as Table 2.1 indicates. The United States continues to lead the lists as leading exporter and importer but the United Kingdom has slipped down the table as its share of world trade has halved over this period. While West Germany and the Soviet Union, among others, have strengthened their position, the outstanding success story is of course that of Japan which has increased its share of world trade from 2.3 per cent in 1955 to 7.2 per cent in 1982. In the future it can be expected that some of the countries now

---

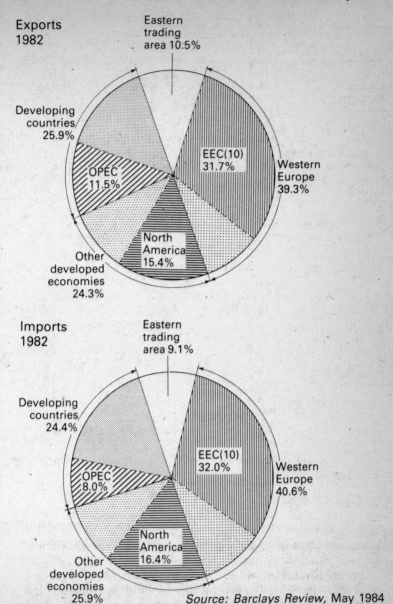

Fig. 2.1 Percentage share of the value of world exports and imports by area

Table 2.1 (a)Top ten exporting countries (% of world exports)

	1955		1982
USA	16.4	USA	11.5
UK	8.8	FR Germany	9.6
FR Germany	6.9	Japan	7.5
France	5.4	UK	5.3
Canada	4.7	France	5.2
USSR	3.6	USSR	4.7
Belgium/Luxembourg	3.0	Saudi Arabia	4.1
Netherlands	2.9	Italy	4.0
Japan	2.1	Canada	3.9
Venezuela	2.0	Netherlands	3.6

Top ten = 55.8%   Top ten = 59.4%
Top twenty = 70.7%   Top twenty = 73.2%

(b) Top ten importing countries (% of world imports)

	1955		1982
USA	11.7	USA	13.3
UK	10.9	FR Germany	8.1
FR Germany	6.2	Japan	6.9
France	5.1	France	6.0
Canada	4.7	UK	5.2
Netherlands	3.3	Italy	4.5
USSR	3.1	USSR	4.1
Belgium/Luxembourg	2.9	Netherlands	3.4
Italy	2.8	Canada	3.1
Japan	2.5	Belgium/Luxembourg	3.0

Top ten = 53.2%   Top ten = 57.6%
Top twenty = 67.7%   Top twenty = 71.7%

Source: Barclays Review, May 1984

undergoing rapid industrialisation like Korea and Taiwan will push their way into the top ten.

The predominance of the industrialised market economies in world trade has already been mentioned and this is further illustrated when world trade flows are examined in Fig. 2.2. Trade between the industrialised market economies in 1982 accounted for 44 per cent of the total value of world exports, and only 15 per cent

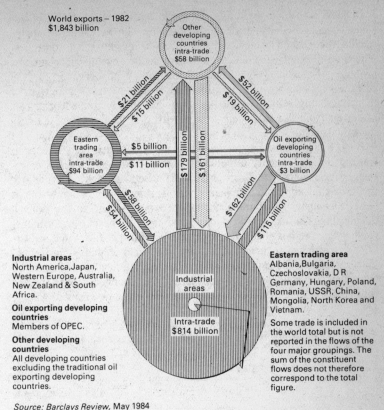

World exports – 1982
$1,843 billion

Other developing countries intra-trade $58 billion

$21 billion
$15 billion

$52 billion
$19 billion

Eastern trading area intra-trade $94 billion

$5 billion
$11 billion

$179 billion
$161 billion

Oil exporting developing countries intra-trade $3 billion

$58 billion
$54 billion

$162 billion
$115 billion

Industrial areas

Intra-trade $814 billion

Industrial areas
North America, Japan, Western Europe, Australia, New Zealand & South Africa.

Oil exporting developing countries
Members of OPEC.

Other developing countries
All developing countries excluding the traditional oil exporting developing countries.

Eastern trading area
Albania, Bulgaria, Czechoslovakia, D R Germany, Hungary, Poland, Romania, USSR, China, Mongolia, North Korea and Vietnam.

Some trade is included in the world total but is not reported in the flows of the four major groupings. The sum of the constituent flows does not therefore correspond to the total figure.

Source: Barclays Review, May 1984

Fig. 2.2 World trade flows

of world exports did not involve some participation in these countries. One important development since the 1950s not shown in Fig. 2.2 is the growth in trading relationships between the members of trading blocs such as the European Economic Community (EEC) or the Asociacion Latino Americano de Integracion (ALADI), and the importance of these will be examined later.

UK trade patterns

The past quarter of a century has witnessed a number of radical changes in the composition of Britain's overseas trade, both by area and by commodity, and these changes are shown in Table 2.2.

In 1960 a third of Britain's trade was with Western Europe, but this was matched by trade with other developed countries, principally the United States and the older Commonwealth countries. The final third of Britain's trade was with the developing countries, notably those of the Commonwealth. With regard to the commodity composition of this trade, the picture is one of a manufacturing nation exporting its goods to pay for essential raw materials from abroad, even though a third of imports were actually manufactured goods.

By 1985, however, Britain has become, quite clearly, a European trading nation, heavily dependent on trade with other EEC countries; trade with most other industrialised nations, particularly those of the old Commonwealth, has declined, in relative terms at least. Similarly the share of Britain's exports going to the non-oil developing countries has declined sharply. These developments reflect the tendency for the markets of Europe and those of the OPEC countries to grow at a faster rate than Britain's traditional markets of the Commonwealth and Latin America, and were to be expected. Of much greater concern is the changed *composition* of this trade. There has been a pronounced shift downwards in the

Table 2.2 Changes in UK trade patterns (by percentage)

	1960		By percentage 1984	
	Imports	Exports	Imports	Exports
Composition				
Food, drink, tobacco	33	6	11	7
Basic materials	23	4	6	3
Fuels	10	4	14	22
Manufactures	33	86	69	68
	100	100	100	100
Area				
Western Europe	30	30	63	57
North America	21	15	14	16
Other developed	10	15	7	5
Soviet bloc	3	2	2	3
Developing countries	36	38	14	19
	100	100	100	100

Sources: Annual Abstract of Statistics 1965; *British Business* March 1985

proportion of export earnings derived from manufactures, while the exploitation of North Sea oil has enabled Britain to become a major exporter of fuel products. At the same time, imports of manufactured goods have risen steadily as a proportion of total imports. These structural changes do *not*, unfortunately, indicate that Britain has performed well as a manufacturing nation, reducing her dependence on overseas supplies of raw materials. Rather they show that while British export of manufactures has grown very slowly through the 1970s and 1980s, the importation of manufactured goods has grown at a dramatic rate over this period.

The decline in Britain's trade performance

The UK share of world exports of manufactures fell from 17 per cent in 1960 to 7 per cent in 1986, reflecting the fact that throughout the 1960s and 1970s the volume of UK exports of manufactures grew at a much slower rate than that of the world as a whole. This relative decline has accelerated in the 1980s; British manufactured export volume was actually down by nearly 2 per cent over the period from 1979 to 1984, yet there was a real growth in world markets of 20 per cent during the same period. At the same time there has been a marked rise in the level of import penetration in most major manufacturing industries. In one industry after another the value of export earnings has been overhauled by the expenditure on imports, from textiles in the 1950s through motor vehicles in the 1970s to electrical engineering in the mid-1980s. In 1983, for the first time in over 200 years, the total value of UK manufacturing exports was exceeded by the value of manufactured imports. Nor was this a temporary aberration, as Fig. 2.3 illustrates.

When, in the late 1950s, the decline in Britain's share of world trade in manufactures first gave serious cause for concern, two explanations were frequently cited.

Firstly, there was the re-emergence of competition from Germany and Japan following the years of reconstruction immediately after the Second World War. During the period of reconstruction, Britain had been able, temporarily, to increase her share of world exports, and a return to more normal circumstances was now to be expected.

Secondly, there was the orientation of Britain's trade to her traditional, but slowly growing, markets of the Commonwealth dating back to the days of imperial preference.

Whatever the initial validity of these arguments, they had

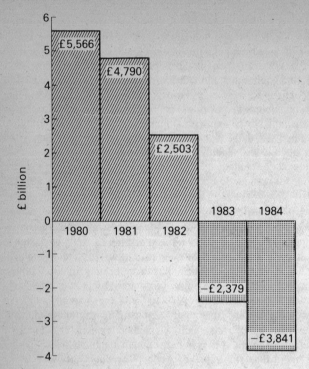

Source: Department of Trade and Industry

Fig. 2.3 UK manufactured trade balance 1980–84

certainly ceased to hold true by the late 1960s. At this time the process of post-war reconstruction was long over and Britain had already shifted the emphasis of her trade towards the faster growing markets of Europe and the industrialised world. The reasons for the decline in British exports of manufactures after 1960 have more to do with the fundamental weaknesses of the British economy than with the geographical structure of her trade.

Price competitiveness
Britain's inflation rate in the 1960s was much higher than the average for the industrialised countries and this problem, coupled with an over-valued pound, helped to price British goods out of world markets. The high prices of British goods reflected a poor record in terms of productivity, new investment and profitability

and the fact that British industrial costs were higher than those of rival manufacturing nations. Competitiveness was only restored by the devaluation of 1967 and by the downward float of sterling in the mid-1970s and in both cases cost-push inflationary pressures were introduced into the economy to perpetuate the high inflation rate.

At the same time, Britain's slow growth rate retarded the modernisation of industrial production methods necessary if competitiveness was to be restored permanently. In any case such competitiveness as was regained by a decline in the exchange rate failed to halt the decline in Britain's trade position. For price competitiveness to have any effect, exports must be elastic in demand, otherwise revenue from exports will fall when prices in foreign currencies are reduced. In addition, domestic products must be able to replace imports if import penetration is to be reversed, or at least halted. In practice, there was some correlation between Britain's price competitiveness and her share of world exports in the 1960s, but from the mid-1960s onwards price competitiveness appears to have become increasingly less important both in determining Britain's share of world exports and in preventing further import penetration. This development is partly due to the tendency for inertia to set in once a market is established so that the larger a country's share of a particular market the more difficult it is for competition to break in. Just as Britain once dominated a number of world markets, despite cheaper competition from elsewhere, she is now in the position of finding it difficult to compete in markets dominated by other manufacturing countries.

The situation is further complicated by the growing importance of oil to the UK economy in the 1980s. One consequence of this development is that the exchange rate of sterling is strongly affected by world oil prices, irrespective of the price competitiveness of Britain's manufacturing sector. On the whole it would appear that the greater the decline in Britain's share of world markets and of her own domestic markets, the *less effective are price reductions* in improving this position. Part of this inelasticity of demand for both exports and imports must be due to non-price competitive factors.

Non-price competition
Much of the lack of price competitiveness of British goods has been associated with the high costs resulting from inefficiency. While a lack of efficiency which results in higher prices can be offset by a

fall in the exchange rate, this inefficiency is likely to spill over into non-price competition where no such compensation is possible. In many industries, reliability, quality, good after-sales service and adherence to delivery dates are more important selling points than low prices. In all these areas British firms have, in general, performed less well than their overseas rivals. While foreign customers cannot be expected to remain loyal to British goods, even the residual patriotism of British customers in buying British has faded. In addition, the greater the share of the British home market gained by foreign companies the greater their ability to compete in terms of supply points, availability of spare parts and choice of products. Though many of these foreign companies were able to break into the British market through their price competitiveness, they are now able to maintain and expand their share of the market through quality and reliability, even when exchange rate movements have made their goods more expensive than the British alternative. The implications of these developments do not augur well for the future of British industry since the developing countries are poised to capture many of the markets for mass-produced cheap goods and Britain, like other industrialised countries, must aim to succeed in those industries where quality and reliability are the most important considerations.

Quite apart from the threat posed to the balance of payments by this decline in Britain's manufacturing trade, there are likely to be serious repercussions for the economy as a whole. Economic growth depends to a large extent on a country's trading performance, a relationship discussed in the last chapter, and if a country's share of world trade declines it will be condemned to slower growth than the rest of the world. This has been the situation facing Britain since the Second World War, but especially since 1979. Had British exports grown in line with world trade since 1979, large current account surpluses would have been accumulated as North Sea oil came on stream. These surpluses could have been used to finance increased overseas investment or a higher level of imports. In either case the economy would have grown faster and permitted higher living standards in the long term. Instead, the decline in British manufacturing trade, accelerated by the overvaluation of the pound between 1979 and 1981, has pushed up unemployment by as much as 80,000 jobs a year and retarded the rate of economic growth. While externally the effect has been to throw a greater burden on the service sector and oil as sources of foreign exchange earnings, the internal impact will result in slow growth, inflation, weak domestic demand and slow expansion in the service industries, the sector with the best hopes for new job creation.

Barriers to trade

When countries find their domestic economies suffering through a rapid growth in import penetration of domestic markets, it is tempting to seek a solution through the introduction of restrictions on imports. These trade barriers may take several forms, but the most common are tariffs, quotas and exchange control.

Tariffs
A tariff is a tax on imported goods. Where a tariff is introduced to stem the tide of imports, the object is to raise the price of the imported product so that it loses its competitiveness against domestically-produced goods. This is illustrated in Fig. 2.4(a) where before the imposition of the tariff the market supply curve is S and the equilibrium market price is £4. The imposition of a tariff of £1 means that suppliers must raise their price to earn the same net revenue as before. The market supply curve therefore shifts to the left, to S_1, leading to a higher market price of £4.80

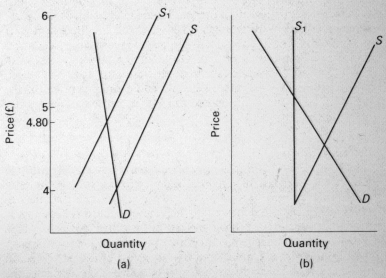

Fig. 2.4

and contraction in the quantity demanded. In order to avoid demand collapsing altogether, suppliers have absorbed part of the tariff themselves. Only if demand is totally inelastic will the supplier be able to pass the entire tariff on to the consumer. Indeed, the extent to which the tariff is successful in reducing demand for the imported product depends largely on the elasticity of demand for that product. It is most likely to be successful where there are close substitutes available from domestic suppliers or where price competition has kept profit margins too low to enable suppliers to absorb the tariff. Tariffs are relatively unsuccessful where demand is inelastic, as when there are no locally-produced substitutes, or where the imported goods are so cheap that even with the tariff they are still much lower in price than the domestically-produced alternative. Of course, some tariffs are imposed, not to cut imports, but to raise revenue for the government, notably the high duties on luxury items with very inelastic demand, such as perfume, wines and spirits, etc.

Quotas

A quota is a specific limit placed on the importation of foreign goods and may consist of a total ban in extreme circumstances. As Fig. 2.4(b) illustrates, the effect of the quota is to shift supply from S to the artificially imposed supply of S_1, so that however much buyers bid up prices, no more can be made available. Quotas are commonly used by Britain and other advanced countries to restrict the import of cheap goods from the newly-industrialised countries of the Far East and to prevent the 'dumping' of excess stocks of goods by East European countries. In addition, Japan has agreed to limit its exports of cars, video and audio equipment and many other goods to the EEC, and to the UK in particular, in a series of 'voluntary' quotas.

Exchange control

Buyers need to be able to obtain foreign currency in order to finance the purchase of imports. Many countries control the level of imports by making it extremely difficult for their nationals to purchase foreign currency or to hold foreign currency accounts. Scarce currencies can be subjected to selective controls which ration them out in payment for high priority imports – a system used by the Soviet Union. The UK abolished exchange control in 1979, the result of a government policy aimed at encouraging the free movement of capital.

Other non-tariff barriers
With the development of free trade agreements in the post-war period, the use of tariffs and quotas has become somewhat restricted. As a result most countries have introduced measures to reduce imports without contravening their international agreements. Among the most commonly used practices are: new regulations on health or safety which immediately outlaw foreign goods; changes in technical specifications to suit domestic producers without giving a warning to overseas competitors; and complex customs formalities to delay the entry of imports. France and Japan, in particular, have been criticised for their use of such measures to restrict imports.

Subsidies
These may be paid to domestic producers to enable them to lower their prices and increase their competitiveness. Such measures have the added advantage that they may also help to boost exports, though other countries may retaliate by imposing tariffs on goods which they perceive as having artificially low prices.

Arguments for protection
The arguments in favour of free trade were discussed in the last chapter – the development of international specialisation and economies of scale, increased world output and higher living standards. None the less, political and strategic considerations make it inevitable that all countries will seek to restrict trade where national interests are jeopardised; controls on the import of dangerous drugs and explosives are obvious examples. The economic arguments for protection are rather more complex and are frequently based on erroneous assumptions. The principal ones are:

1. To protect a declining industry. Once-great industries may use their still considerable influence to pressure the government into introducing trade barriers. Such protectionism is difficult to justify on economic grounds since if the industry has lost its comparative advantage it should give way to more efficient overseas industries. This would release the resources currently being used in the industry for more productive uses elsewhere. There might be a case, however, for giving the industry short-term support while it is being modernised to restore its competitiveness. If this is the situation, investment aid might be more appropriate than a tariff. Where the industry is in long-term decline, social considerations would point to regional assistance for those areas in which the industry is concentrated.

2. *To protect employment.* Two distinct arguments for tariff protection are represented here.

Firstly, there is the argument that the world market is shrinking and unless excess capacity in the domestic industry is utilised to replace imports, unemployment will result. This argument was used in all the industrialised countries in the 1930s and resulted in a series of retaliatory increases in tariffs which left all these countries worse off in terms of trade *and* employment.

Secondly, there is the argument that jobs are being lost because of competition from goods produced by cheap overseas labour. Some writers are equally dismissive of this argument on the grounds that domestic consumers should have the right to benefit from cheaper foreign goods. The workers displaced from home industries can then shift to new industries in which the country has a comparative advantage. It is further asserted that eventually low-paid foreign workers will form their own trade unions to push up wages at the expense of the large profits of their employers.[1] Events in recent years have shown how great is the gap between theory and practice on this issue. In the first place it is futile to talk of displaced workers entering new industries when the rate of job creation falls far short of the rate at which jobs are being lost. In the second place the large profits made out of the labour of workers in the Third World do not necessarily go to local employers; often they go to the multinational companies which distribute the goods. Thus British clothing workers have lost their jobs so that bigger profits can be made by British retailing groups selling clothes produced in Hong Kong, Korea, Taiwan and Thailand. Tariffs may not be the solution but it is pointless to claim that the unemployment caused by the import of cheap foreign goods is not a long-term problem.

3. *To correct the balance of payments.* Tariffs have been used as a policy measure to reduce imports and so eliminate a balance of payments deficit. Their success depends on exports being relatively unaffected by this action. In practice it is likely that other countries will retaliate and impose their own tariffs on the offending country's exports. Placing a tariff on imports is only likely to be successful where a country's imports have elastic demand and where the country's exports are inelastic in demand, or where tariffs are imposed specifically against a country which has a large trade surplus with the country imposing the tariff and where retal-

iation would have little effect. Even in these cases the policy is a dangerous one since the repercussions on the domestic economy of a trade war will almost certainly entail reduced output and national income.

4. To achieve self-sufficiency.   Most countries attempt to protect such industries as agriculture or steel to reduce the country's dependence on overseas supplies of essential materials. Such a motive lay behind the establishment of the Common Agricultural Policy by the EEC with its system of import levies on food products from outside the Community. This tariff argument tends to be political rather than economic in its emphasis on maintaining self-sufficiency as a contribution to the country's independence.

5. Protection against 'dumping'.   Countries frequently attempt to control the level of cheap imports when they regard the lower prices as being the result of unfair competition rather than arising out of the principle of comparative advantage. A primary source of dumped goods is the East European bloc where output is determined by production targets rather than being directly responsive to demand. Excess production is unloaded on western markets at prices which are often below cost but which earn foreign currency. The imposition of tariffs on these goods still leaves them far cheaper than domestic substitutes and so their importation is normally limited by quotas. Another example of unfair competition is the practice of giving large subsidies to exporting industries to enable them to penetrate new markets. While usually associated with the newly industrialised countries, this practice is not uncommon among the advanced countries. In 1985 the American government imposed higher tariffs on British steel on the grounds that the British government was subsidising the export price. Tariffs and quotas against unfair competition are generally regarded as valid because dumping and similar practices impede rather than assist free trade.

6. To protect infant industries.   This is one of the strongest of the arguments for protection. According to this argument some countries are prevented from specialising in those industries in which they would have a comparative advantage because they cannot get these industries off the ground. When the infant industry is established it cannot withstand the competition from foreign industries which already have the benefit of economies of scale and it fails to survive. Protection gives the infant industry the breathing space to attain technical efficiency and scale production and the tariff can be removed once this stage of maturity is reached. Unfortunately the lack of influence of small new industries means that in industrialised countries they are less likely to receive protection than the old declining industries.

7. *To assist development.* This might also be termed the 'infant economy' argument since it is closely related to that made on behalf of infant industries. Developing countries in the early stages of industrialisation have nothing but infant industries and can reasonably claim that short-term protection is necessary to enable the process of economic development to take place.

Free trade and protection in practice

Most of the arguments for protection are at odds with the theory of comparative advantage which shows that all countries benefit from trade. During periods of economic recession, however, most countries are subjected to calls for protection from domestic industries suffering from a lack of demand. The prolonged depression of the inter-war years led to a rising spiral of tariffs as the industrialised nations sought to protect their vital industries but, in so doing, provoked retaliation. During the Second World War the allied nations planned the establishment of an International Trade Organisation (ITO) to complement the work of the World Bank and the International Monetary Fund by promoting a freer system of international trade. There were delays in the drafting of the ITO charter and as an interim measure twenty-three countries signed a multilateral trade treaty to be known as the General Agreement on Tariffs and Trade (GATT) in 1947. The ITO charter was finally drafted in 1948 but the refusal of the United States congress to ratify it[2] led to its being inoperative and the concept of the ITO was finally abandoned in 1950. However, GATT survived and took over the Interim Committee for the ITO which had been established by the United Nations in 1948.

GATT

GATT came into force in 1948 and now has some eighty-eight members. It provides a framework for the conduct of international trade and sets out a number of principles to be followed by member countries to ensure fair trade practice.

The first principle is that trade should be conducted on the basis of *non-discrimination*. All contracting parties are bound by the 'most favoured nation' (MFN) clause in the application of import duties so that a reduction in the duty levied on imports from one GATT member must be applied to all other GATT members. There are two exceptions to the MFN rule. The first is that any system of trade preference in operation before the establishment of GATT, such as Commonwealth trade preference, is permitted to continue. The second exemption allows members of customs and free trade areas to reduce tariffs between themselves without extending most favoured nation treatment to other countries.

The second general principle of GATT is that protection for domestic industry should be provided only through tariffs; such measures as import quotas or import licensing being prohibited. In practice such prohibitions are difficult to enforce and GATT relies on its third principle of consultation to ensure that quotas and other trade restrictions are used responsibly.

The final general principle is that GATT should provide a framework within which negotiations for reductions in tariffs can be held. Under its auspices there have been seven tariff-cutting agreements, the most recent being the Kennedy Round from 1964 to 1967 and the Tokyo Round from 1973 to 1979. The protracted negotiations of the Tokyo Round reflected the growing difficulty in securing agreement to a further liberalisation of trade against a background of the world recession. Indeed, the original aims of the Tokyo Round to dismantle non-tariff measures and provide more assistance to the developing countries were not realised. However, there was agreement on tariff cuts to average 30 per cent over the following eight years and by 1980 average tariffs were in single figures for all the major developed economies.

UNCTAD

In the 1950s and 1960s there was growing dissatisfaction among the developing countries over GATT's preoccupation with the elimination of tariff barriers to the exclusion of a consideration of their particular problems. Pressure for a new initiative led to the establishment of the United Nations Conference on Trade and Development (UNCTAD) as a department of the United Nations in 1964. This followed the 'Joint Declaration of the 75 Developing Countries' proposing a 'dynamic international trade policy' to enable the developing countries to expand and diversify their trade. The 'Joint Declaration' also laid the foundation for the Prebisch Report which was presented at the 1964 UNCTAD conference as an analysis of the trade problems of the developing countries and a plan for action[3]. The report claimed that the poorer countries were handicapped by a steady deterioration in their terms of trade and that their future development required more aid on better terms and fair and stable export prices for their goods, as well as the removal of trade barriers. While the developing countries were enthusiastic about the Prebisch Report, the advanced countries gave it a cool reception and no firm proposals were adopted other than that UNCTAD would remain in being and would reconvene at least every three years. Later conferences were also disappointing in their failure to formulate a plan of action to assist the developing countries – by the late 1970s the industrialised countries were in any case too concerned with their own problems to consider further trade assistance to the Third World.

Customs unions and free trade areas

As well as moves to liberalise the conduct of world trade, the post-war period has also witnessed the growth of trading blocs by countries with close political, economic and geographical ties. Typically these blocs take the form of either a customs union or a free trade area. A customs union is an arrangement between two or more countries whereby tariffs between the member countries are abolished and a common external tariff is established. Such customs unions as the German Zollverein of the nineteenth century and the EEC today are examples of this. Such an agreement requires a supra-national agency to control the workings of the customs union and members are therefore bound by treaty obligations to accept some loss of sovereignty in their dealings with each other. Free trade areas are weaker arrangements in that member states retain the right to determine their own external tariffs. The only commitment made is that of free trade between members and this requires neither a loss of sovereignty nor a supra-national institution. Examples of free trade areas include the European Free Trade Association formed in 1957 by non-EEC West European states and the Association of South-East Asian Nations. While the object of both customs unions and free trade areas is to liberalise trade between member countries, their formation does not signify a move towards freer trade throughout the world since their policies frequently discourage trade with non-member countries. Indeed, a noticeable feature of all the major trading blocs is the growth of the trade between members as a proportion of the total trade of the trading bloc, as shown in Table 2.3.

As well as the examples in Table 2.3, intra-trading has also grown dramatically in such loose trading groups as the 'Pacific Five' (Australia, Canada, Japan, New Zealand and the US). This

Table 2.3 Growth of intra-trade by trading blocs

	Intra-exports as % of total exports	
	1958	1982
EEC*	35.3	51.7
ALADI†	7.5	12.5
ASEAN‡	15.0	18.8

* EEC: Belgium, Denmark, France, FR Germany,
  Greece, Ireland, Italy, Luxembourg, Netherlands
  and the United Kingdom
† ALADI: Argentina, Bolivia, Brazil, Chile,
  Colombia, Ecuador, Mexico, Paraguay, Peru,
  Uruguay and Venezuela
‡ ASEAN: Indonesia, Malaysia, Philippines, Singa-
  pore and Thailand
Source: *Barclays Review*, May 1984

growth in intra-trade represents a tendency towards regional self-sufficiency and isolationism which could hinder rather than promote the development of free trade.

The new protectionism

World economic conditions in the 1970s and 1980s have revived protectionist instincts despite the experiences of the 1930s when trade wars among the major industrialised nations served only to deepen the Depression. The 1970s saw a slowing of world trade expansion after the rapid growth of the quarter century following the end of the last war. Between 1963 and 1973, world trade increased by 8.5 per cent per annum and trade in manufactures by 11 per cent per annum. In the years between 1973 and 1978, both figures were halved while between 1978 and 1983 there was virtually no growth in world trade at all. These difficulties stimulated demands for protection among the industrialised countries while in the developing countries governments were forced into restricting imports in the face of rising foreign debts and declining foreign earnings. The resurgence of protection has not taken the form of crude tariff barriers since these would contravene international agreements and are, in any case, less effective under the floating exchange rate regime of the 1980s than they were in the past. Instead there has been a dramatic expansion in the use of non-tariff barriers going far beyond the traditional controls like quotas and import licences. Many of these developments have promoted bilateral trade arrangements at the expense of multilateral trade. Among the most important barriers in operation are:

1. Voluntary Export Restraints (VERs). These are agreements obtained by the western industrial nations from Japan and the Newly Industrialising Countries (NICs) to protect their own industries. The effect of these VERs is to limit the export of cars, televisions and other consumer durables to Europe. Another example is the Multi-Fibre Arrangement which controls the imports of textiles and clothing from twenty-five developing countries into the EEC.

2. Administrative barriers. These are controls imposed on imports under the guise of measures relating to other aspects of government policy. They include health and safety regulations, customs and other procedures, technical standards, environmental regulations and requirements as to certificates of origin. The effect is that imports are delayed or rejected because of their failure to break through red-tape restrictions.

3. Official persuasion. This occurs when the government obtains undertakings from organisations in both the public and private sectors to limit their imports of raw materials or components. The British government has frequently controlled the level of foreign coal imports by the Central Electricity Generating Board and in 1983 prevailed on Ford to reduce the level of its imports from overseas factories for sale in the UK.

4. Discriminatory public procurement. For many years government departments in the UK have tended to favour British goods even when there have been cheaper equivalent alternatives available abroad. Public corporations like British Rail have been expected to buy British capital equipment as a matter of course even when they might have preferred to look overseas for the best goods available.

5. Counter trading. This term is now used to describe barter trade whereby imports are tied directly to an agreement to buy goods from the importing country. This development is examined in some detail in Chapter 4. The logical outcome of counter trading is that each country buys from another country only to the extent that it can sell to that country. The result would be the total supremacy of bilateral over multilateral trade.

Despite the dangers to the world economy from the growth of protectionism, the western industrialised nations have been pushed towards an extension of trade barriers both by the rising unemployment and sluggish trade experienced by their own industries and by the apparently unfair trading practices of Japan. By the early 1980s it was increasingly being claimed that Japan's huge trade surplus with the rest of the world was the result of her many subtle non-tariff barriers, usually of the administrative control type outlined above. The GATT conference of 1982 was unable to resolve these problems and at the GATT meeting the following year most of the running was made by countries wishing to increase tariffs. Early in 1985 there were growing fears that protectionism could get out of control with the United States Congress demanding a 20 per cent levy on imports and the American government imposing export controls on high technology which could only harm the ability of EEC and other industrialised regions to compete with the Americans in this area. At the same time Mr Nakasone, the Japanese Prime Minister, was pleading with his own citizens to overcome their natural reluctance to buy foreign and increase their imports as a way of reducing Japan's trade surplus[4] and so prevent retaliation from the West. Even the EEC was under attack for its continued protectionism against imported food products which harmed the recovery and growth of the developing countries. It was agreed by the EEC, Japan, Canada and the United States that new GATT talks were vital and these were arranged for 1986. It was hoped then to widen the role of GATT to take in new areas such as banking, insurance and high technology, though for the developing countries the key issues centre around the willingness of the industrialised nations to open their markets to the developing world, while providing safeguards for their own infant industries.

Notes

1. For a brief summary of this view see P. Samuelson, *Economics*, McGraw Hill.
2. Congress was concerned about the risk of higher unemployment in the USA.
3. UN, *Towards a New Trade Policy for Development*, New York, 1964.
4. Estimated to be $44 billion in 1984.

Examination questions

The following questions are taken from the examination papers of various examining bodies which include the areas covered by this chapter in their syllabuses. Those marked with an asterisk (★) are representative of the main types of question asked and specimen answers for these will be found in Part II.

1. The traditional structure of international trade is giving way to a more complex pattern. Discuss. (ICMA Professional Stage, May 1983)

2.★ Since the Second World War the pattern of UK overseas trade has changed drastically. What changes have taken place and why? (FCOT, May 1984)

3. Examine the trends in international trade in recent years in any economy with which you are familiar, explaining the relevance of economic theory to the trends which you discuss. (RSA Stage III, July 1981)

4. (a) Explain the economic case for free trade between countries.
   (b) How may domestic industry be protected from foreign competition?
   (c) What are the economic reasons for such protection? (Cambridge, June 1982)

5. 'Import penetration of the market for manufactured goods in the United Kingdom has gone too far.' Why has this occurred? Do you agree with the opinion expressed? (Cambridge, June 1980)

6.★ Argue the case for and against import controls with respect to the United Kingdom economy. (London, June 1982)

7. What is the case for and against Britain reducing her level of imports through direct controls? (Cert. Marketing, November 1982)

8.★ Distinguish between tariff and non-tariff barriers to international trade. In view of the relative simplicity of operating the tariff system, why has the non-tariff approach become more prevalent? (Dip. Marketing, June 1984)

9.★ When should a developing country adopt free trade policies and when should it not? (ICSA Part III, June 1984)

10. In November 1982, some 80 countries were represented at a meeting of GATT (General Agreement on Tariffs and Trade), held to discuss the increasing degree of protectionism in world trade.

Outline briefly the form this protectionism has taken, and the reasons for individual countries doing so. (Dip. Marketing, June 1983)

11. (a) Explain the term *protection*.
    (b) Discuss the merits and demerits of the policy of protection for conserving foreign exchange in your country. (West African 'A', Paper 2, June 1983)

12. Comment on the growth of protectionism in international trade. (LCCI Higher, Spring 1984)

Chapter Three
The balance of payments

The balance of payments may be defined as a systematic record of all economic transactions between the residents of the domestic or recording country and the residents of other countries, over a given period of time. Residents are defined as those who have a *permanent domicile* in the country in question and include businesses and government bodies as well as individuals. By this definition, diplomatic and military staff, workers temporarily posted abroad and tourists are all regarded as residents of their countries of origin and *not* of the (domestic) country in which they are living for the time being. Again, the definition means that *all* the transactions of domestically-based companies are recorded, including those of overseas branches, but that only the international transactions of a foreign firm's agencies are recorded. This classification of what constitutes residence may be arbitrary, giving rise to anomalies, but this is not too serious as long as the definition is used consistently. The term 'economic transaction' can also give rise to confusion. Economic transactions not only include the exchange of currency for goods and services, but also the transfer of currency or valuable assets abroad as gifts or pensions and the exchange of goods for other goods, as in the case of barter trade. Thus the balance of payments includes the value of all recorded exchanges between one country and another whether or not these exchanges involve the payment of currency.

The balance of payments accounts

It is customary to set out the economic transactions of one country with all other countries as a series of credits and debits. Those economic transactions which involve the receipt of foreign currency are recorded as credits (+) while those which involve the payment of domestic currency are recorded as debits (−). The accounts are set out in three sections.

1. Current account

This is the record of trade in goods and services and other similar payments. It consists firstly of the **balance of trade** which is made up of the value of exported goods (+) and the value of imported goods (−). Only tangible goods are recorded here, and the balance is sometimes called the 'visible' trade balance.

There is also the **balance of invisibles**, made up of several parts.

1. Receipts (+) and payments (−) arising out of the supply and purchase of services such as banking, insurance, shipping and tourism.
2. The receipt of earnings by residents in Britain arising out of interest, dividend and rent payments on capital and property holdings overseas (+), and payments to overseas residents of income from similar holdings in Britain (−).
3. The transfer of gifts, pensions and similar payments in currency between British and overseas residents (inflows +, outflows −).
4. Certain aspects of government expenditure overseas, notably payments for the maintenance of military bases and diplomatic representation.

If the balance of trade and the balance of invisibles are added together, the figure obtained is the **balance on current account**, as shown in Table 3.1.

2. Investment and other capital flows

This section consists of movements of capital into (+) and from (−) the recording country. Again it is divided into several sections.

1. There is the *short-term capital account*, consisting of additions to (+) or withdrawals from (−) balances in British banks by overseas residents and the dealings of those banks in foreign currencies. Also included under short-term capital movements are trade credit given on exports and imports and changes in eurocurrency borrowing in London. Many of these short-term movements in the capital accounts arise from currency speculation, changes in interest rates and alteration in the level of confidence in the economic and political situation.
2. There are *long-term capital movements*, both by the private and the public sector. *Private capital movements* include the

Table 3.1 UK balance of payments 1985 (£m)

Current account	Exports	78,072
	Imports	80,140
	Visible trade balance	−2,068
	Invisible items (net)	
	Shipping	−1,104
	Civil aviation	495
	Travel	617
	Other services	7,494
	Government transfers	−1,211
	Interest, profits and dividends	2,294
	Private transfers	−3,565
	Invisible trade balance	5,020
Current account balance		2,952
Investment and other capital flows	Investment in UK by overseas governments	1,351
	Investment in UK by overseas private sector	6,129
	UK private investment overseas	−22,247
	Official investment overseas	−310
	Trade credit	−139
	Changes in foreign currency borrowing	5,055
	Exchange reserves in sterling	1,741
	Other banking and money market liabilities in sterling	4,107
	External sterling lending by UK banks	−1,666
	Other lending	3,119
Capital account balance		−2,860
Balancing item		835
Total for official financing		927
Official financing		
Foreign currency borrowing by the Government		277
Net foreign currency borrowing under the exchange cover scheme		554
Additions to official reserves		−1,758
Total official financing		−927

Source: CSO Economic Trends 1986

purchase and sale of stocks and shares in foreign governments or companies by individuals or institutions (portfolio investment), whether inflows into the UK (+) or outflows from the UK (−). Private capital movements also include the purchase by companies of a controlling interest in foreign companies (direct investment). *Public capital movements* consist of long-term loans by one government to another, with foreign governments lending to the UK (+) and the British government lending to foreign governments (−). When added together, all these various items make up the **balance on capital account**. Again reference can be made to Table 3.1 to see the make-up of the UK capital account.

3. Official financing

When the balances on the two preceding sections are added together they should yield a figure equal to the net receipt or loss of foreign currency over the year in question, i.e. the **balance for official financing**. This is the key single indicator of how the UK is faring in its external transactions.

The section 'Official financing' shows how a deficit is financed or a surplus used. The main items are:

1. Changes in the level of UK gold and foreign currency holdings;
2. Changes in the level of borrowing from the International Monetary Fund (IMF) and other international monetary authorities.

Accordingly a deficit could be financed either by a depletion of gold and foreign currency reserves or through borrowing from the IMF, while a surplus will result in a rise in reserves or enable the reduction of the country's overseas debts. Net increases in reserves are shown as a (−) while net decreases are shown as a (+) so that if the balance for official financing shows a deficit (−), official financing will show a (+) total for an equal amount, the two balances cancelling out. It is important to note that in the 'Official financing' section, the signs (+) and (−) take on different meanings with (+) referring to a reduction in assets or an increase in liabilities and (−) meaning the opposite.

In practice it is impossible to arrive at a totally accurate figure for the balance for official financing so that a balancing item is inserted to take account of errors and omissions. The 'Official financing' section is assumed to provide the correct total because of the more accurate records kept of gold and foreign currency movements compared to those of the economic transactions between this country and overseas residents. As with the measurement of national income or a population census, the sheer volume of information involved makes errors of measurement of the balance of payments inevitable. On the current account some goods and services are double-counted or not counted at all, while the fact that some transactions take place partly in one year and are completed in the next causes time lags and inaccuracies in the recording of information. On the capital account, private short-term capital movements are very difficult to estimate and constitute one of the main sources of errors and omissions. Problems also arise with respect to the classification into private and government capital. A South American loan taken up by a private institution in Britain will be shown as an official loan in the balance of payments of the issuing country, but as a private loan in the UK balance of payments.

The changing pattern of the balance of payments

The structure of a particular country's balance of payments at any one time reflects the current economic make-up of the country and can be expected to change as the country's economy evolves. Developing countries, for example, are unlikely to exhibit a balance of payments pattern similar to that of an advanced nation enjoying much higher living standards. Several patterns are discernible.

1. The developing country. With only limited industrial capacity, the country must import many essential goods. However, export earnings are unlikely to be sufficient to finance a high level of imports so that the country relies on its current account deficit being offset by a surplus on the long-term capital account. This surplus on capital account arises from developed countries investing in the developing country to build up its capital structure and industrial potential. It is worth noting here how difficult the situation is for an under-developed country with few natural resources and limited potential. Such countries may be unable to attract investment and therefore may be deprived of the foreign currency needed to finance essential imports.

2. The Newly Industrialising Country (NIC). The newly industrialising country is often highly competitive and is able to generate a balance of trade surplus as exports rise and some imports decline. However, the invisible trade balance is usually in deficit since the service sector has yet to develop fully, while there is an outflow of interest and dividends on previous capital inflows. Meanwhile the capital account may move nearer to equilibrium as the country begins to invest abroad itself, even though it continues to attract investment from other developed nations.

3. The developed creditor country. Eventually the developed nation may enjoy a very large surplus on the balance of trade as its export earnings grow. At the same time the development of indigenous service industries and of profits from its own overseas investments reduce the invisible deficit so that the current account as a whole shows a large surplus. In consequence the country can further expand its overseas investments, and the capital account may now move into deficit.

4. The mature creditor country. With higher living standards the country may find its rising imports no longer being matched by continued export growth, especially as it may have lost its competitive edge compared to the newly industrialising nations. However, it may be able to offset the consequent deficit on visible trade by an invisible surplus resulting from receipts from past foreign lending and the earnings of the service sector.

5. The ageing debtor country. Where the developed creditor country's visible trade balance continues to worsen, the point may eventually be reached where invisible earnings are no longer sufficient to outweigh this deficit. The balance of payments then reaches a critical position. The country will have little alternative but to take appropriate measures to reverse the trend towards larger deficits as, unlike the developing country, it cannot rely on future natural improvement to solve the problem.

Not all countries follow the pattern of evolution outlined above. While many of the developed nations of the western world have passed through all these stages, others have stopped at the fourth, or even the third, stage. The situation is complicated by the fact that the structure of exports and imports varies considerably from one country to another so that the balance of payments cannot be expected to evolve in exactly the same way in any two countries. Accordingly, countries whose external trade is based on such vital commodities as oil or essential minerals have tended to enjoy a stronger balance of payments position than have countries dependent for their export earnings on cheap manufactures or basic foodstuffs. Furthermore, economic forces and events differ in their impact on the various types of economy. The 1930s slump led to a greater fall in the prices of basic commodities than of manufactured goods so that the balance of payments position deteriorated most in those countries which relied on raw materials for the basis of their exports. Similarly the oil price rises of the 1970s had several different impacts. The main *oil producers* themselves saw a marked improvement in the current account and were able to use these surpluses to invest in the international financial markets and so run a deficit on capital account. For *non-oil-producing industrial nations* the consequences were less beneficial as the higher price of oil and oil-based products raised the prices of necessary imports. This in turn pushed up the costs of domestically-produced manufactured goods and reduced export competitiveness. Thus the current account suffered as import payments rose and export earnings were hit, both by the rise in export prices and by the general world recession induced by the rise in oil prices. The situation was even worse, however, for the *non-oil-producing developing countries*. Many of these already suffered from a weak current account position and the situation deteriorated further with a rise in the price of essential imports. Unable to push up their export earnings, these countries had no choice but to offset the deficit on current account with an improvement on capital account, either by borrowing on the euro-currency markets or by seeking aid from richer nations (see Ch. 7).

The UK balance of payments

The structure of the UK balance of payments followed the evolutionary path outlined above from developing country to mature creditor nation during the nineteenth century. At the beginning of the twentieth century the visible trade balance was usually in deficit but this was countered by the large invisible trade surplus earned by the substantial British interests built up overseas during the previous century. However, these interests were depleted as they were sold off to help finance both world wars and this severely weakened the ability of the invisible trade balance to subsidise a deficit on the visible balance. In consequence, the post-1945 economy required a greater contribution from the manufacturing sector towards the maintenance of a healthy balance of payments. In practise, though manufacturing exports did rise steadily after 1945, they did so at much slower rate than the growth in the world trade of manufactured goods. Britain's disappointing performance in this respect was considered fully in Chapter 2 and it is only necessary to consider here the implications of this trend for the British balance of payments.

During the 1950s the current account was kept more or less in balance by a healthy surplus on invisible trade which was usually sufficient to make up the difference between visible earnings and payments. In the 1960s, however, Britain's over valued currency and higher than average inflation rate worked together to produce a growing deficit on visible trade which could not be met by invisible earnings. While the devaluation of 1967 and the floating of sterling in the 1970s ensured that the pound was not over-valued through much of the period after 1970, the long-term deterioration of the balance of payments continued due to the inability of the British manufacturing sector to hold its own export markets and to resist import penetration. A cycle of inefficiency, lack of competitiveness, low growth and low investment became established and proved difficult to change, especially in the face of growing and fierce competition from the newly industrialised nations. By 1983, Great Britain was importing more manufactured goods than she was exporting, a situation which had not occurred for 200 years. The principal reason why this deficit on manufactures did not result in a balance of payments crisis was that Britain was now a major oil producer herself and no longer had a massive oil import bill to finance.

Table 3.2 illustrates the principal structural changes in the British balance of payments in recent years, the most important being the impact of North Sea oil and the growing import penetration of manufacturers on the current account. One consequence of the rise in oil prices in 1973 was that all doubts concerning the profitability of exploiting North Sea oil were finally removed[1] and since the mid-1970s this sector has made a growing contribution to the balance of payments (see Table 3.3). Britain's accession to the ranks of the oil producers has not been without its problems, however. In 1979 the worldwide rise in oil prices made British oil that much more valuable and strengthened sterling on the foreign exchange markets, thereby reducing the competitiveness of British manufactured goods and increasing the dependence on oil for balance of payments equilibrium. Indeed, by acting as a buffer against the reality of a declining industrial economy, North Sea oil has delayed the necessity of finding a solution to Britain's poor export performance and the growth in imports of manufacturers. By the time the oil finally runs out, the manufacturing sector may be in irreversible decline unless a greater proportion of the wealth now brought in by oil is channelled into investment in industries with future growth potential.

Table 3.2 UK balance of payments 1970–84 (£m)

	1970	1974	1979	1985
Current account				
Exports	8,121	16,538	40,686	78,072
Imports	8,163	21,773	44,135	80,140
Visible trade balance	−42	−5,235	−3,449	−2,068
Of which: Oil exports	180	711	4,157	16,050
Oil imports	930	4,550	5,228	7,887
Oil balance	−750	−3,839	−1,071	+8,163
Invisible items (net)				
Services	+453	+946	+4,155	+6,291
Interest, profits and dividends	+559	+1,423	+1,034	+2,294
transfers	−194	−441	−2,265	−3,565
Invisible trade balance	+818	+1,928	+2,924	+5,020
Curent account balance	+776	−3,307	−525	+2,952
Investment and other capital flows	+546	+1,606	+1,834	−2,860
Balancing item	−35	+130	+401	+835
Balance for official financing	+1,287	−1,571	+1,710	+927
Allocation of SDRs	+171	—	+195	—
Gold subscription to IMF	−38	—	—	—
Official financing				
Net transactions with overseas monetary authorities (IMF etc.)	−1,295	—	+596	—
Foreign currency borrowing	—	+1,626	−1,442	+831
Additions to reserves (− = increase; + = decrease)	−125	−105	−1,059	−1,758
Total official financing	−1,420	+1,571	−1,905	−927

Source: CSO Economic Trends; 1986 *Annual Abstract of Statistics* 1981

Table 3.3 North Sea oil and gas and UK balance of payments
(£,bn)

	1973–76	1977	1978	1979	1980	1981	1982	1983
Value of sales	+1.5	+2.5	+3.2	+6.2	+9.5	+13.2	+15.4	+18.1
Less imports of goods	−1.1	−0.5	−0.2	−0.2	−0.1	−0.4	−0.5	−0.4
Less net imports of services	−1.4	−0.7	−0.5	−0.4	−0.5	−0.5	−0.7	−0.7
Less IPD due abroad	−0.1	−0.6	−0.7	−1.4	−2.2	−2.4	−2.6	−3.0
'Impact on current account'	−1.1	+0.7	+1.8	+4.2	+6.7	+9.9	+11.6	+14.0
Plus overseas investment in UK CONTINENTAL SHELF	+2.4	+1.5	+0.8	+0.7	+0.8	+1.6	+1.0	+0.5
'Impact on balance of payments'	+1.3	+2.2	+2.6	+4.9	+7.5	+11.5	+12.6	+14.5

Source: Barclays Review, Nov. 1984

Balance of payments disequilibrium

The balance of payments always balances in that disequilibrium on
the current account and capital account will be compensated by
official financing. As an accounting identity the balance of
payments will, in this sense, always balance. However, a country
is said to be in fundamental equilibrium when autonomous income
and expenditure balance out over a given period *without* the need
for import restrictions and *without* resulting in excessive unemployment. Over a number of years a country which alternates
between small deficits and small surpluses is approaching this ideal
condition. Unfortunately, most countries tend to a condition of
fundamental disequilibrium with long periods of permanent
surplus or deficit. There are three main causes of fundamental
disequilibrium – a deficient or excessive level of domestic demand,
a very adverse or highly favourable competitive position, and an
excess of capital movements.

1. The level of domestic demand. If domestic expenditure is greater than domestic output, then the balance of payments will be in deficit. In the case of developing countries this is an acceptable part of the industrialisation and development process referred to above. However, even in these countries, where the excessive demand results in inflation the situation may be less acceptable.

2. The level of competitiveness. Where one country has a higher rate of inflation than that of its competitors, that country will suffer a deterioration in its competitiveness. This higher rate of inflation could be caused by one, or a combination of, factors such as lower productivity, a lower growth rate, the existence of cost-push pressures and a higher level of demand-pull inflation. The experience of the British balance of payments points to such factors interacting with each other to exaggerate the loss of competitiveness and to delay economic recovery.

3. Excess capital movements. Speculative movements of short-term capital to, or from, the country may lead to a substantial surplus or deficit on capital account. These movements usually reflect current or anticipated economic events and may themselves bring about such events. In 1967, for example, Britain's current account deficit led to fears of devaluation and a flight of foreign capital from the country. This made the deficit still worse, brought about a sterling crisis and precipitated the very devaluation that had been feared.

Rectifying a fundamental disequilibrium

Before proceeding to examine the various options open to a government seeking to deal with a balance of payments problem, a brief reference to the balance of payments in the context of government economic objectives as a whole might be useful.

In Chapter 1 mention was made of Mercantilism and its belief in a direct relationship between economic well-being and the size of the balance of payments surplus. Modern economic theory and practice requires that the government seek to maintain balance of payments equilibrium while at the same time promoting a national income level capable of supporting full employment without an excessive rate of inflation. The external and internal positions are closely related, because of the part played by international trade in the determination of national income. In theory a balance of payments surplus will promote economic growth through the foreign trade multiplier, at least up to the point where full employment is attained. On the other hand, a surplus can be detrimental to living standards if *too much* of what is being produced is being diverted abroad. Similarly a deficit may exert downward pressure on national income where imports are crowding out domestically-produced goods. However, in the developing countries, imports may be the only way of supplying essential consumer goods or the capital equipment necessary for industrialisation. The measures adopted to deal with a balance of payments disequilibrium must therefore be related to the *causes* of that disequilibrium, with due regard being given to the country's internal economic situation.

A deficit

A chronic deficit on the balance of payments, unless it be for purposes of economic development, has a deflationary effect on the domestic economy. With the downward foreign trade multiplier operating, a threat is posed to such government objectives as full employment, economic growth and rising living standards. The only advantages for an industrialised nation are that the deficit may help to counter demand-pull inflationary pressures by increasing the supply of goods and services available to the home market. It may also enable the country to enjoy an artificially high standard of living through consuming more goods and services than it produces. In any case such advantages as do arise from a deficit will be shortlived since the deficit cannot be maintained indefinitely. The deficit must be financed either by running down the country's gold and foreign currency reserves or by borrowing from international organisations and other countries. If the deficit persists, both the reserves and international confidence will be exhausted. Steps must therefore be taken to deal with a deficit, and the measures available are of three types.

(a) Direct controls
These consist of those policies involving government limitations on imports or on the movement of foreign currency. These include tariffs, quotas, restrictions on overseas investment, exchange control regulations, travel restrictions and import deposits. The operation of these measures is examined in Chapter 2 and we are concerned here only with their effectiveness in dealing with a deficit. As such, they are crude instruments since they do not tackle the underlying causes of a deficit but aim artificially to close the gap between exports and imports. They are also potentially

dangerous since they invite retaliation and may lead to a trade recession similar to that of the 1930s when the industrialised nations adopted protectionist measures in an effort to maintain demand for their depressed domestic industries. The use of direct controls is thus severely limited, particularly as they are contrary to such international agreements as the General Agreement on Tariffs and Trade (GATT) and to commitments undertaken when joining the European Economic Community (EEC) and similar associations. As an alternative to controlling imports, the government may seek to encourage exports through tax incentives, cheap export credit and other services to exporters. Most countries use these measures to some extent, often going so far as to grant cash subsidies to exporting firms.

(b) Deflationary measures

A principal cause of balance of payments deficits is a lack of competitiveness, so that imported goods are cheaper than home-produced ones while exports are unable to compete with the goods of other exporting nations. Such a situation occurs when the inflation rate is appreciably higher than that of other countries, so that the exchange rate is out of line with the real value of the domestic currency. A very high rate of inflation may be the consequence of an inflationary gap, so that the excess demand for goods and services at the full employment level pushes up prices and sucks in imports. In these circumstances the government could adopt fiscal and monetary measures to close the inflationary gap. This would have the effect of encouraging exports and discouraging imports.

Monetary measures can be used to control demand by restricting the availability of credit. In so doing such measures will help the current account of the balance of payments in two ways – firstly, the reduced demand for goods generally will affect import demand, and secondly, the reduced demand for domestically-produced goods may encourage firms to seek out overseas markets.

Since tighter controls on credit inevitably involve higher interest rates, the capital account will also benefit as capital flows are attracted into the country by the higher returns available.

Fiscal measures, too, can reduce demand by cutting government expenditure and increasing taxation. Fiscal measures have the advantage that they can be applied selectively, such as cuts in government expenditure overseas or higher taxation of goods which are mainly produced overseas. Unfortunately, such measures may have unwelcome side-effects because of the imperfections of the economic system. For example, before the inflationary gap is completely closed and the balance of payments brought into equilibrium, unemployment may rise and economic growth slow down. Furthermore, fiscal measures are unlikely to help the situation when the high inflation rate is due to cost-push pressures like rising fuel or labour costs. Indeed, they may actually make the situation worse by provoking higher wage claims from workers anxious to protect their living standards in the face of higher taxation and cuts in government services. In these circumstances, direct control of prices and incomes might be more appropriate than either fiscal or monetary measures.

(c) Devaluation

This is the deliberate downward alteration of the value of the currency in terms of other currencies from one fixed parity to another. It is therefore a policy option only when a system of fixed exchange rates is in operation. During periods when a system of floating exchange rates prevails the authorities may choose, however, to allow the exchange rate to float down or to depreciate unhindered, or they may even encourage this depreciation. The effect of devaluation or depreciation is to make imports dearer and exports cheaper and, at first sight, this should benefit the balance of payments. To take a simple example, the prices of goods wholly produced in the UK and the USA would have changed after the 1967 devaluation of sterling as in Table 3.4.

While devaluation will make the country's goods more price competitive, the effect on the volume of trade and thus on the balance of payments is not immediately clear. Many potential export goods will not fall in price by as much as the nominal devaluation, notably those produced domestically but made from imported raw materials which now cost more. In the 1967 sterling devaluation, British exports fell in price by only about 7 per cent after a nominal devaluation of 14.3 per cent. Even where devaluation has made the country's goods more competitive, exporters

Table 3.4 Effect of 1967 devaluation

Before devaluation ($£ = \$2.80$)	*After devaluation* ($£ = \$2.40$)
British good priced at £100 = $280	British good priced at £100 = $240
US good priced at $280 = £100	US good priced at $280 = £117

must have sufficient capacity to be able to expand output and to take advantage of the lower prices. All that can be stated for certain is that the terms of trade have deteriorated, so that if there were no change in the volume of trade, export earnings would fall and the national import bill rise. The success of devaluation depends, therefore, on the demand elasticity of exports and imports and the supply elasticity of exports.

Price elasticity of demand refers to the responsiveness of demand to a change in price and is customarily measured mathematically by comparing the proportionate change in the quantity demanded to the proportionate change in price. Thus if the price of a commodity falls by 10 per cent and the quantity demanded rises in consequence by 20 per cent, the price elasticity of demand is 2. If, however, the quantity demanded rose by only 5 per cent after a similar fall in price, price elasticity of demand would be $\frac{1}{2}$. Alfred Marshall[2] was the first economist to illustrate that devaluation has a favourable effect on the balance of payments *if* the sum of the elasticity of domestic demand for imports and the elasticity of foreign demand for exports is greater than unity. Suppose that the elasticity of demand for a country's exports is zero so that a cut in prices has no effect on the overseas demand for that country's goods. The effect of devaluation will be to leave export earnings, measured in local currency, unchanged. If the sum of elasticities is greater than one, the elasticity of demand for imports must be greater than one so that devaluation and higher import prices will lead to the value of imports, measured in local currency, falling, and an improved balance of payments. The effect measured in foreign currency would be that while foreign currency earnings fell by the same percentage as the devaluation, foreign currency payments for imports would fall by more than the percentage devaluation. A few simple examples are shown in Table 3.5.

From Table 3.5 it can be seen that in each case where the combined elasticities of exports and imports exceed unity, the country has improved its balance of trade by devaluing. Only in the last example, where the sum of the elasticities is less than one, does the balance of trade deteriorate.[3] Clearly the greater the sum of the demand elasticities for exports and imports the greater will be the improvement in the balance of trade. Where the balance of payments deficit is very large, or the sum of elasticities barely above one, the percentage devaluation required to deal with the problem will be very high indeed – in only one of the examples shown in Table 3.5 has the deficit of 100 actually been eliminated.

The nature of a country's exports and imports will largely deter-

Table 3.5 The impact of a 20 per cent devaluation with selected elasticities based on initial export value of 400 and import value of 500

Demand elasticity		Post-devaluation (local currency)		Post-devaluation (foreign currency)	
Exports	Imports	Export value	Import value	Export value	Import value
2	0	560	600	448	500
0	2	400	360	320	300
$\frac{1}{2}$	1	440	480	352	400
1	$\frac{1}{4}$	480	570	384	475
$\frac{3}{4}$	$\frac{3}{4}$	460	510	368	425
$\frac{1}{3}$	$\frac{1}{3}$	427	560	341	467

mine the demand elasticity for them. Generally, the demand for services is more elastic than that for manufactures, and the demand for manufactures is more elastic than that for raw materials and foodstuffs. Thus a country like Saudi Arabia would find that devaluation led to a loss in earnings from exports because of the inelastic demand for oil, and a rise in value of imports because most of these are also inelastic in demand. For a country like Britain, however, devaluation offers potential gains from increased sales of exported manufactures, though devaluation in 1967 also led to a rise in import expenditure on essential imports. Even where demand elasticities are favourable for exporters, the *supply* of goods within the country must be sufficiently elastic to enable the country to capitalise on the increased competitiveness arising from devaluation. Since elasticity of supply is greater in the long run than in the short run, there is normally a time lag between devaluation and a full response to the new environment by exporters. This time lag is often called the 'J' curve effect, and may average around 18 months for many countries.

The effects of devaluation on the economy

The immediate effect of devaluation, whatever the eventual impact on the balance of payments, is to cause a deterioration in the terms of trade (see pp. 13–17). This in turn means that the country must export more just to earn the same amount of foreign currency as before, while essential imports will now cost more in local currency. Living standards must therefore drop, at least in the short run, until domestic income is boosted via higher export demand. It is vital during this early post-devaluation period to resist the pressure for higher incomes to offset the fall in living standards, otherwise cost-push inflation will erode the benefits of devaluation. Accordingly it is customary to support devaluation with either a package of deflationary measures or with some form of prices and incomes policy. The other danger to an effective devaluation is that if export supply elasticity is low, exporters may let their prices creep up, so increasing profits rather than trying to boost output.[4]

Whether or not devaluation succeeds in curing the country's balance of payments difficulties there will, unless export elasticity of demand is zero, be increased demand for the country's exports, so that total national output will rise. The extent of the growth in output, and thus of national income, will depend on the size of price elasticity of demand and the size of the foreign trade multiplier. The greater the magnitude of each of these, the greater the eventual increase in national output. Clearly higher exports of goods produced wholly within the country will benefit the economy more than higher sales of goods merely assembled in the country from parts imported from abroad.

A surplus

It might be asked why a country should worry about having a permanent surplus on the balance of payments, since the government need take no action either to protect the exchange rate or to protect domestic producers from damaging import penetration. Indeed, a surplus appears to be highly desirable, leading as it does to a net injection into the circular flow of national income and consequently higher output and employment opportunities. In fact, a situation of chronic surpluses poses three problems:

1. Internally, a surplus means that the domestic population is *not* able to purchase the goods and services its income would support. While there is a consequent stimulus to industrial and commercial expansion, there is a likelihood that, in the short term at least, the economy will experience demand-pull inflationary pressures, especially if there is already full employment.
2. Externally, a series of surpluses results in the country building up large reserves of gold and foreign currency holdings at the

expense of those deficit countries who find their reserves dwindling. Ultimately these deficit countries will be unable to maintain current demand levels as they resort to deflationary measures or devaluation to try to restore equilibrium on the balance of payments. There is thus a threat to world trade stability which could harm the surplus country should there be an increase in trade barriers. To offset a large surplus, the country could export capital in the form of loans to deficit countries (see also Chs. 6 and 7) but in the long run such investment will create its own problems as interest earnings create a growing surplus on the invisibles balance.

3. In a regime of floating exchange rates (see pp. 69–78) a persistent surplus will cause the exchange rate to rise progressively, making exports dearer and imports cheaper.

The cures for a surplus are the reverse of those appropriate to a deficit. The government could relax import controls or introduce fiscal and monetary policies aimed at expanding demand and raising living standards. The result should be that imports rise, exports fall and, with lower interest rates, capital flows out of the country. Where the currency is clearly over-valued and there is a fixed exchange rate system (see pp. 73–78), there may be no alternative but to revalue the currency by altering its value upwards against other currencies.[5] Unfortunately, surpluses have proved as stubborn as deficits in resisting removal. This is due to the fact that nothing breeds success like success. When a country has a permanent surplus, the government can pursue policies aimed at growth without fear of their effect on the external position, so that investment, productivity and incomes are all stimulated to rise. Measures such as revaluation lower the prices of imports, reduce inflationary pressures and raise living standards, making it even more likely that the economic environment will be favourable to increased economic efficiency and a healthy balance of payments.

Notes

1. Though these would return if world oil prices fell to their true market level.
2. A. Marshall, *Money, Credit and Commerce*, Macmillan, 1923.
3. In such circumstances, revaluation would be the appropriate response.
4. Devaluation is thus only able to provide a breathing space for industry to solve its lack of competitiveness.

5. Revaluation will only assist matters when the sum of the elasticities of demand for exports and imports exceeds unity.

Examination questions

The following questions are taken from the examination papers of various examining bodies which include the areas covered by this chapter in their syllabuses. Those marked with an asterisk (★) are representative of the main types of question asked and specimen answers to these will be found in Part II.

1.★ What do you understand by the 'invisibles' section of a country's balance of payments account? Assess the importance of and recent influences on the invisible account of the United Kingdom or any other country with which you are familiar. (IOB 2A, September 1982)

2. What effects does a fall in the domestic rate of interest have on a country's balance of payments? (ICSA Part III, December 1984)

3. Outline the effects on the UK balance of payments (both current and capital accounts) of:
   (a) the development and production of North Sea oil;
   (b) the abolition of exchange control in 1979 (IOB 2A, April 1985)

4.★ What are the various parts which make up the balance of payments? In what sense must a country's international receipts and payments always balance? (Cert. Marketing, November 1983)

5. Discuss in detail the effects of a rise in a country's exchange rate on its balance of payments. (IOB 2A, September 1984)

6. Is a deficit on a country's visible trade account necessarily of concern to its government? Discuss the ways in which a deficit may be corrected. (IOB 2A, April 1982)

7.★ Explain the various methods a government might employ to deal with an adverse balance of payments, commenting on the relative advantages and disadvantages of each method. (LCCI Higher, Autumn 1984)

8. (a) Distinguish between a balance of current accounts and a balance of payments.
   (b) How would you correct a deficit in the balance of payments accounts? (West African 'A', Paper 1, June 1984)

9. In what ways can a deficit on the current account of a country's balance of payments be:
   (a) financed;
   (b) rectified? (IOB 2A, September 1983)

10. Compare and contrast the effects of tariffs and exchange rate depreciation as a means of correcting a balance of payments deficit. (ICSA Part I, June 1981)

11.★ In what circumstances is a fall in the exchange rate most likely to be effective in reducing the deficit on current account? (ICMA Professional Stage, November 1981)

12. Argue for or against devaluation of your country's currency. (West African 'A', Paper 2, June 1984)

Chapter Four
Exchange rates

The term 'international liquidity' can be defined as the means available to the authorities to settle imbalances in international debt. An
adequate supply of liquidity is essential for the development of
world trade and the conduct of the international finance system.
Ideally, this supply would be provided by an international
currency, just as domestic currencies provide the liquidity whereby
payments are settled within countries. Unfortunately there is no
such international currency enjoying the confidence of all trading
nations, so that world liquidity is subject to a number of recurring
problems:

1. The absence of an international currency capable of growing
    at a rate compatible with the needs of world trade results in
    acute shortages of world liquidity at times (Ch. 7). Such a
    shortage of liquid funds has led many countries to resort to
    barter trade as a means of paying for essential imports (Ch. 4).
    It has also led to the establishment of a range of institutions
    and practices aimed at providing more international liquidity
    (Ch. 5).
2. The absence of a single international currency means that the
    domestic currency must frequently be exchanged into other
    currencies acceptable to the exporting country. The 'price' at
    which such exchange takes place will clearly play an important
    part in the prospects for trade. We must therefore consider
    carefully the alternative types of exchange rate system (Ch. 4).
3. The lack of acceptability of some currencies has left many of
    the developing countries deep in debt due to their lack of such
    'harder' currencies.

Barter or counter trade
Barter trade has survived, and even thrived, in international trade

to a much greater extent than it has in domestic trade. The resilience of barter trade is due both to the lack of a universal medium of exchange and to wide variations in the conduct of trade by the various countries of the world. The decision by the Soviet Union to make its currency inconvertible soon after the Russian revolution, and the general shortage of western currency in all the Eastern bloc countries, ensured that these countries would be the backbone of modern barter trade, generally exchanging surplus supplies of raw materials and consumer goods in return for capital goods produced in the West. As a result, many British firms became used to being paid in Hungarian aspirin or Bulgarian jam, especially when the government agency dealing with them suddenly found it had run out of foreign currency and had no choice but to pay in kind. The criticism of barter trade in these circumstances is that it is a means by which one country is able to obtain the goods it needs by insisting on the supplier taking in exchange goods he may or may not want. It has led to the growth of a number of specialist organisations who take over payments in goods and re-export them to other parts of the world. In effect, these organisations are taking over the exporting function of the country indulging in barter trade.

The real growth in this counter trade in recent years has come from the developing countries who have fallen deep into debt and have sought alternatives to paying for vital imports in cash. A number of South American countries became involved in this practice in the 1970s, especially Brazil and Colombia where staple crops can provide surpluses available for export. The practice has now spread to the Far East, where Indonesia insists that major government contracts be accompanied by counter trade deals, while Malaysia has hinted that it may follow the same line. The extent of counter trade is difficult to estimate because of the lack of precise information and guesses vary between 5 and 40 per cent of total world trade. It is certainly on the increase and a number of major banks have established special departments to deal with this business. Similarly, a number of large industrial companies such as ICI, Rolls Royce Aeroengines and Massey Ferguson have special counter trading departments. This growth has come despite the potential disasters awaiting companies who indulge in this type of trading, should they be left with unwanted tons of cooked meat or be unable to realise the expected value of hundreds of gallons of strawberry jam!

The willingness of many companies in the developed world to persevere with counter trading stems from the prolonged recession of the 1970s and 1980s, and the associated difficulty of securing hard cash orders in a buyer's market. Yet while counter trading may offer a short-term answer to a half-empty order book, this practice is fraught with dangers for the efficiency and the conduct of world trade:

1. The likelihood of there being a double coincidence of wants is small; there cannot be many industrial companies actually wanting two tons of cocoa, for example.
2. The goods used by developing countries to pay for imports become themselves a medium of exchange, with the recipient of the goods forced into complicated transactions to unload them. Counter trading may therefore require far more organisation than conventional trade and be more expensive to operate in consequence.
3. Barter trade may not only be more expensive as a trading method, but may also impose conditions on trade, in this way acting as an impediment to the free movement of goods and services. Both GATT and OECD have expressed concern that counter trading could grow into a barrier against free trade.

Exchange rates

A principal feature of barter trading is the difficulty of arriving at a rate of exchange between the two goods being traded. The rate arrived at must be acceptable to both parties involved, otherwise trade will not take place. However, since there will always be several rates of exchange that are acceptable, the one chosen will to a large extent reflect the supply and demand conditions of the products concerned. The alternative to barter trading is the use of a medium of exchange to effect payments. Ideally, a world currency could perform this function between countries just as the local currency acts as a medium of exchange within countries. In the absence of such a world currency, payment must be made for trade in a currency acceptable to both parties and again the question of a rate of exchange arises. Suppose, for example, that the exporter is paid in the currency of the importer. He may then wish to convert this payment into his own currency. To do so he will need to know the precise exchange rate so that the foreign currency payment will convert into his required domestic currency payment. Exchange rates can be determined either by market forces, as with any other commodity, with varying degrees of governmental intervention, or by reference to an external standard, such as gold.

Fixed and floating exchange rates

Where exchange rates are determined by market forces, the attitude of the monetary authorities is of vital significance. If the monetary authorities permit the exchange rate of the country's currency to find its own level, and refrain from intervening to influence that rate, the exchange rate is said to be *floating*. Where the authorities choose to intervene to prevent the exchange rate from fluctuating violently or from moving too rapidly in one direction, a system of *managed floating* is said to operate. If the authorities intervene to counter market forces entirely, thereby maintaining a stable exchange rate (with perhaps relatively small fluctuations around the maintained rate), then a *fixed exchange rate* is said to be in operation. Whether the exchange rate is freely floating or is manipulated to a greater or lesser extent by the monetary authorities, it is still subject to the same forces of supply and demand and no fixed rate is sustainable over a long period if market forces consistently point to that rate being substantially over- or under-valued.

Factors influencing exchange rates

Where the exchange rate is determined purely by market forces, the price of the domestic currency in terms of another (i.e. the exchange rate) is found by the intersection of the demand and supply curves for the domestic currency on the foreign exchange market. This can be illustrated by reference to the exchange rate of sterling against US dollars, as shown in Fig. 4.1.

In Fig. 4.1 the initial equilibrium exchange rate is at P_1 where the demand for sterling from holders of dollars and the supply of sterling from those wishing to obtain dollars are in equilibrium.

The demand for sterling consists of dollars exchanged for pounds by:

1. American importers of British goods and services.
2. American residents transferring capital funds to the United Kingdom.
3. British and other non-American holders of dollars converting their funds into sterling.

The supply of sterling consists of pounds exchanged for dollars by:

1. British importers of American goods and services.

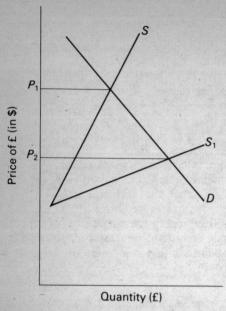

Fig. 4.1

2. British residents transferring capital funds to the United States.
3. Overseas holders of sterling converting their funds to dollars.

A complementary market for dollars priced in sterling also operates with the reverse demand and supply sources to those listed above. In addition there are foreign exchange rate markets for all the major currencies priced in all other currencies.

Any change in the demand or supply conditions operating in the market in question will result in a new equilibrium exchange rate. If, therefore, there was a substantial movement of capital funds from Britain to the United States, this would be shown in Fig. 4.1 as a shift in supply from S to S_1 and would lead to a fall in the value of sterling against the dollar from P_1 to P_2. At the same time, the market for dollars priced in sterling would show a shift in demand for dollars and raise the price of dollars against sterling. To take another example, a deficit in Britain's trade with the United States means that the supply of sterling from British importers will exceed the demand for sterling by American importers causing the price of sterling (in dollars) to fall.

We shall see below that it is often argued that balance of payments disequilibrium is unlikely to persist with a freely operating foreign exchange market. This is because the exchange rate will move to equate the demand and supply for the currency, thereby restoring balance of payments equilibrium. Thus if a country suffers from a deficit on the balance of payments, the exchange rate will fall until, with cheaper export prices and higher import prices, the deficit is eliminated. Similarly, a rise in the exchange rate will remove a balance of payments surplus.

So far it has been established tht exchange rates are determined by the forces of demand and supply operating in the market for a currency. It remains to be seen what factors cause demand and supply to change, e.g. why it is that demand for a currency for investment purposes, or to purchase goods, may change. The principal influences on the market for a currency and therefore on its exchange rate are as follows.

1. Relative price changes in the two countries in question. Where one country has a higher rate of inflation than another, its prices will rise faster than those in the other country and make its products less competitive. Other things being equal, this will result in a balance of payments deficit and downward pressure on the exchange rate.

2. Price elasticity of demand for a country's exports. Countries which export commodities which have a relatively inelastic demand enjoy strong economic bargaining power and are more likely to have a balance of payments surplus. This will be upward pressure on the exchange rate.

3. Interest rates. Short-term capital movements are highly responsive to changes in interest rates. Countries offering higher interest rates can be expected to attract foreign funds and to strengthen the exchange rate.

4. Economic factors within the country. Healthy economies breed confidence so that countries with strong reserves and a favourable balance of payments attract foreign funds, exerting upward pressure on the exchange rate. On the other hand, an economic crisis may result in funds leaving the country, thereby lowering the exchange rate.

5. Political events. Uncertainties about the political future may be expected to damage confidence, leading to capital movements out of the country and a lower exchange rate, especially if there is a danger of a government unsympathetic to foreign capital taking power.

6. Speculation. There is always some uncertainty concerning the future of the exchange rate and speculators may hope to gain by selling a currency in the expectation of its exchange rate falling. Such speculation has an element of self-fulfillment about it since if enough speculators act in the same way they are likely to be proved right.

All these factors are indicators of the likely trends in exchange rates. However, a serious attempt has been made to develop a theory to explain *exactly* what the exchange rate between two countries will be.

The purchasing power parity theory

In its modern form this theory was proposed by Gustav Cassel (1886–1944) and it argues that the exchange rate between two currencies is determined by the domestic value or purchasing-power parity of the two currencies. If, for example, a basket of goods is priced at £100 in the United Kingdom and DM 300 in West Germany, then the purchasing power parity rate of exchange is £1 = DM 3.

While the theory appears logical, it is too simplistic to provide a solid foundation for exchange rate determination. Suppose in the example given above £1 = DM 3, but that the items costing £100 in Britain can now be obtained in Germany for DM 280. The purchasing power parity theory predicts that Britons will now save money by buying German goods and that, as the British trade position deteriorates, sterling will fall against the deutschmark until £1 = DM 2.80, and stability is restored. In practice there are various impediments to trade between countries which enable purchasing powers of currencies to vary from those predicted by the exchange rate:

1. Transport costs and import duties. Thus British and European car companies are able to charge higher prices in Britain because of the difficulties experienced by British buyers in obtaining vehicles abroad and re-exporting them to Britain.
2. Differences of production and supply conditions. For instance, price levels in developed countries tend to be higher than those in developing countries, but the latter are unable to supply the requirements of developed countries with their present industrial output levels.
3. Currency problems. The fact that many currencies are inconvertible, notably those of Eastern Europe, means that there is little relationship between internal and external prices.

However, the theory does serve a purpose. It provides a first approximation of the appropriate exchange rate when normal international economic relations are resumed following upheavals, such as wars. Further, the theory does broadly indicate the changes that are necessary, either in the exchange rate or in the price levels, when inflation rates vary between countries.

Fixed exchange rates

The maintenance of fixed exchange rates involves active intervention by the monetary authorities, nationally or internationally, to prevent the full impact of market forces on the exchange rate. In theory, the authorities could intervene on a daily basis to maintain a *rigidly fixed* rate. In practice, the operation of fixed exchange rates during the quarter-century following the Second World War was restricted to ensuring that the exchange rate *would not deviate excessively* from a designated (par) rate of exchange.

In Fig. 4.2 the par rate of exchange of sterling against the dollar is £1 = $2.80. The exchange rate is allowed to fluctuate by up to

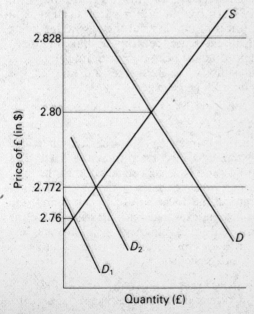

Fig. 4.2

1 per cent either side of this par rate, i.e. to an upper limit or 'peg' of $2.828 and to a lower peg of $2.772. Initially the equilibrium exchange rate is £1 = $2.80 so there is no need for government intervention. However, if there is a fall in demand for sterling and the demand curve shifts to the left (D_1) the equilibrium rate is now below the lower peg at $2.76. The Bank of England[1] would now intervene in the market to support sterling by buying pounds and selling dollars, so shifting demand to the right (D_2) and raising the equilibrium rate to $2.772. If, on the other hand, the pound threatened to break through its upper peg, the Bank of England would sell pounds, so shifting supply to the right and causing the equilibrium rate to fall.

We have already noted that there is a limit to the extent that a fixed exchange rate can be maintained. For instance, if a country runs a permanent balance of payments deficit, there will be a continual downward pressure on the exchange rate, and gold and foreign currency reserves will be depleted on two fronts: in financing the deficit and in supporting the currency. Eventually the monetary authorities will have no alternative but to devalue the currency to a rate sustainable by market forces. In the case of a strong currency, upward pressure on the exchange rate will strengthen the country's reserves and prompt revaluation as a means of reducing the prices of imports and thereby raising living standards. The principal difference between floating and fixed exchange rates in terms of adjustment is that floating rates can change steadily and smoothly while fixed rates are adjusted less frequently but by much larger percentages.

Fixed versus floating rates

Historically the international monetary system has alternated between fixed and floating exchange rates from the fixed rates operating under the various forms of gold standard until the early 1930s, through the floating exchange rates of the 1930s and early 1940s, on to the fixed rates of the dollar-based post-war period, and finally to the system of floating exchange rates prevailing since the early 1970s. Both fixed and floating rates have their advocates and any comparison of the two systems necessarily requires an examination of the merits of each system.

Advantages of floating exchange rates

The main arguments in favour of floating exchange rates centre around the greater freedom such a system gives to the working of economic forces and to the operation of government policy.

1. They automatically restore equilibrium on the balance of payments. Where a freely floating exchange rate is in operation, the balance for official financing should, by implication, be zero. Any deficit on *current account* will push the exchange rate down and make investment in the country more attractive, thereby creating a surplus on *capital accout*. Thus a drop in exports will reduce demand for the country's currency and so lower the price of that currency. This in turn will enable foreign investors to buy more financial assets in that currency for the same expenditure of their own currency and lead to an increase in capital flows into the country. A surplus will have the opposite effect, so that in both cases the position on capital account should cancel out the current account balance.

In addition, the *current account* will, to some extent, be self-adjusting; a deficit leads, through the lower exchange rate, to an increase in demand for the country's (cheaper) exports and a fall in demand for its (dearer) imports. Clearly price elasticity for export and import demand are important in determining the precise effect. In fact, for the current account to improve, it is *necessary* that the Marshall–Lerner elasticity condition holds, i.e. that the price elasticity of demand for exports plus the price elasticity of demand for imports together be greater than one. If the condition is *not* fulfilled, then a lower exchange rate will cause the current account to fall further into deficit.

2. They eliminate the need for large holdings of official reserves. Because the balance of payments is self-adjusting, countries need not maintain reserves at a level so high that they can cope with a prolonged period of deficit. At the same time the absence of permanent surpluses in a group of countries ensures a more even spread of world liquidity, rather than the accumulation of large unused reserves in a small group of surplus countries. The need for reserves is further reduced by the fact that central banks are no longer required to support their currencies on the foreign exchange markets.

3. They remove external constraints from government economic policy. This follows from the two preceding advantages. Since the exchange rate operates to maintain balance of payments equilibrium, the government has no need to adopt measures to cure a deficit such as prolonged deflation of domestic demand or exchange control. In consequence, fiscal and monetary policies can be suited to the needs of the domestic economic situation with less fear of the external repercussions.

4. The exchange rate changes smoothly. Natural movements in the rate, either up or down, prevent the exchange rate from getting out of line with its true market value. This helps avoid large devaluations or revaluations of the currency and the upheavals these bring, both internally and externally.

5. They may reduce speculation. These natural movements should also help reduce speculation on the foreign exchange market, and the instability so caused. This follows from the fact that under the fixed par value system it becomes obvious in which direction, if any, a country must change its exchange rate. A deficit country can only lower its exchange rate, or resist any change at all. A speculator moving out of the currency will therefore either win, or not lose. He could only lose if the change is opposite to that anticipated[2]. With a floating system the exchange rate *can* move by small amounts in *all* directions so that a loss becomes possible.

The arguments against floating exchange rates stem from the greater uncertainties attached to international trade by less stable currency values.

1. They increase uncertainty. Because trade contracts often take a long time to complete, exporters and importers alike wish to be able to predict future currency values. With floating rates, such predictability is lost and recourse must be made to the forward exchange market. Although this market enables traders to know for certain the rate they will receive for their own, or another currency, it is costly to use and cannot eliminate entirely *long-term* uncertainty.

2. They hinder the attainment of price stability. If exchange rates are unstable, import prices and consequently domestic costs are also prone to fluctuation. In particular, a downward floating exchange rate will make imports more expensive and this will increase the inflationary pressures operating within the economy.

3. They may increase speculation. One advantage of floating exchange rates is that a massive overnight change in the rate is highly unlikely. This might be expected to deter speculators from putting pressure on a currency since they have no hope of making the large instant gains identified with devaluation or revaluation. On the other hand, the absence of a lower limit, below which the rate will not be permitted to fall, may allow a decline in the exchange rate to gain momentum as speculators and investors alike withdraw their funds. This may cause a draining of confidence and result in the rate falling still further. Indeed, recent evidence points to the fact that floating rates can move substantially over a very short time period, as in the case of sterling in 1976/7 and 1984/5.

Advantages of fixed exchange rates
The principal claim made for fixed exchange rates is that they promote stability in the international financial system, leading to a number of advantages.

1. *They promote the expansion of world trade.*   Fixed exchange rates enable traders to predict with greater certainty both prices and profits. They therefore contribute to an atmosphere in which foreign trade is encouraged.

2. *They promote stability in the international capital markets.*   Since capital may safely be left in overseas financial centres with reasonable confidence as to its future value, investors are more likely to consider making overseas loans. At the same time, speculators are able to make only limited gains from exchange dealings unless they are able, by concerted action, to engineer a major devaluation or revaluation[3].

3. *They impose discipline on government economic policy.*   In order to avoid excessive strain on the exchange rate, governments must ensure that their economic policies do not lead to high rates of inflation or to severe balance of payments disequilibrium.

Disadvantages of fixed exchange rates
Unfortunately the maintenance of a fixed exchange rate does impose severe restraints on the freedom of action of governments, with potentially harmful consequences for the domestic economy.

1. *Large official reserves are required.*   The monetary authorities are required to intervene regularly to maintain the exchange rate within its permitted range of adjustment from par. When the rate is experiencing downward pressure, this will involve using large quantities of foreign currency to support the rate. Large reserves are also required to finance balance of payments deficits, which may be a persistent feature of the economy when the exchange rate is fixed.

2. Exchange rates are misaligned. There is a tendency for exchange rates to move seriously out of alignment over a long period and the major devaluations and revaluations which follow can themselves operate to destabilise the international trading system.

3. Economic policy is dictated by external pressures. Where the exchange rate is under pressure, the government is forced to adopt measures to restore confidence in the currency. Thus instead of policies designed to promote economic growth and full employment they are forced to adopt deflationary measures to assist the balance of payments and to support the exchange rate. This was a familiar problem for successive British governments throughout the 1950s and 1960s when a series of sterling crises necessitated frequent changes in economic policy, leading to the familiar 'stop–go' cycle.

When considering the relative merits of floating and fixed exchange rates it is apparent that the advantages of the former tend to be the disadvantages of the latter and vice versa. In practice, the fixed exchange rate system which prevailed for a quarter-century after 1945 sought to obtain some of the flexibility of floating rates by allowing rates to deviate from the par rate between the limits imposed by the upper and lower pegs. Similarly, most governments are today reluctant to allow the currency to float without some intervention for fear that a violent movement in the rate should have undesirable consequences for the internal economy. They also have to be aware of the effect of internal policies on the exchange rate since events in the exchange market could have severe repercussions for domestic policy. If, for example, the government is seeking to promote growth and higher living standards through stimulating demand, any resultant inflationary pressures may lead to a fall in the exchange rate, raising the cost of imports and thereby giving a further twist to inflation. Most governments have therefore tended to operate a system of managed or 'dirty' floating whereby the exchange rate is theoretically free to float but where the government intervenes to prevent too drastic a movement, especially if it feels that the rate is being driven too far out of line with its 'natural' rate.

The gold standard

The alternative to exchange rates linked to market forces or being fixed by government action is to link the exchange rate to some external standard. Historically, the most important of these has been the gold standard. Under the gold standard a country keeps the value of its monetary unit equal to the value of a defined weight of gold. By an Act of Parliament of 1870, £1 (sovereign) weighed 123.27447 grains troy, made up of eleven parts of gold to one of base metal. This relationship between the currency and gold was fixed, so that the price of one ounce of gold was £3.17.10½ (£3.89). A free market in gold operated with gold coins in circulation and bank notes exchangeable on demand for gold.

Great Britain was on the full gold standard outlined above from the early eighteenth century until 1914, except for the period during and just after the Napoleonic Wars from 1797 until 1821. Only in the last quarter of the nineteenth century, however, did most of the major European countries embrace the gold standard; this period was the great era of the gold standard. When two currencies are on the gold standard, the exchange rate between them is based on the relative gold content of each currency. Thus the exchange rate of £1 = \$4.6867 meant that the gold sovereign weighed 4.6867 times the weight of a gold dollar. Exchange rates will not vary by more than the cost of shipping gold from one country to another, otherwise arbitrage gains could be made from buying a weak currency and converting it first into gold and then into a strong currency.

The gold points
If a British importer owed money to a New York company, he must either exchange sterling for dollars on the foreign exchange market or buy gold from the Bank of England and ship it to New York. Assuming that he chooses whichever is cheaper, the exchange rate of the dollar against sterling cannot rise beyond the point where obtaining dollars is more expensive than buying gold and paying to ship it to the United States. Since the cost of transporting gold is relatively low, the rate of exchange between currencies on the gold standard can move only between narrow limits. These limits are known as the *gold points*. The point at which it becomes cheaper for British importers to ship gold to the United States is the *gold export point* for London and the *gold import point* for New York. When it becomes cheaper for American importers to ship gold to Britain, the *gold export point* for New York and the *gold import point* for London have been reached. When the exchange rate between sterling and the dollar stands at one of these gold points, gold will move in the appropriate direction until equilibrium is restored. Similar gold points would serve to limit the movement of exchange rates between all gold standard countries.

The operation of the gold points ensures that exchange rates move only within narrow limits around the so-called 'mint par of exchange' – the rate based on the gold content of the two currencies. However, if the exchange rate of one currency falls against other currencies on the gold standard to the point where gold is consistently flowing out of the country, the government may eventually have no alternative but to devalue the currency against gold.

The gold standard and the internal economy

When a country is on the gold standard, adequate reserves of gold must be maintained to cover *bank-notes* in circulation so that the money supply would be directly related to the country's level of gold reserves. *Bank deposits* would also be limited by the stock of gold, since banks would be subject to liquidity requirements and if the gold stock were running down the central bank would adopt deflationary measures to reduce bank deposits. An inflow of gold, on the other hand, would lead to expansionary monetary measures being adopted. In both cases, monetary policy is directly related to the external position irrespective of the state of the domestic economy.

The gold standard and the balance of payments

In theory the gold standard operates to ensure that the balance of payments always returns to equilibrium. When a country suffers a *deficit*, gold reserves fall and this leads the central bank to adopt deflationary monetary measures to reduce credit and the level of bank deposits. Such policies will lead to deflation, reducing demand for both home-produced and imported goods. As a result, prices will fall and with them the rewards offered to factors of production in the form of wages, interest and rent. Again imports will be discouraged by the availability of cheaper home-produced substitutes and exports will be stimulated by lower costs and prices. The net result is that home consumption of imports falls, cheaper exports become more attractive, and the balance of payments moves back towards equilibrium.

Where, on the other hand, a country enjoys a *surplus* on the balance of payments, the stock of gold in the country would rise and the central bank would adopt expansionary monetary measures resulting in higher demand and a rise in prices. The net result is that home consumption of imports rises, dearer exports become less attractive and the balance of payments moves back towards equilibrium.

The gold standard in practice

The great advantages claimed for the gold standard by its supporters were that it acted *automatically* to maintain stable exchange rates, a stable internal currency and balance of payments equilibrium. A key point which they missed was that the world supply of gold was required to keep pace with changes in world trade to ensure the stability of currencies and an adequate supply of world liquidity. In fact, both in the sixteenth and the nineteenth centuries the discovery of new sources of supply led to a fall in the value of gold and to a rise in prices. On the other hand, a shortage of new gold supplies in the twentieth century meant that world liquidity did not grow fast enough for the needs of world trade.

Another serious problem arose from the failure of the gold standard to operate with the smoothness predicted for it. Before 1914 it seemed to work quite well in maintaining balance of payments equilibrium but failed dismally in the far less favourable economic circumstances following 1918. For the gold standard to work effectively, countries on the gold standard had to allow gold movements to act freely on their price levels so that an inflow of gold would raise, and an outflow lower, the price level. Since such gold movements could have harmful effects on the domestic economy, most countries interfered with the working of the gold standard to help deal with domestic problems.

Even where, as in the case of Britain, countries did try to adhere to the requirements imposed by a gold standard regime, they were not very successful. The Cunliffe Committee of 1918 recommended a return to the gold standard abandoned at the outbreak of the First World War. By 1925 Britain felt strong enough to return to the gold standard but the ever-present concern over gold reserves meant that instead of the full gold standard which had operated until 1914 the gold bullion standard was adopted. This meant that internally the pound was no longer freely convertible into gold and no gold coins circulated. However, 400 oz gold bars were exchangeable for £1,669 so that traders could still settle their debts in gold. Yet even this diluted form of the gold standard proved difficult to maintain. Although prices did fall in Britain along orthodox gold standard lines following deficits in the balance of payments, wages proved more resilient and the gold standard therefore failed to achieve the automatic restoration of balance of payments equilibrium expected of it. The pound was under almost continuous pressure in the late 1920s and after the Wall Street crash in 1929 and a flight of capital from London in 1930 the government eventually had no choice but to leave the gold standard in 1931.

Most other countries followed Britain and through the late 1930s a system of floating exchange rates prevailed over much of the world. However, world trade suffered deeply, partly through lack of confidence in this uncontrolled system of exchange rates and partly because of the onset of world recession. Only at the end of the Second World War did the establishment of the International Monetary Fund, together with a system of fixed exchange rates, enable a return to a more orderly pattern of international transactions.

Notes

1. Using the exchange equalisation account in which UK gold and foreign currency reserves are kept.
2. There is evidence to support the view that speculation contributed significantly to the devaluation of sterling in 1967.
3. For example, if the speculator sells pounds for dollars and then sterling strengthens, his dollars will buy back less pounds than he started with.

Examination questions

The following questions are taken from the examination papers of various examining bodies which include the areas covered by this chapter in their syllabuses. Those marked with an asterisk (★) are representative of the main types of question asked and specimen answers for these will be found in Part II.

1. In the absence of official intervention in the foreign exchange market, what factors are likely to influence changes in a country's exchange rate? (IOB 2A, April 1983)

2.★ (a) By means of a diagram explain how an equilibrium rate of exchange is determined in a free market for foreign exchange. *(5 marks)*
   (b) Explain how the equilibrium rate of exchange may be affected by:
     (i) the actions of speculators;
     (ii) change in relative prices of imports and exports;
     (iii) changes in income levels;
     (iv) foreign investment;
     (v) government overseas expenditure.
       (RSA Stage III, June 1984)   *(15 marks)*

3.★ Discuss the arguments for and against a floating exchange rate. (London, January 1980)

4. Analyse the principal consequences for the United Kingdom of a rising value of the pound sterling on foreign exchange markets. (London, June 1982)

5.★ What factors are responsible for determining the rate of exchange of a country's currency? (*10 marks*)
What effects may a fall in the rate of exchange have on the economy? (*10 marks*)
(RSA Diploma for Personal Assistants, June 1982)

6. (a) Analyse the economic forces which determine your country's exchange rate. (*13 marks*)
(b) How may changes in the exchange rate affect the domestic economy? (*12 marks*)
(Cambridge, Nov./Dec. 1983)

7. How, and in what way, might speculation affect foreign exchange rates? (London, January 1985)

8. The recent fall in the value of the pound sterling, notwithstanding a very high surplus on the balance of payments, has given rise to much discussion as to the merits and demerits of a strong pound. Discuss with reference to the various factors which influence exchange rates. (FCOT, May 1983)

9.★ For what reasons and in what ways might the monetary authorities seek to affect the level of a country's exchange rate? (IOB 2A, May 1984)

10. Why and how might the government wish to influence the external value of sterling under an international system of floating exchange rates? (AEB, June 1984)

11. 'Both fixed and floating exchange rates provide automatic adjustment to balance of payments disequilibria'. Discuss. (AEB, June 1985)

12. How do variable exchange rates help in dealing with balance of payments imbalances? (ICSA Part I, June 1985)

Chapter Five
The IMF and international liquidity

The collapse of the gold standard and the recession in world trade which followed had served to reduce international financial confidence to a very low level in the 1930s. As the Second World War drew to a close the western powers were anxious to avoid a return to this era. Following proposals by Britain in the Keynes Plan of 1943[1], and by the United States in the White Plan[2] of the same year, the Bretton Woods conference was held in July 1944. The aim of the conference was to establish an international financial regime that would be conducive to the growth of world trade, through the provision of stable exchange rates and the free convertibility of currencies. After the chaos of the pre-war period it was generally accepted that there was a need for a well-structured system of international liquidity with a new international monetary institution, an international currency and a direct link between the exchange rate structure and gold. The British proposals, particularly those concerning the provision of international liquidity, went further than those of the United States, but it was the latter which prevailed in the final agreement. The Bretton Woods Charter came into force in December 1945 and established both the International Monetary Fund and the International Bank for Reconstruction and Development.

The International Monetary Fund (IMF)

The primary objective of the IMF is to promote a freer system of world trade and payments. This in turn could be expected to encourage economic growth and a general rise in both levels of employment and real incomes. The formal objectives of the IMF are specified in Article 1 of the Articles of Agreement as follows:

1. To promote international monetary co-operation.
2. To facilitate the expansion of trade and so promote and maintain high levels of employment and real income.
3. To promote exchange rate stability and avoid competitive exchange depreciation.
4. To assist in the establishment of a multilateral system of payments and the elimination of foreign exchange restrictions.
5. To make the IMF's resources available to members and so enable them to correct balance of payments maladjustments without adopting measures harmful to national or international prosperity.
6. To shorten the duration and lessen the degree of disequilibrium in the international balances of member countries.

The Charter therefore required two key roles of the IMF:

1. It had to provide its members with a code of international behaviour and to ensure that this code was followed.
2. It was responsible for the provision of additional liquidity to members when they fell into deficit.

As we shall see later, the Fund has since widened its interpretation of these roles into giving much broader assistance to member countries. The Fund began operating in 1947 and today most countries of the world are members, the principal exceptions being Switzerland and all the communist countries apart from Yugoslavia and Romania.

Constitution

The IMF is, at least in theory, a subsidiary body of the United Nations Organisation which is why Switzerland felt unable to join without risk of prejudicing its policy of strict neutrality. In practice the Fund enjoys full autonomy and is run by a Board of Governors and an Executive Board.

The *Board of Governors*, on which all member countries are represented, meets annually and is the supreme authority of the Fund. The Board of Governors considers new admissions to membership and changes in quotas, as well as constitutional changes, but delegates most of its powers to the Executive Board. *The Executive Board* has twenty members, of whom five are appointed by the member countries with the largest quotas (at present the United States, Germany, Japan, the United Kingdom and France), and the remainder are elected by other member countries grouped into constituencies. The Executive Board appoints as its non-voting chairman a Managing Director, who heads the appointed staff responsible for day-to-day administration of the Fund.

There is a system of weighted voting which applies both to the Board of Governors and to the Executive Board. Each member has a basic allocation of 250 votes plus one vote for each 100,000 units of its quota, so that the larger a member's quota the greater its voting power. Since the size of a country's quota is based on its importance to the world economy in such matters as the volume of trade and the level of international reserves, the voting system is clearly weighted in favour of the more powerful and wealthier member countries. Votes are carried by a simple majority, except in the case of such vital matters as alterations in the articles of the Fund or increases in quotas, in which case larger majorities are required. In the case of quota changes, for example, the change must be approved by 75 per cent of the total voting power as well as by the member concerned.

Exchange rates

As a prerequisite to the attainment of its objectives, the IMF instituted a system of fixed exchange rates. Each member country undertook to establish and maintain an agreed par value against gold. This did not mean a return to the gold standard, however, since there was no requirement for countries to make their currency convertible into gold. The one exception was the United States which undertook to convert dollars at a fixed price into gold. All other countries fixed their par value against the dollar, which effectively underpinned the new arrangements. Exchange rates were not to be rigidly fixed but were to be allowed to fluctuate within a range of 1 per cent either side of the par value, as outlined in Chapter 4 in the section on fixed rates. A member country was permitted to change its currency's par value in the face of severe pressure on the rate brought about by balance of payments disequilibrium. A change of up to 10 per cent either side of parity could be made merely by notifying the Fund, while a change of between 10 and 20 per cent was possible after a brief consultation with the Fund. A change of over 20 per cent required Fund approval and due notice had to be given, though in practice events often moved too quickly for a negative decision to be practicable, as when sterling was devalued by 30 per cent in September 1949. The devaluation of the pound was one of many devaluations between 1947 and 1949 resulting from the fact that many of the original parities were out of line with the changed economic circumstances of the early post-war period. Between 1949 and 1967, however, the exchange rates of the main industrial nations were fairly stable, apart from the devaluation of the French franc in 1958 and revaluations in West Germany and the Netherlands in 1961.

If the IMF wished to insist on a stable exchange rate regime, it followed that the Fund must be willing to give support to member countries with temporary but serious difficulties on the balance of payments; otherwise these difficulties would threaten the maintenance of their par rate of exchange. This assistance is given through the operation of the general account.

The general account

Each member of the IMF is required to subscribe to the Fund a sum equal in value to its quota, a quarter in gold and the remainder in the member's own currency. Initially the total of all quotas was about $9 bn. The admission of new members, together with several increases in quotas, has led to this figure growing to SDR 89.2 bn, following the eighth quota increase in 1984.

These subscriptions enable the IMF to honour the *drawing rights* which member countries enjoy. Technically the drawing country buys currencies which are needed to effect settlements and pays for them with its own currency. For example, if the UK were short of French francs to pay France or some other country, it could buy from the IMF and pay for them in sterling. In consequence a drawing results in an increase in the Fund's holdings of the drawing member's currency and a decrease in the holdings of the currencies purchased.

In Fig. 5.1 the relationship between a country's quota and its drawing rights is illustrated. Drawings are made in equal blocks or 'tranches' equivalent to 25 per cent of the drawing member's quota.

Gold tranche

Initially the Fund holds 75 per cent of the drawing member's quota in that country's currency and 25 per cent in gold. Foreign currency equivalent in value to the gold tranche can be drawn automatically. In addition, should the Fund have originally held less than 75 per cent of the country's quota in its currency because other members have drawn this currency, the country is in credit and may draw this 'super-gold tranche' automatically too. A country's unused gold and super-gold tranche drawing rights are known as its reserve position in the IMF general account.

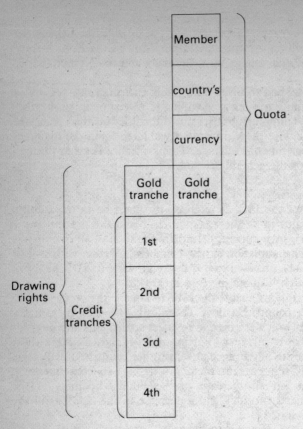

Fig. 5.1 IMF quota and drawing rights

Credit tranche

Further drawings are known as 'credit tranches' and the country is expected to show evidence that it is seeking to cure the problems which led to the application for assistance. The first credit tranche, which takes the Fund's holding of the country's currency to 125 per cent of its quota, is granted almost automatically but the second, third and fourth credit tranches can only be drawn with increasingly more detailed evidence of a programme designed to cure the country's deficit. The maximum drawing is when the Fund holds 200 per cent of the country's quota in that country's currency.

Repayment of drawings in the gold tranche and the credit tranches have to be made within three to five years. Interest payable on drawings is not related to market rates but to the size of the drawing and the length of the loan. While interest charges are not penal, the fact that they exist at all reflects the IMF's concern that recourse to drawings should be undertaken with a view to early settlement, as well as with a proper sense of responsibility. The primary aim of the Fund in this context is to ensure that members are assisted to overcome *temporary* balance of payments difficulties, without being encouraged to rely on permanent assistance to the exclusion of finding a solution to their underlying payments problems.

Since it first began operations, the IMF has added several other credit facilities to the general drawing right. Of particular importance are:

1. **The standby agreement.** Many drawings in the higher credit tranches take this form. Under this arrangement the applicant is expected to submit a programme of action. The drawing of each instalment of the credit is subject to the observance of the key elements of the programme in such areas as trade policy, the balance of payments, foreign debt and the exchange rate. As long as these criteria are met, the country in question can draw each instalment as and when required.
2. **The compensatory financing facility** was introduced in 1963 to extend the IMF's support to members with balance of payments difficulties. This facility applies especially to primary producers and is intended to provide short-term support needed as the result of a temporary drop in export earnings following a crop failure or similar misadventure.
3. **The bufferstock facility** was introduced to help finance the holding of stocks by producers when high production levels have resulted in falling commodity prices.
4. **The extended credit facility** was introduced in 1974 to help countries unable to guarantee repayment of credits within the normal period of three to five years, giving credit facilities of up to ten years in certain circumstances.
5. **The oil facility** was also introduced in 1974 to provide finance for members experiencing balance of payments difficulties caused by the sharp rise in the price of oil. Originally introduced for one year, this facility was frequently extended until 1979.
6. **The supplementary financing facility** replaced the oil facility

Table 5.1 IMF lending (as at
30. 11. 84) (SDR m.)

Credit tranche	31,890.9
Compensatory financing facility	13,366.5
Bufferstock facility	557.7
Oil facility	6,902.5
Supplementary financing facilities	7,154.0
Extended credit facility	10,776.9
Total	70,648.5

Source: International Financial Statistics, IMF
1985

in 1979 and provides a similar drawing facility. In both cases
the assistance given is in addition to that normally available to
a member from IMF funds.

The evolution of the international monetary system

For the first twenty years or so after its formation the regime
established by the IMF appeared to work well. Exchange rates
were fairly stable in the 1950s and 1960s and world trade grew
steadily. Such was the post-war recovery of the major European
industrial nations that by 1961 they were able to join the United
States and Canada in making their currencies fully convertible.
Thus all their currencies were exchangeable against the United
States dollar and the dollar itself was convertible into gold.

The level of international liquidity was also maintained at a
healthy level by the existence of two 'reserve currencies' – the
dollar and sterling. All IMF members were prepared to accept
settlement for international indebtedness in dollars while a significant number were also prepared to accept sterling. This latter
group, the so-called 'sterling area', included the British Commonwealth (except Canada) and a number of other countries with
British political or trading connections. The development of the
dollar and sterling as reserve currencies flowed from the traditional
strengths of the two currencies and the importance of the United
States and Britain as major trading nations. The possession of
reserve currencies was considered advantageous to the United
States and Britain since a major part of their overseas indebtedness

could be financed without resort to their official reserves. On the other hand, the fact that there were so many dollars and pounds held in the banks of the world meant that large official reserves were needed to cover the possibility that major creditors might wish to convert their dollars or pounds into other currencies. Both currencies were also prone to the activities of speculators moving short-term balances ('hot money') from one financial centre to another.

Currency 'swaps'

By the 1960s the first strains in the system were beginning to show as problems arose over the level of international liquidity, which was not rising as fast as the level of world trade. The system was still underpinned by gold (which had remained at an official price of $35 per ounce since 1931) supplemented by each country's holdings of foreign currency, notably dollars. To improve the flow of international liquidity, currency swaps were introduced in 1961. These are arranged through the Bank for International Settlements in Switzerland and involve the exchange of national currencies between central banks, together with a contract to reverse the transaction at the same exchange rate at some future date, usually three months. Currency swaps have enabled participating countries both to ease balance of payments difficulties and to bolster reserves when trying to support their currency's exchange rate.

General Agreements to Borrow (GAB)

In 1962 the so-called Group of Ten (Belgium, Canada, France, Italy, Japan, the Netherlands, Sweden, UK, USA and West Germany) agreed to provide the IMF with $6 bn of their currencies. Members of the group could draw on this fund should they be in balance of payments deficit. Switzerland joined the GAB scheme in 1963 and in 1983 the fund was increased from $7 bn to $19 bn in order to enable *all* IMF members to use this facility in times of deficit.

Special drawing rights

Despite the increased world liquidity generated by the facilities outlined above, the growth in world liquidity continued to lag behind the expansion of world trade. Therefore in 1966 the Group of Ten proposed an increase in world reserves through the introduction of special drawing rights (SDRs). This proposal was accepted by the IMF at its annual meeting in 1967 and the first issue of SDRs was made in 1970. SDRs are, in effect, non-repayable credits issued to each member of the IMF in proportion to its IMF quota. When a country needs to finance a balance of payments deficit it may use its allocation of SDRs to obtain currencies from other countries, subject only to the limitation that over a five-year period the country maintains an average of 30 per cent of its cumulative allocation over the period. In effect, therefore, 70 per cent of the SDR allocation represents unconditional extra liquidity, and 30 per cent represents a borrowing facility which can only be used over a short period.

The other limitation attached to SDRs is that no country can be required to hold them to a value more than three times its net cumulative allocation. A country entitled to make use of its SDRs may do so either by buying back its own currency from another participating country or by applying to the Fund to obtain another currency. In this latter case the Fund channels the transaction through its special drawing account and designates which countries are to accept the SDRs in exchange for the denominated currency. Originally one SDR unit was valued at 1/35 oz of gold (i.e. one dollar at the pre-1971 parity) and was therefore in effect 'paper gold', adding to the total of world liquidity. Subsequently the demonetisation of gold in the 1970s was to lead to the SDR being valued in the form of a basket of currencies, originally sixteen but (since 1981) now only five.

The total issue of SDRs has been far less than might have been predicted after the original issues of $3 bn in each of the years 1970–72. Unfortunately the rapid rise in world inflation rates in the early 1970s deterred further allocations for fear that these might fuel inflationary pressures, and the only subsequent allocations have been those of SDR 4 bn a year between 1979 and 1981. On

Table 5.2 The composition of the SDR unit

Currency	%
$US	51.0
Deutschemark	16.7
Yen	14.0
£ sterling	9.6
French franc	8.7
	100.0

the other hand, the SDR has established its position as the official unit of account of the IMF. Since the mid-1970s its use has grown to such an extent that even issues of public bonds have been denominated in SDR.

The collapse of the Bretton Woods system

In the late 1960s the international monetary system, based on fixed exchange rates and underpinned by the American dollar, was showing increasing signs of strain. The history of this period is examined in detail elsewhere[3], with only the key events outlined here.

By 1967 the position of sterling as a reserve currency was under attack as a result of fundamental weaknesses in Britain's external position. A persistent balance of payments deficit, coupled with a flight of short-term capital, led to a serious drain of official reserves and culminated in a 14 per cent devaluation at the end of that year. Devaluation did lead to some improvement in the balance of payments but failed to restore full confidence in sterling. Accordingly in 1968 the UK and all other sterling area members entered into the *Basle Agreement* aimed at stabilising the exchange rate of sterling balances held by sterling area countries. In return for a dollar guarantee from Britain in respect of 90 per cent of their sterling reserve balances, the members of the sterling area agreed to maintain a certain proportion of their total official reserves in sterling. The agreement was underwritten by the Bank for International Settlements which placed at the disposal of the UK a standby credit of $2 bn to finance any rundown of sterling balances occurring as a result of this agreement. Despite the improvement in confidence which followed this arrangement, it was becoming increasingly clear that the pound was too weak to perform adequately the functions of a reserve currency and in the 1970s successive British governments worked to phase out this role[4].

Events at this time were in any case eroding the possibility of *any* currency successfully performing the role of a reserve currency. While the Basle Agreement relieved, at least temporarily, the pressures on sterling, the problem of the US balance of payments deficit remained. Unlike the UK, the United States could not devalue its currency without threatening to undermine the entire working of the Bretton Woods system. Since, on the other hand, most surplus countries were consistently unwilling to revalue *their* currencies, the disequilibrium in world payments continued to grow until it reached a critical point in 1971. The pressure on the dollar arising from balance of payments deficits was increased by the movement of substantial funds from America to other financial centres, which in turn prompted further speculation against the dollar. In May 1971 there were token revaluations of the stronger European currencies but, in the absence of more decisive action, the American deficit continued to increase and there was a very real threat of a run on the US gold reserves. In August 1971 the American government suspended convertibility of the dollar, and in December of the same year an attempt was made to establish a new regime of exchange rates under the Smithsonian Agreement.

The Smithsonian Agreement 1971

Essentially this agreement aimed to replace the system of Bretton Woods convertibility with a dollar standard. The principal features of the arrangement were:

1. The dollar was no longer to be convertible into gold.
2. The official price of gold was raised from $35 to $38 an ounce. This rate was to be used by central banks in transactions between themselves while a free market price would operate for private transactions.
3. In recognition of the greater volatility of exchange rates, the 1 per cent margin either side of parity permitted previously was replaced by a $2\frac{1}{4}$ per cent margin.
4. The US dollar was to remain an intervention currency with all other currencies pegged to it.
5. To help the introduction of the new system, the other members of the Group of Ten agreed to a revaluation of their currencies as indicated in Table 5.3.

It was generally hoped that the Smithsonian Agreement would mark a return to a stable international monetary regime, especially since the new arrangement reduced the potential pressure on the United States dollar. In fact this new regime was to last no more than fifteen months before the final collapse of the post-war system of fixed exchange rates. The first blow came in June 1972 when renewed problems with the British balance of payments resulted in the British government floating the pound. Although Ireland followed the lead of sterling and allowed the punt to float with the pound, most sterling area countries now detached their exchange rate from sterling. In retrospect, the floating of sterling can be seen as the first step in the eventual demise of the sterling area. The second blow came during the latter part of 1972, when fears for

Table 5.3 Smithsonian
Agreement revaluation
against US dollar (Dec. 1971)

	%
Belgium	11.6
Canada	floating
France	8.6
Germany	13.6*
Italy	7.5
Japan	16.9
Netherlands	11.6*
Sweden	7.5
United Kingdom	8.6

* Includes revaluation of May 1971

a further devaluation of the dollar led to a speculative run on it. This run was not halted by a further revaluation of major currencies against the dollar in February 1973 and in March the Group of Ten, together with Switzerland and the smaller EEC members, agreed that the major industrial nations should cease to peg their currencies to the dollar. This new agreement ushered in the era of floating exchange rates, though some countries continued to peg their currencies against each other (notably the members of the European snake). In addition, many small countries pegged their currencies against the dollar, sterling or other major international currencies.

Post-1973 floating

Ironically, almost at the moment the new regime was introduced, the pressures which had brought down the Smithsonian Agreement began to recede. To begin with, the devalued dollar was making American goods more price-competitive, while later in 1973 the OPEC decision to increase the price of oil greatly increased the demand for dollars as the principal currency for the settlement of oil debts. This latter event had the effect also of increasing the demand for sterling, though to a lesser extent. Yet despite the greater stability now accorded to the dollar, hopes that some system of fixed exchange rates might be restored failed to materialise as higher oil prices and their impact on the world economy acted to increase inflationary pressures, making exchange rate stability difficult to achieve.

Another unresolved issue concerned the role of gold. The *market price* of gold had soared since the ending of dollar convertibility and in such circumstances no central bank was prepared to part with gold at its *official* price ($42.2 an ounce since February 1973), so that transactions in gold had dried up since the ending of dollar convertibility. In 1974 it was agreed that central banks should value their gold reserves at the market price and in 1975 the United States held two auctions to sell off large parts of its official gold reserves. Finally the *Jamaica conference* of the IMF in January 1976 agreed to the demonetisation of gold and to the sale of part of the gold holdings of the IMF in order to assist the liquidity of developing countries.

The system of floating exchange rates has perhaps worked rather better than its critics had feared but not as well as its supporters had hoped. The crises in the international monetary system predicted by critics of floating rates did not materialise, despite a world recession, oil price rises and severe international debt problems. In large part, stability was maintained by the monetary authorities *managing* their currencies rather than allowing them to float freely. Nevertheless exchange rates have on occasions proved to be extremely volatile, especially since the volume of internationally mobile speculative balances has grown substantially since the early 1970s. Also 'managed floating' has meant that exchange rate movements have not been sufficient to eliminate balance of payments problems, one of the supposed key advantages of floating rates (see pp. 74–7 above). The events of 1985, when speculative support pushed the American dollar sharply upwards, confirmed the fear that the markets can indulge in panic behaviour in the absence of specific intervention points and can threaten confidence in major currencies. Yet, despite these misgivings about floating rates, there is at present no widely accepted alternative. There seems to be little likelihood of a return either to gold or to a convertible currency as the commonly accepted standard for international payments and the best hope for a new 'international currency' is the somewhat under-used SDR.

Expansion of world liquidity

In order that both world trade and the settlement of international debts may operate smoothly, it is essential that there is an adequate supply of international liquidity. This means that the growth in trade must be accompanied by a complementary growth in the level of international reserves. Experiences under the gold standard pointed to the destabilising effects on trade and the system of payments when the supply of liquidity grows erratically and led Keynes to propose at the Bretton Woods conference that some form of additional liquidity be devised. In the event it was not until the late 1960s that SDRs were introduced to supplement traditional reserves, although such innovations as currency swaps and the GAB had already been introduced to help use *existing* liquidity more effectively. The current supply of world liquidity consists as follows.

1. Central bank gold holdings. From Table 5.4 we see that gold constitutes 8 per cent of official reserves. Despite being effectively demonetised at the 1976 Jamaica conference, gold is still acceptable in settlement of international debts, and holdings are maintained by most countries. Gold holdings serve both to bolster confidence and to finance trade in conditions of uncertain exchange rates, as with the Soviet Union and its allies.

2. Convertible foreign currencies. While the importance of gold as a proportion of total reserves has declined since 1948, that of foreign currencies has increased from 28 to 78 per cent. Total world reserves grow in consequence of balance of payments deficits by countries with internationally acceptable currencies, such as the United States. Since the early 1970s the decline of the reserve currencies has reduced the relative importance of dollar and ster- ling holdings, though holdings of other strong currencies have grown rapidly. A further increase in currency holdings has occurred through leakages from the various eurocurrency markets.

3. IMF reserve positions. The subscription of quotas (in gold and their own currency) by member countries increases international liquidity since these quotas can then be used by other members to settle international indebtedness. While increases in quotas over the years from 3 to 10 per cent have added to the IMF's reserve position, it has been estimated by the IMF that one-sixth of these currency holdings are of little value since they are not generally acceptable in settlement of trade transactions, notably those of some developing countries.

4. SDRs. As we have seen, each issue of SDRs represents a once and for all incease in the supply of world liquidity, and SDRs now constitute 4 per cent of official reserves.

Table 5.4 Official reserves 1948–85 (SDR m.:% of total in [ ])

	1948	1958	1969	1977	1985
Gold	34,500 [69]	38,000 [66]	38,900 [50]	36,021 [14]	33,207 [8]
Reserve positions in IMF	1,600 [3]	2,600 [5]	6,500 [9]	18,089 [7]	39,931 [9]
Foreign exchange	13,400 [28]	17,000 [29]	32,000 [41]	203,660 [76]	341,054 [79]
SDRs	— [—]	— [—]	— [—]	8,133 [3]	17,293 [4]
Total	49,500	57,600	77,400	262,200	431,485
Ratio of reserves to imports (%)	n.a.	62.5	33.0	27.0	25.0

Sources: International Financial Statistics (various issues); IMF *Annual Report* (various issues)

The IMF uses the ratio of reserves to imports as a rough guide to the adequacy of reserves and Table 5.4 shows that this ratio has declined steadily since the 1950s. It is necessary, however, to qualify the apparently substantial decline in reserve adequacy to what may be regarded as the 'danger' level of a reserves/import ratio of only 25 per cent:

1. The advent of floating exchange rates in the 1970s has to some extent reduced the *need* for official reserves.
2. The growth of the eurocurrency markets has provided alternative sources of liquidity for central banks and made it easier to recycle the excess liquidity held by oil-producing countries.
3. It is in any case impossible to be sure that a decline in the reserve/input ratio constitutes a 'problem'. This presupposes that the initial, higher ratio was 'just right', whereas it might have been higher than necessary!

Quite apart from the alleged problem of the inadequacy of the *level* of world liquidity, there may be problems with its *distribution*.

The tendency for reserves to become concentrated in the hands of the industrialised and oil-producing countries has helped contribute to the debt problems of the lesser developed countries (LDCs). It has been suggested[5] that a large-scale expansion of SDRs would enable the LDCs to rebuild their reserves without increasing their overseas debt and without imposing any strain on other countries. However, fear of the inflationary effects of further SDR increases has so far prevented this solution being adopted.

Notes

1. *Proposals for an International Clearing Union*, Cmd 6437, 1943.
2. *United States Proposal for a United and Associated Nations Stabilisation Fund*, HMSO, 1943.
3. B. Tew, *The Evolution of the International Monetary System 1945–1977*, Hutchinson, 1977.
4. UK sterling liabilities fell from SDR 8.2 bn in 1974 to SDR 3.3 bn in 1977.
5. John Williamson, *A New SDR Allocation?*, Institute for International Economics (MIT Press), 1984.

Examination questions

The following questions are taken from the examination papers of various examining bodies which include the areas covered by this chapter in their syllabuses. Those marked with an asterisk (★) are representative of the main types of question asked and specimen answers for these will be found in Part II.

1.★ Assess the present role in the international monetary system of:
   (a) gold;
   (b) special drawing rights (SDRs);
   (c) the US dollar.
   (IOB 2A, May 1984)

2.★ (a) Outline the main changes that have occurred in the composition of international liquidity since 1971.   (*15 marks*)
   (b) To what extent has the existence of floating exchange rates reduced the need for international liquidity?   (*10 marks*)
   (IOB 2A, April 1982)

3.★ Discuss both the desirability and the feasibility of a return to worldwide fixed exchange rates such as operated under the so-called Bretton Woods system. (IOB 2A, September 1982)

4.★ Following the breakdown of the so-called Bretton Woods system in the 1970s most major currencies were allowed to float. To what extent have the theoretical advantages of floating exchange rates been borne out in practice? (IOB 2A, September 1984)

5. Discuss the arguments for and against a return to a system of fixed exchange rates between the major world currencies such as that which prevailed under the Bretton Woods agreement up to 1971. (IOB 2A, April 1980)

6. What do you understand by the concept of international liquidity? Assess the importance of the International Monetary Fund (IMF) in ensuring an adequate supply of international liquidity in recent years. (IOB 2A, September 1983)

7. Examine the advantages of floating exchange rates in the light of United Kingdom experience since 1972. (AEB, June 1982)

8. Outline the ways in which the International Monetary Fund (IMF) has assisted countries experiencing balance of payments difficulties in recent years. How effectively has IMF support served the needs of such countries. (IOB 2A, April 1985)

9. Identify the components of international liquidity and discuss the advantages and disadvantages of each of them in its role as a component. (IOB 2A, September 1985)

Chapter Six
Capital movements and the eurocurrency markets

International capital movements relate to the transfer of money capital rather than capital goods. Such movements therefore refer to the transfer of financial claims from the residents of one country to the residents of another.

Types of capital movement and their importance

Short-term capital movements. These include transfers of financial assets of less than one year to maturity, such as bank deposits and bills of exchange, as well as transfers of currency.

Long-term capital movements. These result from investment overseas in assets with maturity dates of more than a year, notably stocks and shares, convertible debentures and other long-term loans. These long-term capital movements are classified either as 'portfolio investment' or as 'direct investment'.

Portfolio investment refers to capital movements where the investors have no control over the use to which their funds are put, as in loans to foreign governments or the acquisition of a minority shareholding in a foreign company.

The term *direct investment* is used when the investor does have control over the use of funds as, for example, in the establishment of an overseas subsidiary or the purchase of a controlling interest in a foreign company.

Since capital movements figure in the balance of payments accounts of a country, such movements clearly contribute to a country's external position. However, the impact goes much further, involving the following items.

1. The balance of payments. These effects have already been discussed in Chapter 3. A country with a net outflow of capital funds will experience a decline in official reserves, unless this negative item in the accounts is offset by a current account surplus. Where the net outflow is the consequence of rapid movements of short-term funds (hot money), severe downward pressures may be exerted on the exchange rate. Similarly, massive inflows of funds may increase the upward pressure on a country's exchange rate. To offset these large inflows, the country may encourage foreign access to the domestic capital market or it may encourage overseas investment by the private sector.

2. *The money supply.* Capital flows may affect both domestic liquidity and the conduct of monetary policy. Countries with capital outflows will suffer deflationary pressures unless the public sell holdings of government debt to finance the acquisition of foreign assets. In the case of capital inflows they will add to the country's official reserves unless they are reinvested abroad or used to finance a higher level of imports. Where reserves do rise, the effect on the domestic money supply depends on how the monetary authorities finance the purchase of this additional foreign currency. If the government borrows from the public, there will be no increase in the money supply. Where, however, the banking sector holds the debt, there will be a growth in banks' reserves and thus a multiple credit creation. West Germany's money supply grew by 40 per cent in 1971, largely as a result of capital inflows.

With regard to monetary policy, conflicts may arise in the implementation of government objectives. The adoption of tight monetary controls to dampen domestic demand will involve higher interest rates and this will cause an inflow of foreign funds which results in a growth in the money supply – the very thing the government was seeking to avoid.

3. *The domestic capital market.* Where there is a net outflow with capital funds diverted to foreign investment, the domestic capital market may be short of funds. This may push up domestic interest rates and deter investment or at least inhibit the attainment of the government's investment targets.

4. *Political effects.* Where outflows of long-term capital reduce the investment funds available to the domestic economy, the government may well feel obliged to restrict such outflows to support its policies of economic growth and industrial development. While an inflow of long-term capital undoubtedly assists in the development of the country's economy, foreign ownership of key sectors in the economy may result in difficulties in the execution of government policy. In particular, multinational

companies with worldwide interests may attempt to influence government policy to favour their own corporate aims rather than those of the economy as a whole; they may even threaten withdrawal from the country in question unless given favourable treatment. This topic is discussed in more detail in Chapter 9.

The evolution of capital issues

Throughout the nineteenth century, world financial markets were dominated by the sterling bond and in 1914 over half of the gross long-term investment of the major creditor nations was held by Great Britain. In the previous half-century, Britain had annually invested about 4 per cent of her national income abroad, a figure unequalled by any country since then[1]. Despite having to liquidate some of these investments to help finance the First World War, and losing others through debt repudiation by some East European and Middle East governments after 1918, Britain remained the leading creditor nation throughout the inter-war period. New investment was, however, dominated by the United States, and the New York bond market now took over the role previously played by the London market. American overseas investment came to an abrupt halt with the 1929 crash and the Depression which followed it. When American lending overseas was resumed after 1945 the greater part of it consisted of government loans to assist in European reconstruction. During the 1950s private investment in Europe resumed but it was now principally direct, rather than portfolio as had previously been the case. Nonetheless there was still a considerable demand for foreign loans, much of it centred on the New York market because of the various restrictions imposed on foreign issues by European governments anxious to ensure an adequate flow of capital funds to the domestic economy. For European borrowers, the New York market offered the twin advantages of low interest rates and low direct issuing costs. At the same time, European investors were attracted by the security of capital issues denominated in dollars so that it was often easier to raise a loan for a European borrower in New York even when the funds also came from Europe.

So popular did loans denominated in dollars prove to be that in 1964 the net private capital outflow was $6,000 m., comprising direct investment outflows and foreign lending on the New York market. This deficit on the capital account put a strain on the United States' balance of payments and invited a response. In 1964 an interest equalisation tax (IET) was levied by the US government on purchases of foreign securities by United States residents. The imposition of IET dramatically reduced European borrowing on the New York capital market as American investors virtually ceased to support foreign issues, making them difficult to market. Attention now switched to Europe, but the existing European capital markets were not really capable of absorbing the extra demand for funds. The result was the establishment of a new market for foreign issues based in London. What was peculiar about this market was the near-complete absence of British subscriptions to the issues made, due to the heavy penalties placed on overseas investment by British residents. In fact, London merely acted as a go-between for international capital in what was to become the London Eurobond Market.

The two main differences between a eurobond and a conventional foreign issue are the composition of the underwriting syndicate and the rules governing the issue of the loan. *Foreign bond issues* are underwritten by a domestic syndicate and are therefore subject to the rules of the issuing authorities in that country, so that their coupon rates reflect those of domestic issues. *Eurobond issues* are underwritten by an international syndicate and are not subject to the rules of the issuing body of any country. Accordingly their coupon rates may be quite different from those on domestic issues in the same currency.

From the information in Table 6.1 it can be seen that the number and value of eurobond issues expanded rapidly in the 1960s and early 1970s and then declined quite rapidly from 1973. This decline was accompanied by a very rapid growth of the eurocurrency markets, where the development of medium-term lending attracted many borrowers who would previously have sought eurobond finance.

Eurocurrencies

A eurocurrency is a deposit in a currency held in a bank situated outside the country of origin of the currency. Thus a *eurodollar* is a dollar deposit at a bank outside the United States, while a *eurosterling* is a pound deposit at a bank outside the United Kingdom, and so on. Markets in the eurocurrencies evolved as banks lent out these deposits either in the same currency, in their own domestic currency or in the currency of a third country. If, as is often the case, these loans are redeposited in the eurocurrency market, claims in the currency now exceed the original deposit in the

Table 6.1 The early growth of international bond issues* ($ USm. equivalent)

	1963	1964	1965	1966	1967	1968	1969	1970	1971	1972	1973	1974	1975
Foreign bonds													
Deutschemark	40	58	123	—	10	674	531	89	308	500	374	263	600
Swiss franc	143	85	78	94	153	238	196	193	661	815	1456	703	3500
Other	206	121	175	284	240	223	100	96	560	745	655	160	8100
Total	389	264	376	378	403	1,135	827	378	1,529	2,060	2,485	1,126	12,200
Eurobonds													
Dollar	102	485	726	921	1780	2554	1723	1775	2203	3908	2467	996	
Deutschemark	—	200	203	147	171	914	1338	688	786	129	1001	313	
Other	62	34	112	74	51	105	95	503	635	1298	721	752	
Total	164	719	1041	1142	2002	3573	3156	2966	3624	6335	4189	2061	
Total international bonds	553	983	1,417	1,520	2,405	4,708	3,983	3,344	5,153	8,395	6,674	3,187	

Source: World Financial Markets, Morgan Guaranty Trust Co.
* Excluding foreign issues in New York

currency's country of origin. The primary distinguishing feature of the eurodollar market compared to the domestic money market in the United States is that transactions are conducted exclusively by banks operating outside the United States and using a different interest rate structure from that in America; similar features apply to all the other eurocurrency markets. There are now markets for all the world's leading eurocurrencies throughout the world, with the exception of Africa and Latin America. The London markets, the largest of all, have now become a complete financial system and in size of deposits now exceed the market in banks' sterling funds.

The growth of the eurocurrency markets

Commercial banks had already been accepting foreign currency deposits for at least fifty years when this practice grew in scale in the 1950s, with a rapid growth in the volume of dollar deposits held with European banks. It was not when dollar deposits were initially accepted but when the European banks began to lend these deposits to other European banks, rather than to the United States money market, that the eurodollar market can be said to have first appeared.

The development of the eurocurrency markets in the late 1950s was due to the coincidence of several favourable factors:

1. There had been, as mentioned above, a considerable growth of dollar deposits held by European banks. Much of this came from Eastern bloc banks who found it useful to hold their dollar deposits in London for fear of them being blocked by the United States government if held in America. Furthermore, many other dollar deposit holders preferred to keep these funds with European banks to take advantage of higher interest rates, or more favourable tax treatment, in Europe. In addition, the general acceptability of dollars in international trade finance made many large companies wish to hold dollar balances for financial and commercial use.
2. The unregulated nature of these markets aided their growth. The European banks were able to offer higher interest rates than American banks who were subject to regulation Q of the Federal Reserve System. This imposed ceilings on time deposits with American banks but did not apply to time dollar deposits owned by foreign accounts. Furthermore, the lack of regulation meant that no reserve requirements were imposed on the eurocurrency markets. This in turn contributed to finer

rates of interest being quoted since virtually all deposits could be on-lent without a proportion being lodged with central banks. Thus higher deposit rates could be offered than on the domestic market while lower rates were charged to borrowers. The ability to offer these competitive rates was bolstered by the economies of scale obtained in the eurocurrency markets through a concentration on wholesale transactions.

3. The return of external convertibility of the major currencies in 1958 and the lifting of many exchange controls in Europe resulted in many European residents taking advantage of the competitive lending rates offered by the eurocurrency markets. Convertibility also encouraged the development of euromarkets in other currencies, notably sterling, deutschemarks and Swiss francs.

4. The eurocurrency markets proved useful to central banks which had to keep a high proportion of reserves in very liquid assets. They therefore found the eurocurrency markets a lucrative outlet for temporary deposits. Indeed, it has been estimated that central banks were, in the early days of the markets, the most important sources of funds, with perhaps as much as two-thirds of all eurodollars being owned by central banks in the early 1960s.[2]

Such was the success of the eurodollar market in particular that the larger American banks rapidly expanded their network of branches overseas to meet the needs of American companies who could borrow funds more cheaply than in the United States. Furthermore, when dollars were short in the USA the London offices of American banks could lend back eurodollars to their head offices and thus avoid some of the problems posed by tight monetary restrictions. Even when the US authorities removed the restrictions imposed on the outflow of dollars in the early 1970s, the eurodollar market continued to grow because of the competitive edge on interest rates enjoyed through the absence of reserve requirements.

A further boost to growth came after the oil price rise of 1973 which resulted in the surplus of the oil-producing countries rising from $7,000 m. in 1972 to $60,000 m. in 1974[3]. Much of this surplus was deposited in the eurocurrency markets which seemed to be a more attractive proposition for short-term funds than the more uncertain eurobond market. The surpluses of the oil-producing nations were matched by corresponding deficits in other countries – notably the non-oil-producing developing countries –

who were forced to borrow from the commercial banks through the eurocurrency markets to supplement their liquidity. In effect the banks took over the role of the bond market at this time by recycling the oil producers' surpluses as roll-over credits to the developing countries.

The multinational corporations have themselves become major operators in the eurocurrency markets since they offer both a high degree of liquidity and high rates of interest and are therefore ideal for short-term surplus funds. In addition, eurocurrency deposits act as a hedge against exchange rate changes.

Between the early 1960s and the early 1980s, gross lending in the eurocurrency markets grew at a rate of 30 per cent per annum and reached $2,000 bn in 1982. Nearly three-quarters of this total consisted of eurodollars, while the next market in terms of size was that for deutschemarks, followed by Swiss francs and yen. The eurosterling market's growth has been hindered by the very low reserve requirements imposed in Britain so that the competitive edge on interest rates over that on the domestic market is minimal. The level of new eurocurrency lending fell after 1982 both because of reductions in balance of payments deficits and because of growing concern about the level of international debt.

Operations in the eurocurrency markets
The advantage of a eurocurrency deposit is that it usually offers a higher interest rate than does a deposit in the domestic financial market. A secondary advantage is that the depositor can hold a foreign currency deposit in his own rather than in the country where the currency originated. Such deposits are usually time

Table 6.2 The growth of the eurocurrency markets ($bn)

Year	Gross eurocurrency lending
1964	26.7
1968	46.0
1973	374.3
1977	850.0
1982	2,200.0
1983	2,260.0

deposits on a short-term basis, most frequently up to a month to maturity. The main borrowers of these deposits are large commercial companies, governments and banks. While the eurocurrency markets offer relatively cheap sources of short-term loans for both companies and governments, the largest borrowers are banks seeking to ensure they have adequate amounts of particular currencies for their needs.

Despite this preponderance of short-term credits in the markets, medium-term eurocurrency loans have become increasingly important in recent years and have attracted customers away from the eurobond market. These medium-term loans may be for as long as seven years and are lent at rates which vary over the life of the loan in accordance with changes in market rates. In the case of very large loans it is not uncommon for a group of banks to form a syndicate to spread the risk of the loan.

The eurocurrency markets and domestic monetary policy

The growth of the eurocurrency markets has improved the efficiency of the financial markets by increasing the opportunities for both depositors and borrowers of large funds. Accordingly, dollars holders can choose to deposit their funds either in the United States or with banks offering dollar deposit facilities outside the United States. Similarly a company wishing to borrow dollars could obtain them either in the United States or from the eurodollar markets in London and elsewhere.

The growth of the credit facilities generated by the eurocurrency markets raises questions about the effect on credit creation within countries, with resultant problems for the conduct of monetary policy. Eurodollars, for example, will be on-lent, generating further eurodollar deposits and loans when they are deposited with banks outside the United States. This credit creation is limited, however, since banks outside the United States retrieve only a small proportion of the eurodollars they lend out, the bulk going back to the American markets. The relation between the eurodollar market and domestic currency markets is more complex. If eurocurrency funds in the United Kingdom are converted into sterling, they may be used to purchase short-term government assets, such as Treasury bills or local authority loans, and similar assets in the secondary money markets. If interest rates in the secondary markets are more competitive than the Treasury bill rate, then funds will flow to those markets, thereby expanding the money supply. The extent to which this process will occur depends on domestic interest rates generally, so that if they are high in Britain, dollars will be attracted to the London eurodollar market and ultimately feed through into an expansion of the sterling money markets.

The implications for government monetary policy of this interaction between eurocurrency markets and domestic money supply depend on the nature of the controls adopted by the government to achieve its monetary objectives. Where the government attempts to control money supply growth by *direct* controls on the level of credit, business may seek further funds in the eurocurrency markets, thus circumventing the controls. Where, however, the policy is indirect, perhaps using higher interest rates to slow credit demand, eurocurrency market rates will also rise to eliminate the potential gains of borrowing in the eurocurrency markets and lending on the domestic money market. Nonetheless, higher interest rates in the eurocurrency markets are likely to attract short-term credits from outside the country, in this way expanding the eurocurrency markets and possibly the domestic money supply. Taken together, these factors reduce the effectiveness of monetary policy and, especially in the case of smaller countries, restrict the degree of independence enjoyed by the country in directing its monetary strategy.

The eurocurrency markets and international liquidity

The part played by the markets in helping to manage the problems generated by the oil surpluses of the 1970s has already been mentioned. The effect of the operation of the eurocurrency market on international liquidity is as follows. When private markets have a surplus of a currency, they present their excess holding to the central bank for conversion into domestic currency. If the central bank retains this holding, there is a once and for all increase in international liquidity. However, if the central bank then reinvests this currency in private eurocurrency markets, then the excess supply is reconstituted and the process continues indefinitely (unless the central bank reinvests the excess funds in the country of origin of the currency). When the central bank of a developing country borrows funds deposited on the market by a surplus country, there is a direct expansion of liquidity since the surplus country acquires assets to add to its reserves (the loan backed by the deficit country) while the borrowing of the deficit country is *not* regarded as adversely affecting its reserve position. Despite the short-term advantages of being able to supplement liquidity via the markets, this practice has raised fears for the international control of liquidity and the stability of the world financial system. Of particular concern has been the extent to which a few countries have become indebted to the eurocurrency markets, increasing the likelihood of them being unable to meet their international financial obligations. This eventuality would, in turn, impose excessive strain on the international financial system and pose a threat to world trade. In such circumstances the need for some form of regulation of the activities of banks and governments in the eurocurrency markets has become increasingly pressing.

The regulation of the markets

As early as 1971 the major central banks agreed to limit their participation in the markets by redepositing dollars with New York rather than in the eurocurrency markets. However, the oil crisis of 1973 led, as we have seen, to a further wave of borrowing by deficit countries to support their reserves and to finance their deficits. At this time the international operations of commercial banks were not subject to the prudential regulation associated with their domestic activities, such regulation being concerned both with the conduct of monetary policy and the supervision of the banking system. This resulted in failures on the part of banks too heavily involved in the eurocurrency markets, notably that of Herstatt in 1974. In the following year a committee of supervisors from the ten major industrial countries was set up to recommend guidelines for the supervision of international banking. National banking supervisory authorities are now responsible for supervising the overseas activities of banks domiciled in their country. In the case of foreign subsidiaries of banks, supervision is shared between the country of origin of the parent bank and the country in which the subsidiary is situated. Nevertheless such supervision has not ended the banking failures, as the failure of the Banco Ambrosiano in 1982 showed, and many banks have carried on increasing their lending to developing countries for fear that financial collapse in any one of these countries will bring them down too.

Regulation of the activities of *central banks* has also been attempted. The World Bank monitors the borrowing of developing countries, while the Bank for International Settlements records the overseas assets and liabilities of the developed countries (excluding in both cases Eastern bloc states). It is often pointed out, with considerable justification, that the present monitoring arrangements are inadequate, otherwise the problems encountered by Poland, Nigeria, Mexico and other developing countries would not have

111

occurred. On the other hand the most strenuous monitoring arrangements are unlikely to prevent countries continuing to borrow to avert economic catastrophe. The best hope would appear to be that of the monitoring bodies keeping commerical banks informed of the level of borrowing, with the banks themselves exercising the necessary caution in their activities. Such a solution seems the only likely one when some of the most important offshore fund and eurocurrency centres, such as Hong Kong and the Caymans, have no central bank through which regulation could be compulsorily enforced.

Notes

1. See S. Kuznets, *Modern Economic Growth. Rate structure and Spread*, Yale University Press, 1966, pp. 331–4.
2. O. L. Altman, 'Eurodollars', *Finance and Development*, March 1967.
3. As estimated by the Bank of England.

Examination questions

The following questions are taken from the examination papers of various examining bodies which include the areas covered by this chapter in their syllabuses. Those marked with an asterisk (★) are representative of the main types of question asked and specimen answers for these will be found in Part II.

1. (a) Define and distinguish clearly between
        (i) Sterling balances   (6)
        (ii) Eurosterling   (6)
    (b) What problems have arisen from the growth of *either* sterling balances *or* eurocurrencies?   (13)
    (IOB 2A, April 1980)

2. Account for the growth of the eurocurrency markets. Is there a case for the international control of these markets? (IOB 2A, September 1981)

3.★ For what reasons are rates of interest paid on deposits in the euromarkets usually higher than comparable rates paid on domestic deposits? How far does this factor explain the rapid growth in the euromarkets? (IOB 2A, April 1983)

4.★ What factors have contributed to the rapid growth of the eurocurrency markets in recent years? To what extent has this growth been a cause of concern to the world's monetary authorities? (IOB 2A, April 1984)

5.★ What is a eurodollar? Why are changes in eurodollar interest rates of importance to the foreign exchange markets? (IOB 2A, September 1984)

6.★ Your customers, European Consortium Limited, wish to establish a manufacturing and trading enterprise in Holland to service their EEC and Scandinavian needs. During a visit to their office you discuss with the finance director various methods of raising short-, medium- and long-term finance for the operations in Holland.
Required:
Brief notes explaining the various methods of obtaining finance, other than sterling, which will satisfy your customer's needs. (IOB 2B, September 1982)

7. Identify the main types of lenders and borrowers in the eurocurrency markets and discuss the characteristics of the markets which have attracted these participants over the past decade. (IOB 2A, September 1985)

8. Examine the relationship between rates of interest for a currency in the domestic money markets and the euromarkets. Other things being equal, what effect would a change in domestic interest rates have on:
(a) the spot foreign exchange rate?
(b) the forward exchange rate? (IOB 2A, April 1986)

Chapter Seven
The international debt problem

International debts arise when countries borrow from abroad to finance a deficit on the current account of the balance of payments or to provide capital for investment projects. Such borrowing is a useful facility for all countries but is essential for developing countries if they are to achieve their full potential. When a country is in the early stages of development its exports are unlikely to be sufficient to pay for the importation of those raw materials and capital goods vital for growth, while official reserves are generally too small to finance a series of deficits. At the same time overseas capital is necessary to augment the limited domestic funds available for industrial development – a need which continues even when the country has already made substantial progress in developing its resources. For these reasons overseas borrowing is an instrinsic part of the process of economic development and should be supported by the advanced industrial countries because of the long-term benefits they can expect to derive from access to the new markets of the developing world. The international debt crisis of the 1980s arose not from fears concerning overseas borrowing as such, but out of the rapid growth of the international debts of the developing countries after 1973 and the effect this growth had on the structure of international debts. These developments give cause for concern because of the dangers they pose for the stability of the international financial system.

The growth of international debt

Between the end of 1973 and the end of 1983 there was a fivefold increase in the external debt of the non-oil-developing countries (LDCs). The sharpest increases in this debt followed the oil price rises of 1973–74 and 1979–80, and these two events were undoubtedly among the principal causes for this debt expansion. In 1973–74, oil prices quadrupled while they doubled again in 1979–80. In both cases the immediate consequence of the price rise was that non-oil-producing countries experienced a severe worsening of their balance of payments. The oil-producing countries, on the other hand, accumulated large surpluses and the failure of some of the oil producers to expand substantially their imports of goods and services had a deflationary effect on the world economy. Most of these unspent surpluses were invested in the major industrial countries so that the currencies of the industrial nations did not depreciate sufficiently to increase their price competitiveness and thereby generate pressure for the elimination of trade imbalances.

Faced with cost-push inflationary pressures and balance of payments problems, the industrial countries reacted by introducing deflationary fiscal and monetary measures to reduce domestic demand. This served to further reduce the level of economic activity as the world moved into the worst recession since the 1930s. The effect of the recession was to bring down the prices of non-oil primary products, which account for 45 per cent of the export earnings of the LDCs, and cause a further deterioration in their terms of trade against the rest of the world. Thus in both 1974 and 1980 the industrial world passed on the worst effects of the oil price rise to the LDCs who found their bill for essential imports rising, while their export earnings fell. Confronted by the consequent balance of payments difficulties, the LDCs were forced to seek borrowing facilities; but the resources of the IMF had not grown sufficiently to cope with the demands now being made upon them. Instead, the LDCs had to turn to the major banking centres of the United States, Britain, Switzerland, West Germany, France, Japan and other countries where the eurocurrency markets had funds available. So began the process in the mid-1970s whereby oil surpluses were recycled to debtor countries by the international banking system through the mechanism of eurocurrency credits. This solution was to prove less successful in dealing with the second wave of debt expansion after 1980.

The other principal factor in the growth of the international indebtedness of the developing countries during the mid-1970s arose out of the activities of those developing countries known as the 'newly industrialising countries' (NICs). While definitions vary as to which countries should be included in this group, the OECD identifies them as Argentina, Brazil, Greece, Hong Kong, Mexico, Portugal, Singapore, South Korea, Spain, Taiwan and Yugoslavia.

Table 7.1

	1972	1973	1974	1975	1976	1977	1978	1979	1980	1981	1982	1983	1984
Non-oil developing countries' balance of payments current account deficits ($ billion)		11.3	37.0	46.3	32.6	28.9	41.3	61.0	89.0	110.0	86.8	67.0	
Average crude oil prices ($ per barrel)	2.65	3.79	11.9	11.26	11.89	13.01	13.06	18.91	31.39	35.03	34.23	29.90	29.20
Terms of trade* of non-oil developing countries		116.3	110.8	100.0	107.3	115.6	108.3	105.9	95.5	90.3	84.6	87.0	

* Export prices ÷ import prices (1975 = 100) *Source: Barclays Review, May 1984*

This group is distinguished from other developing countries on the grounds that its members are passing through the transitional stage from developing country to industrial nation, as evidenced by their rapid industrialisation and a high rate of economic growth. They can therefore be compared to Britain in the early nineteenth century or the United States towards the end of the same century. Like the United States between 1870 and 1890 these countries were enjoying a high annual rate of economic growth (over 5 per cent throughout the 1960s) but did not possess the domestic capital resources to sustain this growth, and they therefore sought to obtain investment funds from overseas.

In the early 1970s the majority of funds for development came from three sources:

1. There was official assistance provided by the advanced countries, often with some underlying political motive behind the aid.
2. There were export credits given for the purpose of buying specific goods from the lending countries and backed by the government of the lending country. An example is the support for export credit given in Britain by the Export Credits Guarantee Department (ECGD).
3. There was the multilateral assistance given by the International Bank for Reconstruction and Development (IBRD) and its affiliated organisations, the International Development Association (IDA) and the International Finance Corporation (IFC).

The IBRD, commonly known as the World Bank, was established at the Bretton Woods conference in 1944 to help finance the reconstruction of areas devastated during the war, and to aid the development of the poorer nations of the world. Since the late 1940s, its activities have been exclusively devoted to the problems of the developing countries, which it assists by providing loans to governments or to government-backed organisations to cover the foreign exchange costs of capital projects. The funds of the IBRD are raised through the subscriptions of member countries and from loan issues floated on the world's capital markets. Unfortunately the strict commercial criteria applied to requests for loans make it very difficult for the LDCs to obtain assistance from the IBRD. In consequence the IDA was established in 1960 to finance projects which make a contribution to development but may not be revenue-producing. The IDA is financed by the wealthier members of the World Bank and gives loans for up to fifty years, interest free, with repayments only being made after ten years. The role of the IFC differs somewhat in that it invests, without government guarantee, in productive private enterprises in association with private investors. By the mid-1970s the sources of finance outlined above were not adequate to deal with the demands of the developing countries and the NICs turned for assistance to the banks of the advanced countries. The international banks were happy to take on this business since lending to the governments or government-sponsored organisations of these countries offered the prospect of a profitable and relatively risk-free area of diversification. The growth and changing structure of the debt of the developing countries is illustrated in Table 7.2.

The problem of the debt

From 1979 onwards a succession of countries, probably as many as forty, have fallen into arrears in repaying their borrowing and in meeting scheduled interest payments. This development was largely unforeseen, since the rapid growth in the international debts of developing countries after the oil price rise of 1973–74 had been absorbed fairly comfortably by the international financial system.

Table 7.2 Total debt of developing countries by source of lending at selected year ends (SDR bn: % of total in [ ])

Source of lending	1971		1975		1979		1982	
Official development aid	24	[27]	34	[19]	53	[13]	63	[10]
Export credits	27	[30]	42	[23]	100	[25]	148	[24]
IMF, World Bank and subsidiaries	10	[11]	22	[12]	47	[12]	76	[12]
Banks	11	[12]	49	[28]	131	[31]	210	[33]
Private borrowing and bond issues	9	[10]	11	[6]	31	[8]	55	[9]
Other	9	[10]	22	[12]	43	[11]	74	[12]
Total	90		180		405		626	

Source: OECD, *External Debt of Developing Countries*, 1982 Survey, Table 1

The causes of the crisis after 1979 lay in the cumulative effects of the growth in the debt and the different circumstances attending the second rise in oil prices.

The causes of the problem

Several factors, most of them inter-related, conspired to bring about the current debt crisis.

1. The unregulated growth of bank lending. The success of the mid-1970s expansion in bank lending to the developing countries probably bred a sense of complacency among the international banks about the security of these operations. This confidence was reinforced by the widespread belief that default by governments, unlike that by commercial borrowers, was almost unthinkable. In fact the banks were in a far weaker position than many of them realised since they had no collateral for the loans granted and were unable to impose controls on further borrowing by debtor countries. In addition, the banks were often ignorant of the true extent of their commitment. This was partly because of the inadequacy of official statistics as to the size of the debts, and partly because of the lack of communication within banks so that several departments might simultaneously be granting loan facilities to a country in isolation from each other. Another problem arose from the fact that the large amount of interbank lending in the eurocurrency markets obscured the extent to which a particular bank was exposed to the possibility of default by any one country.

2. The level of interest rates. During the first oil price rise, interest rates rose only moderately everywhere, including the United States whose rates influence those of the rest of the world. The second rise in oil prices brought a sharper rise in American interest rates and, even though nominal rates have since fallen somewhat, real interest rates are much higher than they were at any time in the 1970s, as Table 7.3 shows. Much of this is due to the policies of the Reagan administration producing a large budget deficit which has had to be financed by attracting loanable funds from all over the western world. It has been estimated that every 1 per cent on dollar interest rates costs the LDCs $2.5 bn net per annum, after allowing for the interest on their own short-term balances.[1] The debts of the LDCs are sensitive to short-term changes in interest rates for two reasons:

1.   Many of the debts have not been repaid or freely renegotiated at maturity but have been rolled forward on a short-term basis

Table 7.3 Dollar interest rates and inflation (% per annum)

	3 months eurodollar rate	US inflation	Real interest rate
1970	8.5	5.9	2.6
1971	6.6	4.3	2.3
1972	5.4	3.3	2.1
1973	9.3	6.2	3.1
1974	11.0	11.0	0
1975	7.0	9.1	−2.1
1976	5.6	5.8	−0.2
1977	6.0	6.5	−0.5
1978	8.8	7.6	1.2
1979	12.0	11.3	0.9
1980	14.0	13.5	0.5
1981	16.8	10.4	6.4
1982	12.2	6.2	6.0
1983	9.6	3.2	6.4
1984	12.0	5.0	7.0
1985	8.0	4.5	3.5
1986	7.6	2.5	4.5

to avoid default. As each slice of debt becomes eligible for renewal, the coupon attached to it is based on current rates.

2. Much of the debt, even that which is long-term, carries short-term interest rates such as the London Inter-bank Offer Rate (LIBOR). Higher interest rates in New York, therefore, immediately translate into increased debt service costs for debtor countries and delay the reduction of the debt.

3. Deflationary policies by industrial countries.   The restrictive fiscal and monetary policies of the industrialised countries after each oil price rise have had serious consequences for the developing countries, a problem discussed on pp 115–17. Referring back to Table 7.1, it can be seen that the world recession following the second rise in oil prices was much more serious than that of 1974–5, and was not followed by so strong an upturn. In consequence the terms of trade of the LDCs show little sign of recovering to their pre-1979 level, a problem reflected in the retarded level of export earnings and slow or non-existent growth of many of these countries. Ironically for some of the developing countries notably Mexico, Indonesia and Venezuela, the *decline* in oil prices after 1982 was the cause of *their* debt problems, since they had already embarked on ambitious expansionary projects in anticipation of higher export earnings.

4. The oil-finance cycle. The process by which the balance of payments surpluses of the oil-producing countries have been recycled, via the eurocurrency markets, to finance the deficits of the LDCs, has provided a short-term respite for the debtor nations but has contributed to what David Lomax has called the oil-finance cycle.[2] The cycle begins with the rise in oil prices, with the subsequent balance of payments deficits of oil-importing countries leading to a recession. The recession causes the prices of oil to fall as world demand for oil drops in the face of lower economic activity. As a result, the balance of payments surpluses of the oil-producing countries start to fall, as they did from $110 bn in 1980 to $60 bn in 1981. The banks are now deprived of the funds which they need to support the debt of the developing countries. This will result in a liquidity crisis unless the fall in oil prices is strong enough to provoke economic recovery in the industrialised nations and, in turn, among the developing countries. Even if there is a recovery, the higher demand for oil which follows will push up oil prices and the whole cycle begins again. While this cycle persists there will be repeated fluctuations in energy prices, in the rate of inflation, in interest rates and in exchange rates which will have a twofold effect on the developing countries. One is a direct effect in that they must export more and more of their basic commodities to finance their imports of oil. The other is an indirect effect in that they keep being pushed into recession by the deflationary measures of the industrialised countries in response to higher oil prices. In consequence, the LDCs suffer higher unemployment, a fall in investment due to the uncertainty of interest rates and a fall in growth. Such economic conditions are clearly not conducive to the reduction of their international debts.

The extent of the problem

The growth of international indebtedness of the non-oil-producing developing countries posed, by the early 1980s, two major threats:

1. There was the possibility that some of the largest debtors might default on their debts and send a shock-wave through the international banking system.
2. There was the risk of a banking collapse brought on by banks straining their liquidity in an attempt to shore up the debt structure of countries threatening to default.

International economics

Table 7.4 External debt of non-oil-developing countries

	1977	1978	1979	1980	1981	1982	1983	1984
Total external debt ($ bn)	280	334	395	475	560	633	669	711
Debt as % of GDP	23.7	24.1	23.3	23.9	27.1	32.5	36.7	37.5
Interest payable ($ bn)	12.7	18.1	25.9	39.0	54.7	63.0	59.2	63.7
Interest as % of exports	5.7	6.9	7.7	9.1	12.0	14.3	13.2	13.0
Debt service as % of exports	14.8	18.1	18.1	17.2	21.3	24.5	21.6	21.1

Source: IMF, *World Economic Outlook*, 1984

With regard to the likelihood of default, the high interest rates now being paid by debtor countries were forcing up the cost of servicing the debt. At the same time the protracted recession of this period had the effect of increasing the size of the debt, both as a percentage of gross domestic product and as a percentage of exports. These impacts are shown in Table 7.4.

By 1981, debt service payments by developing countries equalled approximately half their current account receipts compared to less than a third in 1977. This difficulty was aggravated by the fact that much international lending was accounted for by a dozen or so countries. Of the $159 bn increase in eurocurrency lending to LDCs between 1978 and 1982, two-thirds went to six countries – Argentina, Brazil, Chile, Mexico, Philippines and South Korea. Of the total LDC external debt of $669 bn outstanding in 1983, over $300 bn was owed by Latin American countries, with Brazil owing $92 bn, Mexico $87 bn and Argentina $44 bn. For these countries, the servicing of the debt had assumed alarming proportions by 1982, as Table 7.5 illustrates.

During 1982 the real threat of default came when Mexico entered a financial crisis following the fall in the price of oil and was unable to repay her scheduled debts. A rescue operation was mounted by

Table 7.5 Latin American debt

	1973	1983
Debt as % of exports	176	243
Debt as % of GDP	23	39
Interest as % of exports	11	28

Source: *Barclays Review*, May 1984

the IMF and over fifty international banks to raise $10 bn of new credits and enable the Mexican debts to be rescheduled. This was to become a model for many subsequent rescheduling operations examined in the next section.

The willingness of so many banks to assist in the Mexican crisis is understandable when it is considered that by 1982 a number of banks, particularly in the United States, were very worried about the effect on themselves of default by a major debtor nation. They were in the position of being owed so much already that they could not afford the consequences of letting a default occur, so they had to lend debtor countries the money to meet interest payments due on earlier loans. These further loans would in turn create their own problems at a later date. By 1982 a number of banks were anxious to reduce their level of lending to the developing countries for fear of default, and perhaps the biggest danger at this time was that the banks might precipitate the very thing they feared most by attempting to stop new lending. The immediate crisis was averted largely by the intervention of the IMF and the rescheduling of debts.

The rescheduling of debts

In 1981 the banks arranged for the rescheduling of $10 bn of debts, approximately 2 per cent of the outstanding debt. Rescheduling involves a reduction in the level of capital repayments and a consequent lengthening of the repayment period. The effect is to ease the immediate burden for the borrowing country of servicing its debts while increasing the hopes of the lending banks that the debts will eventually be repaid. Rescheduling agreements tend to be very complex, involving as they do so many banks, and it was the escalating demands for rescheduling in the latter half of 1982 which prompted many banks to wish to pull out of financing operations for the developing countries.

A solution to the crisis was found in the intervention of the IMF. Although the lending facilities of the IMF were sufficient only for it to make token advances to the major debtors, its key contribution was in co-ordinating rescheduling operations and in insisting on borrowing countries adopting economic policies aimed at solving their problems. This made it easier for the banks to continue to participate in the rescheduling of the debts. The IMF's own ability to assist borrowing countries was aided by the 50 per cent increase in quotas agreed at the end of 1982. This was just as well since rescheduling took on epidemic proportions at the end of that year, and in 1983 $100 bn, some 15 per cent of all LDC debt, had to be rescheduled, as we see from Table 7.6.

While undoubtedly successful in solving the immediate crisis and in averting a threat of default, the rescheduling operations brought their own problems. The austerity programmes imposed on the borrowing countries as part of the rescheduling package have often been onerous to the point of being almost impracticable. Mexico, for example, was only able to meet the criteria laid down by the IMF in 1982 at the expense of a contraction of national income, cuts in food subsidies and a higher public sector deficit. In 1984

Table 7.6 Rescheduling as a percentage of non-oil-developing country debt

	Amount rescheduled ($bn)	Debt ($ bn)	Rescheduling as % of debt
1973	0.4	130.1	0.3
1974	1.5	160.8	0.9
1975	0.5	190.8	0.3
1976	0.5	228.0	0.2
1977	0.4	278.5	0.1
1978	2.3	336.3	0.7
1979	3.9	396.9	1.0
1980	6.1	474.0	1.3
1981	10.1	555.0	1.8
1982	10.6	612.4	1.7
1983	104.0	664.3	15.5

Source: Barclays Review, May 1984

the demands made on Jamaica before the IMF would give assistance resulted in the budget deficit being cut in half, redundancies in the civil service and the removal of food subsidies. By the middle of 1984 many of the debtor nations were exhibiting an unwillingness to bear further economic hardship as the price for rescheduling their debts. The stronger stance taken by Argentina and Venezuela in their rescheduling negotiations in 1984 resurrected fears of a major debt crisis in the mid-1980s.

The Cartagena agreement and the 1984 crisis

In June 1984, representatives of eleven Latin American nations met at Cartagena in Colombia to agree a common policy on the restructuring of the area's foreign debts of over $350 bn. The Cartagena meeting resulted from a common belief among the attending nations that they were getting rather less than fair treatment from the industrialised world in the resolution of their debt problems. Several arguments could be put forward in support of this view:

1. There was the 1984 annual report of the Bank for International Settlements (BIS) which criticised the economic policies of the United States as 'bound, sooner or later, to exert a serious destabilising influence on the world economy'. In particular, these policies had led to higher world interest rates which were eating up the benefits of improved exports and balances of payments in Latin America. The report pointed out that to get the ratio of debts to exports down to the 1973 level of 175 per cent at current Latin American growth rates would take fifteen years with interest rates of 11 per cent, but only eleven years if rates were reduced to 10 per cent. A 1 per cent hike in interest rates would, on the other hand, be enough to wipe out Mexico's tourist earnings for a year.

2. There was the attitude of the western governments in abdicating any responsibility for the current state of affairs through their encouragement of banks giving non-performing loans and their refusal to take joint action to deal with the loan problem. This attitude was evidenced by opposition to Third World demands for a new allocation of special drawing rights and by pressure from the United States for the IMF to cut back on its enlarged access facilities. Only in 1983 had the IMF agreed to borrowers drawing up to 125 per cent of their accounts each year when under special difficulties.

3. There was the harsh stance taken by the IMF itself in demanding fierce austerity measures as the price of its support

for a restructuring agreement. These austerity programmes brought hardship to the peoples of the debtor countries, retarded the growth necessary to enable the debtor countries to solve their problems and, coupled with the prevailing high interest rates, meant that the debtor nations were paying for the economic policies of the western world.

The conference at Cartagena produced a consensus document outlining a package of measures designed to enable the debtor countries to reorganise their debt payments. The final declaration stressed that each country would carry on with its individual debt negotiations but that recent experience had shown that the problem was now too serious to be left to isolated dealings with banks or the international institutions.

The first part of the document covers the debtor countries' analysis of the debt problem. The policies of the industrialised countries were held largely to blame because they had changed the original terms of the loans by pushing up interest rates. Protectionism in some industrialised countries was also attacked since it stood in the way of the debtor countries being able to increase their exports. It was recognised, however, that part of the fault lay with the over-enthusiasm of Latin Americans generally for investing their capital overseas; the flight of capital from Latin America had been $30 bn in 1983 alone. Governments of the countries attending the conference were urged to stop the region being a net exporter of capital and to encourage more investment from overseas.

The document then went on to outline a number of specific proposals for the reorganisation of the debt. Among the most significant were:

1. That in renegotiations and new dealings, banks should use interest rates no higher than the cost of obtaining money in the markets.
2. That costs should be brought down to a minimum and commissions abolished along with penalty payments during renegotiations.
3. That arrangements to mitigate the effect of high interest rates, such as the extension of loan terms or greater assistance from the IMF, should be introduced.
4. That repayments should be held to a percentage of total export revenues; a ratio of 20 per cent was suggested.

The views expressed at Cartagena were given support by the World Bank in its annual report at the end of 1984. The report identifies four major problems left unresolved by the austerity plans agreed by the IMF, the debtor countries and the international banks:

1. that some developing countries have been required to follow contradictory policies;
2. that where developing countries have achieved a trade surplus, the industrial nations have reacted by introducing protectionist measures;
3. that long-term growth has been slowed; and
4. that the rescheduling of debt has merely pushed repayment further into the distance.

The report argued that current policies were too negative and that there should be a greater emphasis on export and industrial growth and less on restraint. Finally, the World Bank report attacked the sharp cutback in aid to the developing countries at a time when it is needed most.

The pessimism of the World Bank contrasts with the confidence expressed at the IMF annual meeting soon after that the debt crisis was under control and that by 1990 the ratio of foreign debts to exports for the seven largest debtors could fall by 40 per cent. Yet early in 1985 the IMF cut off its loans to Brazil after that country was unable to meet the prescribed IMF targets for inflation and monetary growth.

The future

The difficulties which emerged in rescheduling Brazil's $45 bn bank debts early in 1985 indicate that the crisis is far from over and have led to renewed speculation concerning the possibility of default. On practical grounds it might be thought that default could present only a short-term remedy since the finance acquired by default will eventually run out and the country will have to seek to renew its borrowing facilities. However, the key is the interest rate. As Malcolm Crawford has pointed out, 'in a simple debt-default trade-off model, it is advantageous for the debtor to default if the rate of interest on his debts exceeds the average expected annual increase in his outstanding debt in future'[3]. While the law of contract and its enforcement prohibits private debtors from exercising this option, sovereign states are subject to no such restraint and may base their decisions on the debt-default trade-off calculation. On the other hand, the repudiation of debts could be expected to result in retaliation from those countries whose banks have suffered through default. Such retaliation would include the seizure of assets of the defaulting country, such as bank funds, aircraft, ships and cargoes. There is also the risk of trade sanctions which would harm the debtor country's exporters.

Default has therefore rarely been considered a possible policy instrument by debtor nations because of the need to take account of the private business sector. However, in a recent paper, Anatole Kalesky has argued that default by some Third World countries is quite likely in the foreseeable future[4]. He considers that outright default is unlikely but that the larger debtors may exploit their potential power to achieve 'conciliatory default' whereby trade and official creditors continue to be accommodated but private debts are repudiated. In part this willingness to default is due to the increased self-sufficiency of many of the developing countries in oil, food and other raw materials which has resulted from the economic hardship of recent years. But it is also the result of the slow growth, already referred to, giving predictions such as that for Latin America where output per capita will still be 7 per cent lower in 1987 than it was in 1982; and predictions that the industrial nations will not grow fast enough to enable the LDCs to expand their exports sufficiently to reduce their debt burdens.

In these circumstances, conciliatory default is an attractive proposition since many westerners would still be willing to trade with and invest in the country provided that default was limited to the banks. Furthermore, governments in the advanced countries might find it politically less dangerous to maintain a friendly attitude to defaulting countries rather than inflict punishment on them. This possibility of default is also important because it affects the process of renegotiation of debts. The more attractive default becomes as a way of solving the debtor country's problems, the weaker the bargaining position of the banks and the IMF in new negotiations. Indeed, there has already been some relaxation of conditions imposed on loan rescheduling arrangements by the IMF.

The great fear of default arises from the uncertainty of the effect of such a default on the international financial system. The nine major US 'money centre' banks have lent to the six main debtor countries amounts which are 79 per cent greater than their shareholders' total equity, so that they would clearly be at risk. However, the US authorities could be expected to intervene to protect the system, and there are 15,000 other banks in the United States with little or no exposure to Third World debts. Similarly there are central banks in all the other advanced countries which could be expected to support their banks if default threatened them. Widespread banking collapses would be unlikely although individual banks might encounter difficulties. None the less the risk of disruption in the international banking system, however slight, cannot be ignored. It is to be hoped that in the future a greater emphasis will be placed on the role of the international institutions, notably the IMF and the World Bank, in the finance of investments in the developing countries. This will require a much greater willingness on the part of the industrialised world to recognise that their own interests can best be served by increasing the level of economic activity within the developing world. A major increase in the level of SDRs to increase world liquidity, which would incur no direct costs for themselves, would be a move in the right direction.

Notes

1. See 'International Indebtedness – The Banking Crisis of the 80s?', Sir Timothy Bevan, *Barclays Bank Review*, May 1984.
2. See *National Westminster Bank Quarterly Review*, November 1982.
3. 'Third World Debt is Here to Stay', *Lloyds Bank Review*, January 1985.
4. *The Costs of Default*, 20th Century Fund paper by Anatole Kaletsky, Priority Press Publications, New York 1985.

Examination questions

The following questions are taken from the examination papers of various examining bodies which include the areas covered by this chapter in their syllabuses. Those marked with an asterisk ($\star$) are representative of the main types of question asked and specimen answers for these will be found in Part II.

1.$\star$ Over the past year, several countries have revealed figures of international indebtedness which have cast serious doubts on their national solvency, and the willingness of lending countries to extend further credit. What is likely to be the effect on world trade in general, and for such countries in particular? (Dip. Marketing, June 1983)

2.$\star$ Distinguish between the roles of the IMF (International Monetary Fund) and the World Bank (International Bank for Reconstruction and Development). Why may they both be seen as of increasing importance? (ICMA Foundation, November 1983)

3. Discuss some of the longer-term consequences of the *1973* rise in the price of oil. Illustrate your answer by specific reference to a particular country. (London, January 1985)

4.★   What problems have been posed for international liquidity requirements by the large balance of payments surpluses accruing to oil-producing countries in recent years? To what extent have the eurocurrency markets helped in overcoming these problems? (IOB 2A, September 1982)

5.   Analyse the effects of a rise in the price of oil on the rate of inflation and on the balance of payments (current and capital accounts) of TWO of the following:
   (a) the United Kingdom;
   (b) a country which is a member of OPEC (Organisation of Petroleum Exporting Countries);
   (c) a non-oil-producing developing country. (IOB 2A, September 1981)

6.   Can one reasonably argue that it would be in the self-interest of advanced countries to increase capital flows to the developing countries? (Oxford Entrance Examination, November 1981)

7.   'The use of foreign capital for development purposes in West Africa solves some problems but at the same time creates a few others.' Discuss this statement. (West African 'A' Level, Paper 2, June 1984)

8.   Explain why international trade tends to operate to the detriment of less developed countries and suggest actions which might improve their trading position. (AEB, June 1985)

Chapter Eight
The European Economic Community

In the years immediately following the end of the Second World War there was considerable interest in the ideal of European unity, as evidenced by the establishment of the Organisation for European Economic Co-operation in 1948 and the Council of Europe in the following year. Both organisations were intended to promote harmony between European nations; the former through greater economic co-operation and the latter by a common acceptance of the rule of law and a respect for human rights. While all the western European states were ultimately to join these organisations, the driving force for European unity came from those countries most closely united by historical ties – Belgium, the Netherlands, Luxembourg, France, Italy and West Germany. The first three had even constituted one country for a time during the nineteenth century, and in 1947 they combined again to form the Benelux customs union. They, with their larger neighbours, were hopeful that closer political and economic ties would both reduce the pressures which had led to so many past conflicts and speed up the process of European reconstruction. Accordingly, the 'Six' established the European Coal and Steel Community (ECSC) in 1951 as a 'common' market in coal and steel, i.e. a market in which there would be no discrimination between members as regards trade in coal and steel. The ECSC was given a supra-national institutional structure with an executive body empowered to take decisions binding on member states. Those in Europe strongly committedd to political unification hoped that the ECSC would lead to the formation of a European Defence Community involving the integration of Europe's armed forces under a unified command structure. While French unease at this proposed submerging of national identities prevented such a European Defence Community from ever forming, the mere hint of such a possibility was enough to deter Britain from joining the ECSC until 1954 and to leave her suspicious of closer European ties.

During the 1950s the European economies were sufficiently strengthened that attitudes towards unity changed. Instead of defeated, war-ravaged nations seeking unification to re-establish European influence, they were now confident, healthy states who regarded further unification as a means of achieving accelerated economic expansion rather than as an end in itself. When the Six signed the Treaty of Rome in 1957, the object was the formation of an economic unit of comparable size, wealth and influence to that of the United States. This European Economic Community (EEC) would enable Europe to compete on equal terms with the United States and to resist further Americanisation of the European economy. While the Treaty of Rome contained clauses providing for eventual political unification, the implementation of these was regarded as neither imminent nor of paramount importance. None the less this apparent commitment to political unity was enough to deter Britain from applying for membership at that time.

The institutions of the Community

As the development of the EEC could not be predicted at the outset, the Treaty of Rome established an institutional framework which could both administer the work of an international economic organisation and could be adapted, if necessary, to become the institutions of government in a European super-state. In practice, little progress towards political unification has been achieved and the growth of the Community to include Great Britain, Denmark, Ireland and Greece has diluted strength of the movement for unification. The accession of Spain and Portugal to full membership in 1986 further increased the scope for a divergence of aims among the various member states. In consequence the institutions of the EEC have continued to be primarily concerned with the various economic problems of twelve independent but economically-linked states.

The Commission

This body has two members from each of the larger states and one each from the remainder. It is customary in the case of Britain for one commissioner to be named by the Conservative Party and one by Labour, whichever is in office. Commissioners usually have political backgrounds but must suspend their political activities during their term of office[1], a period of four years renewable for a further two. From among the commissioners are chosen the President and Vice-President of the Commission, these posts being rotated among member countries. The commissioners head the departments of the Commission which reflect the various areas of activity of the EEC and which co-ordinate policy, execute decisions, enforce regulations and carry out day-to-day administration. Policy decisions taken by the Commission are referred for approval to the Council of Ministers.

The Council of Ministers

This is the senior executive body of the Community and consists of a minister from each member state. Membership is not restricted to a specific person or post so that national governments are represented by different ministers at different times, depending on the topic under consideration. The ministers most commonly attending are those responsible for foreign affairs, finance, agriculture and trade, while there are regular meetings of heads of government. The presidency of the Council is rotated among the member countries on a six-monthly basis, the role of the president being crucial in the reconciliation of differences and in the establishment of compromise. The Council considers proposals placed before it by the Commission and has the final say on whether the proposals should be enacted. Disputes over such controversial issues as the Community budget, agricultural policy and fisheries policy are common and progress is frequently difficult. While voting strength is weighted in favour of the larger countries, a two-thirds majority is required on all decisions to protect dissenting countries. Since, however, policies must be generally acceptable to each of the member states if they are to be enforceable, decisions tend to be based on compromise in an effort to obtain unanimity. Meetings are much publicised, with national governments frequently threatening reprisals where they feel that policy is moving against their interests, and compromises reached are often regarded as unsatisfactory by all parties.

The parliament

The title of this body is somewhat misleading since, although elected by universal suffrage, it is not a parliament in the true sense of the word. Ministers are not members of the parliament and nor are they responsible to it. In addition, the parliament may not legislate on its own initiative so that its primary role is as a place for debate and the airing of grievances. In exceptional cases it may also reject ministerial legislation. The parliament's greatest strength lies in the area of the budget as it may approve it, amend it (e.g. increases in certain areas of expenditure) or reject it outright. If the last course is taken, parliament and the Council of Ministers must seek a compromise. In other matters the parliament has the right to criticise legislation and to question the Council of Ministers, but it may not alter legislation. Its only sanction is the dismissal of the Commission, which can be effected by passing a censure motion having the support of a two-thirds majority. Such an event is highly unlikely due to the fragmented party system within the European parliament and the fact that voting patterns are as likely to be based on national groupings as on ideological lines.

The court of justice

The court is a supreme court of twelve judges appointed by the member countries for a six-year term and assisted by four advocates-general. The court deals with disputes between member states, disputes between member states and the institutions of the Community and disputes between individuals or corporate bodies and the institutions of the Community. Typical disputes settled would include complaints against countries or companies which were not obeying the regulations of the Commission. Like any other international court, it has no power to enforce its decisions and depends on acquiescence by the parties to the dispute. The court has no authority to intervene in the internal civil or criminal proceedings of member countries.

Other institutions

In addition to the bodies outlined above, there are over seventy consultative organisations covering such areas as economic policy, transport, energy, employment, education and training, equality of opportunity, social issues, nuclear research and consumer affairs. The work of many of these institutions will be examined in subsequent sections.

The economy of the Community[2]

Central to the role of the EEC in drawing member countries closer together have been the steps taken to promote economic unity within the Community. The purpose of economic unity is that each member state should achieve greater prosperity than it could realise as a separate unit. This is also the aim of the customs union or protected free trade area established for industrial goods (see pp 40–41) and the regulated market established for agricultural produce (see pp 137–43).

The EEC goes much further, however, since it seeks to increase the efficiency of the productive system of the Community. This involves the adoption of policies which will enable the development of international economies of scale through the free movement of labour, capital and enterprise. But the relaxation of barriers between member states is not enough; there must also be a harmonisation of policies and regulations among members to ensure that resources are not drawn to particular locations for purely non-economic reasons. In addition, the opening-up of markets makes the economy of each member country more sensitive to developments in the others and it is therefore desirable that all of them pursue compatible short-term economic policies. Such harmonisation, and if necessary unification, of policies involves a degree of co-operation far beyond that likely to be achieved on a purely voluntary basis and has required the development of supranational regulatory agreements binding on the members. Ultimately, full harmonisation can only come through economic and monetary union, a process requiring free agreement by all member states. To date, progress in the various areas of economic harmonisation and unification has been patchy, as can be seen from a review of the main areas of Community action.

1. Free trade
The general principle is that goods should be able to move freely throughout the territory of the Community. Quotas for industrial products were abolished on 31 December 1961, and customs duties were abolished on 1 July 1968 for the original six members and on 1 July 1977 for the Nine. Though customs duties and quotas have been formally abolished, barriers to trade have not entirely disappeared:
1. The member countries retain their differing tax structures, which distort competitive conditions; the wide variations in taxes imposed on motor cars and alcoholic drinks are examples of this.
2. The Community has attempted to outlaw technical barriers to trade, except where legitimate concerns over safety or health are involved. Yet such barriers persist as a way of preventing the entry of goods from other Community countries.
3. Obstacles to trade are posed by the complex customs formalities maintained by each country. While these may have their origins in bureaucratic regulations, their survival may well

be due to a residual resistance to free trade. Ironically, Community regulations on trade may also contribute to the 'red tape' slowing down the movement of goods.

2. Free movement of labour

Significant progress has been made towards the free movement of labour in that work permits are no longer required by individuals wishing to obtain work in member countries other than their place of birth. However, cultural and language barriers still present very real obstacles to mobility. Nevertheless the Community has attempted to negate many of the hindrances formerly posed by differences in social security rights, in working conditions and in recognised qualifications, by promoting standardisation of regulations and the comparability of qualifications.

3. Free movement of capital and enterprise

The Treaty of Rome, Article 67, provides for the free movement of capital 'to the extent necessary to ensure the proper functioning of the common market'. This qualification recognises that capital movements may affect the working of the economy in a variety of ways and that national governments will wish to ensure that such movements are consistent with short-term economic policy. A directive issued in 1960 contained four lists of capital movements and required unconditional liberalisation of movements in lists A and B, and conditional liberalisation of those in lists C and D.

List A: direct investments, personal capital movements, movements associated with trade in goods
List B: operations in securities dealt with on stock exchanges
List C: issues of securities on capital markets
List D: movements of short-term capital between banks

While no changes in official policy have occurred since 1960, the movement of short-term capital, as well as long-term, has grown rapidly, especially through the growth and expansion of the eurocurrency markets (see pp 104–12).

As regards the free movement of enterprise, Article 52 of the Treaty specifically provides that there should be no barrier to the establishment of a business outside the country of origin of the enterprise, as long as local legal obligations and responsibilities are observed. In practice, the psychological and other barriers to the mobility of enterprises have, as with the mobility of labour, proved too great. Apart from transnational expansion by multinational companies, few enterprises have attempted to transfer their centre of operations.

Nevertheless, despite reservations regarding progress in these areas of the Community's work, intra-community trade has grown faster than the trade of each member state with the rest of the world. The importance of intra-community trade to each member is illustrated in Table 8.1.

4. Agricultural policy

From its foundation, the Community was keen to promote increased agricultural production, especially since the Community was the largest importer of agricultural produce in the world. With agriculture the single most important industry in the Community, employing as it did some 10 per cent of the working population, increased agricultural production was clearly a politically attractive policy.

The objectives of the Community's agricultural policy are set out in Article 39 of the Treaty and are:

1. to increase agricultural productivity by promoting technical progress and by ensuring the rational development of agricultural production and the optimum utilisation of the factors of production, in particular labour;
2. to ensure a fair standard of living for the agricultural

Table 8.1 Intra-community trade

| | % of total exports | | % of GDP | |
	1958	1982	1958	1982
FR Germany	36	48	6	13
France	28	49	3	8
Italy	34	46	3	10
Netherlands	57	72	22	35
Belgium/Lux	53	71	17	43
United Kingdom	20	41	3	9
Ireland	84	71	21	33
Denmark	58	49	16	13
Greece	50	46	4	5
EEC	35	52	5	13

Source: Economy of The European Community, Commission of the European Communities, 1984

community, in particular by increasing the individual earnings of persons engaged in agriculture;
3. to stabilise markets;
4. to assure the availability of supplies;
5. to ensure that supplies reach consumers as reasonable prices.

In effect, the Community was intent on achieving self-sufficiency through support for improved productivity and through the creation of an environment conducive to the expansion of the various sectors of agriculture, notably price stability.

Initially the Community gave priority to the objective of raising living standards for those engaged in agriculture. This meant either granting direct financial aid to farmers with low incomes or raising prices. In the first case, farmers are subsidised by taxpayers[3] while in the second it is consumers who foot the bill. The option chosen was that of higher prices, and this gave rise to the pricing system adopted by the Common Agricultural Policy (CAP) which came into full effect in 1968. Under this system, prices were fixed in units of account, so that in principle there was a single pricing system throughout the Community in agricultural products. The CAP is directed by the European Agricultural Guidance and Guarantee Fund (EAGGF). which is part of the Community budget. The EAGGF has two sections:

1. The guidance section, which finances schemes to improve the efficiency of agricultural production, e.g. by encouraging larger production units and other structural changes. In 1983 this expenditure amounted to ECU 812.7 m., only about 5 per cent of total community expenditure on agriculture.
2. The guarantee section, which finances all expenditure on price support policies of the CAP. This expenditure amounted to ECU 15,662.3 m. in 1983, about 95 per cent of total Community expenditure on agriculture.

The guarantee section is responsible for running the system of price-fixing which has both internal and external effects. Internally a target price is set which is the price the farmer should receive plus the cost of transporting the products to the consumer. In order to help prices reach the target price, an intervention price is set 5 per cent below the target price and if market prices fall to this level the CAP's intervention agencies buy up surplus production. Externally, imports are controlled by the imposition of a threshold price below which imports will not be accepted into the Community. Import prices are raised to this level by the imposition of a levy

Table 8.2 Distribution of guidance section expenditure 1983

	ECU m.	%
Projects for improvement of structures	186.8	23
Social-structural measures	133.7	16
Regional measures	380.1	47
Market-related measures	81.6	10
Structural measures – fisheries	30.5	4
	812.7	100

Source: *Midland Bank Review*, Winter 1984

on imports when the world price is below the target price. The working of the system is illustrated in Fig. 8.1.

In Fig. 8.1 (a), Community output (Q_1) is less than demand (Q_2) at Community prices (P_2). Imports are allowed to make up the shortfall in output, but since the world price is only P_1, an import levy of P_2-P_1 is imposed to bring imports up to the Community price.

In Fig. 8.1 (b), Community output (P_2) is greater than demand (Q_1) at Community prices (P_2). Excess production is taken up by CAP buying into intervention or by subsidising exports with an export subsidy of P_2-P_1. It is assumed that all products bought into intervention are later exported.

In Fig. 8.1 (c), Community output (Q) is limited by quota to match demand and Community prices. Since the Community price is P_2 while the world price is only P_1, an import levy, set at P_2-P_1, keeps out imports. No subsidy is required for Community output.

The green pound

When the CAP was first established, the emphasis was on growth and stable prices and there was little thought given to the possibility of excess production and undisposable surpluses. One threat to stable prices was the alteration of exchange rates between member countries and this led to the introduction of *green rates* in 1969. The green rate is the rate of exchange between the ECU and a member country's own currency for agricultural purposes, and in 1969 the devaluation of the French franc was followed by France being allowed to keep its pre-devaluation exchange rate for agri-

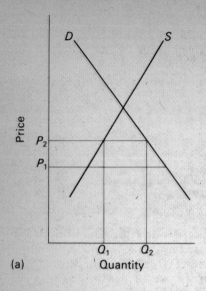

(a)

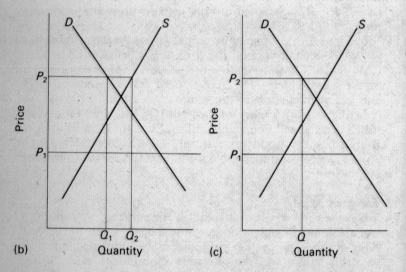

(b)

(c)

Fig. 8.1

cultural prices, thus protecting French consumers from the full inflationary effects of the devaluation. The UK was accorded similar treatment when the exchange rate of sterling fell sharply in the mid-1970s. The system of green rates is further complicated by the fact that a member country may have different green rates for different products. Furthermore, green rates distort trade and therefore have had to be supplemented by monetary compensatory amounts (MCAs) to compensate for the artificial difference between the green rate and the market rate. The development of the MCA system has protected Community farmers from the effects of exchange rate movements but has tended to create national rather than Community prices and policies. Indeed, the stronger countries have been unwilling to revalue their green currencies so that farmers' subsidies are even higher than they would be if prices were based on market exchange rates.

Impact of the CAP
The effects of the development and sustained importance of the CAP have been several:

1. The objective of self-sufficiency in major food products has been achieved, as Fig. 8.2 shows.
2. Over-production in some cases has reached staggering proportions as evidenced by wine lakes and butter mountains.
3. The subsidy system has kept in existence some small marginal dairy farms and has also resulted in large efficient farms receiving substantial handouts.
4. The CAP has continued to dominate the Community budget, taking 66.4 per cent of total spending in 1983 and preventing the development of funding in other areas of concern for the Community.
5. The CAP conflicts with the principles espoused by GATT and in the future a failure to reform the system could result in retaliation from the rest of the world.

Despite the difficulty in achieving change in the face of opposition from powerful vested interests, some reforms have been introduced, mainly since the mandate of 30 May 1980 calling for structural changes to policy.

1. In 1981, 'Guidelines for European Agriculture' was published and aimed specifically at a reduction in grain output by keeping prices down, with the aim being to bring prices into line with the rest of the world by 1988.

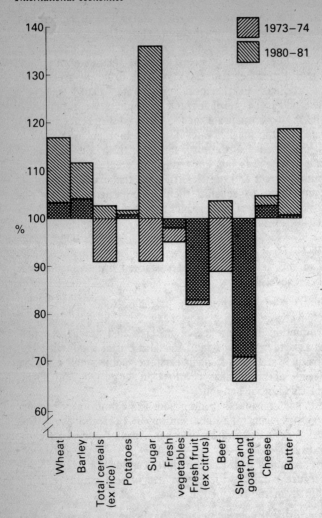

Source: Midland Bank Review, Winter 1984

Fig. 8.2 Degree of self-sufficiency in the EEC

2. In addition, *co-responsibility levies* have been introduced for milk and cereal products. Under this scheme, any excess in production over the stated limit leads to prices being reduced.
3. In 1984 a quota system was introduced for dairy farming.

While this may help reduce excess output, it may actually harm the efficient high-output farmer more than his inefficient counterpart.

One barrier to further progress remains the desire to protect the poorer agricultural communities of member countries, especially since one of the aims of the CAP originally was to help such groups. Perhaps the future lies in a rationalisation of agriculture in the Community with a stronger emphasis on regional aid for those who can never hope to compete with the major farming regions.

5. *Industrial policy*
The Community has itself identified three main areas of positive industrial policy:

1. Action against cartels and monopolies under Articles 85 and 86 of the Treaty. Generally, EEC regulations are similar to the legislation passed in Britain, though Britain is also bound by EEC regulations which go further than its own domestic policies. While the regulations are rarely invoked, they enable the Commission to prohibit both cartel agreements and intended mergers and to impose fines on firms which contravene the Commission's ruling. Competition policy has also aimed to control assistance by member states to their own industries where this militates against competition between domestic producers and those of other member states.

2. Specific intervention in particular industries to assist their development. Coal and steel spring to mind since the EEC grew out of the European Coal and Steel Community, established itself to foster the development of these two industries. While early policy in the ECSC aimed at expansion, recent years have seen the Community being forced to deal with the problems posed by excess capacity. The Treaty of Rome made no provision for a positive industrial policy, and progress in industrial policy in other areas has been very limited, despite the obvious case for the Community taking the lead in industrial development.

3. The encouragement of co-operation between enterprises of different member countries and the launching of genuine Community projects. Here again successes have been few. Although there has been a rapid growth in the number of agreements between enterprises and in the number of sales subsidiaries formed, transfrontier mergers have been very few. With regard to industrial projects involving enterprises from

several member states, the only notable successes have been the European Space Agency and the European Airbus, neither of which were set up through the Community's machinery. This situation contrasts strongly with the growth of co-operative projects between European and American enterprises and between European and Japanese enterprises, e.g. those between CII and Honeywell-Bull and between British Leyland and Honda.

Progress on an industrial policy has, on the whole, been disappointing. As Professor Maillet has put it, 'Enterprises have taken only limited advantage of the opportunities made available for transfrontier regrouping or reorganisation and governments have missed opportunities for developing new industries opened up by the change of dimension from the national to the Community scale'[4].

6. Energy policy

Because of its heavy dependence on energy imports (see Table 8.3) the Community has always sought to improve the development of energy sources, initially through the ECSC and Euratom, and latterly through a joint Commission on energy.

Energy policy was relatively late in developing because of the

Table 8.3

	Energy consumption in 1983		% dependence on energy imports		
	per capita (toe)	total (mtoe)	1963	1973	1983
FR of Germany	4.0	276	23.7	56.5	51.2
Belgium	4.1	41	52.0	88.0	73.3
Denmark	3.2	17	96.8	99.6	86.6
France	3.2	174	53.6	79.6	61.8
Greece	1.6	16	—	—	64.9
Ireland	2.2	8	74.8	84.4	62.6
Italy	2.2	125	72.3	84.3	81.2
Luxembourg	7.7	3	99.7	99.6	98.7
Netherlands	3.3	57	67.7	22.0	7.2
United Kingdom	3.4	191	29.7	53.1	−17.4
EUR 10	3.2	876	41.6	64.3	41.9

Source: The Economy of the European Community, 1984

predominance of cheap energy sources until the 1970s and it remains an area in which surprisingly little has been achieved; energy still being primarily an issue dealt with on national lines. On the positive side the Community has formulated a Community system for intervention in support of the coal-mining industry. It also grants financial aid for Community research and development projects on new techniques for oil and gas exploration, and contributes to various research projects on new sources of energy.

7. *Regional policy*

Regional disparities in incomes and standarda of living are of concern to the Community for three main reasons:

1. They are the underlying causes of some loss of overall economic efficiency.
2. There is need to ensure that the regional policies of individual member states are compatible.
3. Regional disparities are a potential source of division and social conflict within any community.

Consequently the *Regional Development Fund* was set up in 1975 to assist poorer regions and areas worst hit by the recession. The Fund aids investments in industry and services which create new jobs or maintain existing employment, such as the construction of a new factory or the modernisation of an exisiting production unit. The Fund also assists the financing of infrastructure investments directly linked to the development of industrial activities or which revitalise ailing agricultural areas, for example the building of roads or the improvement of electricity or water supply. The work of the Community's regional policy is closely related to that of its Social Fund which co-finances training and retraining schemes and job-creation projects.

The budget

The Community budget is minute by national standards. In 1984, Community expenditure accounted for approximately 2.5 per cent of the member states' total public expenditure and represented only 0.8 per cent of their collective gross domestic product.

In examining the breakdown of Community expenditure, the most notable feature is the predominance of agricultural spending, already referred to in the section on the CAP. The very low level of resources allocated to industry, energy, research and transport reflect the virtual non-existence of Community policies in these fields. One area where there has been more rapid expansion is in the provision of regional aid to poorer areas, first given in 1975. Such a development was inevitable given the changing balance of the Community with the accession of the poorer Mediterranean countries to membership, first Greece and then Spain and Portugal. In 1985 the European summit to confirm Spanish and Portuguese entry also established £960 m. of new funds for Integrated Mediterranean Programmes (IMPS) and agreed to increase regional and social development by £1,500 m. over seven years. The evolution of the budget is shown in Fig. 8.3.

The proportion allocated to regional policy includes budgetary refunds (see below). The expenditure on co-operation and development went mainly on food aid and assistance to Mediterranean, Asian and Latin American countries.

The revenue from which the budget is financed comes from four main sources:

1. Customs duties on industrial products imported from non-Community countries.
2. Agricultural levies charged at the external frontiers of the Community to bring the price of imported foodstuffs up to the Community level.
3. Levies on sugar and isoglucose by which producers pay part of the cost of disposing of excess quantities.
4. A proportion of value-added tax (VAT). In 1970 the rate was fixed at 1 per cent of VAT receipts, unless a higher figure were ratified by national parliaments. None the less this figure has proved insufficient to finance Community expenditure and in 1984 the ceiling was increased to 1.4 per cent.

The budget has been the source of much friction within the European Community. This is because the pattern of expenditure does not represent the economic structure of member states, whereas the revenue does. The result is that large discrepancies can occur between what a member receives from the Community and what it contributes to the Community. While it would be self-defeating for the Community if each member expected to take out exactly what it put in, there have been some startling deficits, especially in the case of Britain. From her accession, Britain was a net contributor, and by 1980 was making 37 per cent of the net contribution of the Community, by far the largest of any member despite being the third poorest. This situation occurred because of the large proportion of total expenditure allocated by the Community to agriculture. This meant that while Britain, with its

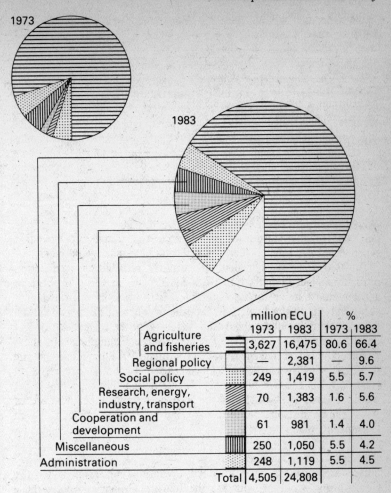

	million ECU		%	
	1973	1983	1973	1983
Agriculture and fisheries	3,627	16,475	80.6	66.4
Regional policy	—	2,381	—	9.6
Social policy	249	1,419	5.5	5.7
Research, energy, industry, transport	70	1,383	1.6	5.6
Cooperation and development	61	981	1.4	4.0
Miscellaneous	250	1,050	5.5	4.2
Administration	248	1,119	5.5	4.5
Total	4,505	24,808		

Source: *European File* 18/84

Fig. 8.3 The development of the overall European Community budget (actual expenditure)

relatively high level of imports of industrial products, contributed 25 per cent of total revenue, her small and efficient farming community attracted only 5 per cent of the large Community agricultural support. At the same time, the failure of Community policy to develop in other areas meant that although Britain received 26

Table 8.4 Overall Community budget: revenue
1986

	ECUm.	%
Customs duties	9,700	27.7
Agricultural levies	2,699	7.7
Special contributions	204	0.6
VAT	22,184	63.2
Miscellaneous	263	0.8
	35,050	100.0

Source: European Commission

per cent of the Community's regional and social support, this represented only $7\frac{1}{2}$ per cent of the total Community budget.

In 1980 a series of ministerial summits resulted in a reduction of Britain's net contribution from £1,200 m. to £350 m. and an agreement to strive for an equitable distribution of the burden of contributions in the future. In fact the problem of excessive British contributions soon recurred and led to another review of budget liabilities in 1984. In June of that year the Council of Ministers agreed new corrective measures to modulate VAT payments by any member state whose budgetary burden becomes excessive in relation to its relative prosperity. It was hoped that these measures would reduce by two-thirds the gap between the UK's share of VAT contributions and what she received back through Community spending.

The European Investment bank
There are a number of financial operations undertaken by the Community which are outside the budget. Principal among these are the borrowing and lending activities of the European Investment Bank (EIB). Following the terms set out in the Treaty of Rome, the EIB promotes the balanced development of the Community by aiding the financing of projects which modernise and develop industry, which introduce new technology, and which develop new sources of energy and protect the environment. In 1984, total loans granted by the EIB amounted to ECU 6.0 bn. from funds raised on the world's capital markets. Other organisations offering loans for industrial development within the Community are the ECSC, Euratom and the New Community Instrument – this last

body being concerned increasingly with aid to small and medium-sized companies.

The European Monetary System

An ultimate objective of the EEC is to attain economic and monetary union. Economic union would involve the member countries adopting a common strategy on all key economic issues as a prelude to complete unification of economic policy-making and the establishment of one budgetary and fiscal regime. Monetary union is the establishment of a common currency, a unified money supply and pooled official reserves under the control of a central bank with the ability to direct monetary policy for the Community as a whole. These two elements are inextricably linked since any group of countries wishing to form an economic unit must maintain stable exchange rates (or have a single currency), which in turn requires consistency in the development of their respective economies. To achieve this, economic policies must be dovetailed and common economic objectives must be pursued.

The Treaty of Rome is very general in its provision for a common macroeconomic strategy and not until the late 1960s was there a serious attempt to specify the aims of the Community in this respect. In 1969 the heads of government agreed that in 1970 plans should be formulated for eventual economic and monetary union. This was followed by the 1970 Werner report, which saw economic and monetary union as implying fixed exchange rates between member states, consistency of monetary and budgetary policy throughout the Community, and a unified balance of payments. The Werner report went on to set out the blueprint for what is effectively a single economic unit. In 1971 the Council resolved to work towards European Monetary Union by 1980 and recorded its agreement to the establishment of a mechanism for medium-term financial assistance to supplement the agreement of February 1970 on short-term monetary support.

A further impetus to greater European monetary co-operation came with the dollar crisis of 1971 and the Smithsonian Agreement, which together weakened the Bretton Woods system of fixed exchange rates. Fluctuations in exchange rates between member countries' currencies threatened the stability of the Community and led to the introduction of the 'snake' in March 1972. While Community currencies would continue to be able to fluctuate by $2\frac{1}{4}$ per cent either side of parity against *non-member* currencies, they would fluctuate by no more than 1 per cent against each other, thereby creating a 'tunnel' within the broader limits of the Smithsonian Agreement. In addition to Community currencies, those of Norway and Sweden were also associated with the snake, but the growing divergence of inflation rates and balance of payments problems among member countries led the snake to break down almost immediately. Sterling was withdrawn in June 1972, together with the Irish pound; the Italian lira followed in 1973, the French franc in 1974 and the Swedish krona and Norwegian krone in 1977. The reasons for the collapse of the snake lay in the growing economic problems of the 1970s – high inflation rates, rising unemployment and exchange rate instability. In such circumstances most countries reverted to national economic and monetary policies to try to solve their internal problems. In 1974 the Marjolin working group summed up the lack of success in making further progress towards monetary union as 'adverse events, a lack of political will, and an inadequate understanding of the nature of an economic and monetary union and of the conditions to be fulfilled if it is to come into being and be able to operate'[5].

Interest in European Monetary Union revived during the late 1970s. By now the instability of the dollar and the serious problems besetting the member countries were posing both external and internal threats to the continuing operation of the Community. A new initiative was proposed in 1977 in the Jenkins Report which stressed the simultaneous need for stronger co-ordination of economic policies by member states and the implementation of measures to complete the common market. A series of Council meetings in 1978 culminated in the agreement of December 1978 which created the European Monetary System based on the Jenkins Report and the Schmidt Plan.[6]

The EMS came into effect in March 1979, its key features being:

1. The creation of a European Currency Unit (ECU), the value and composition of which are defined in terms of a basket of currencies. The function of the ECU is to serve as the *numeraire* for the exchange rate mechanism, thereby providing a basis for measuring divergence between currencies and acting as a means of settlement between Community monetary authorities.
2. The provision of an exchange rate and intervention mechanism. Each currency has an ECU-related central rate and fluctuations of exchange rates between currencies are limited to $2\frac{1}{4}$ per cent either side of the central rate, except in the case of

Table 8.5 Composition of the ECU
(1984)

German mark	0.719
Pound sterling	0.0878
French francs	1.31
Italian lire	140.0
Dutch guilder	0.256
Belgian francs	3.71
Luxembourg franc	0.14
Danish krone	0.219
Irish pound	0.00871

countries with floating currencies which are allowed margins of up to 6 per cent. There are also divergence thresholds which are fixed at 75 per cent of the maximum spread of divergence.[7] When a currency crosses this threshold, the authorities of the member states concerned are required to take appropriate measures to correct the divergence or, if all else fails, to adjust central rates.

3. The establishment of a European Monetary Fund to provide financial support for member countries with payment difficulties.

4. The co-ordination of exchange rate policies vis-à-vis the rest of the world.

Since its inception, the EMS has had some success. The intervention mechanism has the advantage that stabilisation is the responsibility of *both* the country with the strong currency *and* the country with the depreciating currency. Thus if intervention becomes necessary, the central bank of the strong currency buys the weak currency and the central bank of the weak currency sells the strong currency. If it does not possess sufficient reserves, it borrows the currency required from the other central bank. These very short-term credit facilities are arranged through the European Monetary Cooperation Fund (EMCF) and are expressed in ECUs. The lending central bank acquires a claim in ECUs while the borrowing central bank incurs a debt for the same amount. Originally it was envisaged that the ECU could be used to settle all debts between member central banks but as yet progress has failed to get beyond the point where 50 per cent may be settled in ECUs. For the rest the creditor central bank may demand another reserve asset. Nor has progress been as great as was hoped with regard to the establishment of a European Monetary Fund with central bank powers. Since the EMS was established, member states have deposited 20 per cent of their dollar and gold reserves with the EMCF in return for ECU credits. This exercise has still to get past the rudimentary stage, however, since there has as yet been no physical transfer of reserves, the deposits being in the form of three-month revolving swaps. Nevertheless the IMF has made allowance for deposits against ECUs by no longer showing 'gold reserves deposited with the EMCF' as part of a member country's official gold and foreign currency reserves.

A more marked success has been the ECU. Apart from its role as an embryo reserve currency for the EMS, it has become the sole unit of account for the Community. Since 1979 current accounts have been opened by some European banks denominated in ECUs and by 1982 this facility was widely available for deposit and savings accounts. Some multinational companies have gone so far as to use the ECU as in internal accounting currency. As a denomination for loans, too, the ECU has made spectacular progress. In 1981 five ECU capital loans were floated to a value of ECU 190 m.; in 1983, twenty-one loans totalling ECU 1,935 m. were raised, including one for the World Bank of ECU 150 m. By 1984 an ECU clearing system had been established, based on the Bank for International Settlements.

The failure of the EMS to develop fully into European Monetary Union is the result of a lack of progress in the harmonisation of economic policy by member states. Countries have proved unwilling to surrender too much of their capacity to make independent decisions and this is particularly the case with Britain where successive governments have feared a loss of control over economic policy. Indeed, Britain still remains outside the EMS for fear that membership would pose too great a strain on the economy. One particular fear was that the instability of the sterling exchange rate might necessitate almost constant intervention by UK monetary authorities to prevent excessive divergence. Existing members, too, have not followed the spirit of the EMS, often preferring to seek adjustments in the EMS central rate rather than take politically unpopular decisions. As in other areas of Community activity, member countries have been unable to put the interests of the Community as a whole before national considerations and few seem willing to work towards greater convergence of economic policies, without which economic and monetary union is a far-off dream.

Notes

1. This led to the appointment of Lord Cockfield as a British commissioner being queried as he remains a member of the British legislature.
2. Much of what follows is extracted from *The Economy of the European Community*, 2nd edn, compiled by P. Maillet, Office for Official Publications for the European Communities, 1984.
3. The system operated in the UK until her accession to the Community.
4. Op. cit. p. 33.
5. Op. cit. p. 48.
6. Which proposed a replacement for the snake (the Boa).
7. The divergence threshold for a currency with a weighting of 20 per cent in the ECU is reached when it deviates from the ECU central rate by:

$$\frac{2.25 \times (100 - 20) \times 0.75}{100} = 1.35 \text{ per cent}$$

Examination questions

The following questions are taken from the examination papers of various examining bodies which include the areas covered in this chapter in their syllabuses. Those marked with an asterisk (★) are representative of the main types of question asked and specimen answers for these will be found in part II.

1. Within the EEC, tariff barriers have been progressively reduced; but non-tariff barriers have appeared to be increasing in numbers and complexity. Distinguish between these two forms of restrictions to trade, with examples, and consider the implications which could arise in the case of a product of your choice. (Dip. Marketing, June 1982)

2.★ What advantages have accrued to the UK in terms of international trade as a result of EEC membership? *(10 marks)* Is our continuing membership economically desirable, in view of a trend towards increasing trade barriers in recent years of recession? *(10 marks)*
(RSA Diploma for Personal Assistants, June 1984)

3. What do you understand by the theory of purchasing power parity? Discuss the implications of this theory for the operation of the European Monetary System. (IOB 2A, April 1982)

4. Explain why official market intervention to stabilise agricultural prices can lead to excessive stocks of certain commodities. (London, January 1981)

5. 'The European Economic Community (EEC) gives greater markets to West Germany and safeguards French farmers. And that is all.' Discuss. (London, January 1983)

6.★ Discuss the economic arguments for and against British withdrawal from membership of the European Community. (London, June 1983)

7. (a) List the main economic aims of any trading bloc with which you are familiar. *(8 marks)*
   (b) Explain any THREE problems associated with the operation of a trading bloc. *(12 marks)*
   (RSA Stage III, June 1984)

8.★ Outline the main features of the European Monetary System (EMS). What do you consider to have been the successes and failures of the system? (IOB 2A, September 1983)

9.★ Your customers, Europe Forever Limited, call to see you to discuss the renewal of their existing facilities for the coming twelve months. As a large import/export organisation, they are always interested in movements of foreign currency. Among the subjects they raised during your discussions is the rise in the use of European Currency Units (ECU). They are interested in this type of currency and want to discuss the use of currency certificates of deposit and eurobond issues, both of which they think might be expressed in ECUs.
   Required:
   A brief explanation for your customers of the salient features of:
   (a) an ECU and the reasons for its rise in popularity over recent years. *(6 marks)*
   (b) a currency certificate of deposit; and *(7 marks)*
   (c) a eurobond *(7 marks)*
   (IOB 2B, April 1984)

10. Discuss the economic arguments for and against customs unions. (AEB, November 1983)

Chapter Nine
The multinational companies

A multinational company is a business enterprise legally domiciled in more than one country and whose commercial activities are of a scale large enough to have a considerable impact on the economies of both the parent country from which it originates and the overseas host country in which it has established its operations. It is customary to distinguish between the multinational company which has a substantial proportion of its investment located overseas and the international campany which is based in one country but is heavily engaged in overseas trade. Some writers have argued that a company cannot truly be called multinational unless the extent of its international activities is such that its original nationality becomes irrelevant. This position is rarely, if ever, attained. The term transnational company is often used to describe those companies which have at least reached the stage of having large-scale operations located overseas. Another definition of the multinational is that at least a quarter of its total business must be conducted outside its country of origin.

Origins and growth

In the eighteenth and early nineteenth centuries, Europeans established trading companies in the colonial empires to extract raw materials to be sent to the home country for processing in return for their own manufactured goods. No significant manufacturing subsidiaries were established, however, since first Mercantilism and later Liberalism expected the home country to supply the manufactured goods – though for different reasons. The *Mercantilists* wished to protect home industries while *liberal free trade* extolled the virtue of international specialisation. By the end of the nineteenth century, however, the growth of protectionism and higher wage rates in the advanced countries led to many European and

American companies establishing overseas subsidiaries to avoid tariff barriers or to benefit from sources of cheap labour. This process was continued and extended in the twentieth century as companies competed across national boundaries for the new mass consumer markets; for example, American car producers had become multinationals long before the Second World War.

The greatest period of multinational growth occurred after the Second World War. In the early post-war period, American manufacturers rushed in to fill the vacuum left by the devastation of European industry, and they greatly expanded their export markets in Europe. Once the process of reconstruction got under way, however, European countries were anxious to protect their industries during the recovery period and so they imposed exchange control and import tariffs to restrict the flow of imports. American companies were loath to lose these markets and the recession in the United States which followed the Korean War made the continued expansion of overseas markets essential. As a result, more and more American companies sought to avoid the regulations imposed on their goods by establishing European subsidiaries. This development was generally welcomed by European governments who foresaw benefits in new employment opportunities and increased capital investment. The continued growth and stability of the European democracies made investment in Europe attractive throughout the 1950s, especially after the establishment of the EEC.

The foundation of the EEC provided a stimulus to further multinational growth, both European and American. The Treaty of Rome actively encouraged the growth of European multinationals through the removal of barriers to the movement of capital between member countries. At the same time, the ability of outside companies to sell in Europe was threatened by the EEC policy of a common external protective tariff, which meant that continued access to this important market could only be assured by the formation of subsidiary companies domiciled in Europe. A number of British companies responded by establishing European subsidiaries but it was the great American corporations which dominated the multinational expansion of the early 1960s. By the end of the decade, however, capital investment was also moving in the opposite direction as an increasing number of European companies took advantage of the weakness of sterling and the dollar to penetrate the British and American markets via operating subsidiaries located in those countries. With European labour now as expensive as American, there was less multinational expansion in Europe after

1970 and the emphasis now shifted to the Far East, where American and European companies established manufacturing subsidiaries in the more stable countries of the area. Here they were joined by Japanese companies in making use of unskilled labour at cheap rates of pay as mass-production techniques were applied to an increasing number of industries. The growing prosperity of the Asian economies enabled the development, by 1980, of Hong Kong, Korean and Taiwanese multinationals – themselves able to make use of local or neighbouring supplies of cheap labour.

Multinational operations may take many forms. The commonest form in the last century was the **vertically** integrated company with the parent company producing goods in its home country using raw materials supplied by the overseas subsidiary – Brooke Bond and Unilever are examples of this type. In the middle of the present century the **horizontally** integrated company, such as General Motors or IBM, became more common, with the parent company having a number of overseas subsidiaries all producing the same or similar products in different countries. Of increasing importance in recent years has been the **reverse vertical** operation where the parent company produces its goods in less developed countries to benefit from cheap labour or other cost advantages and then exports these goods back to the home or other markets; the manufactures of electrical and audio goods such as Philips or Grundig have long operated on these lines. Multinational companies are not limited to the manufacturing sector since many service industries have ventured overseas to provide support for the activities of manufacturing multinationals. In the case of banking, the prohibition on large branch networks in some states has led to overseas activities being the principal outlet for expansion by American banks.

Structure and operations

The operations of a particular multinational will influence the way it is managed and the organisational structure appropriate to it. A company like Coca-Cola, for example, produces the same product all over the world and can therefore have a far more centralised marketing operation than a company which has to cater for different needs in each centre in which it operates. While there are several organisational structures which can be adopted by a multinational, the suitability of a particular structure depends upon the type of operation of the company.

Some companies prefer a highly centralised structure with senior staff in all countries being nationals of the company's home country and all key policy decisions being made at head office. While this maintains the supremacy of the parent company, such a structure may well lack sensitivity to local market needs and will always be seen as a foreign firm. It is most appropriate where local management expertise is virtually non-existent or where the world market for the product or service is fairly homogeneous, as in banking.

An alternative form of organisation is where each overseas subsidiary is regarded as an independent operation, staffed and managed by nationals of the country within which the particular subsidiary operates. This form of organisation is quite common when the parent company has taken over an existing local firm rather than set up a new company. It is most appropriate where the company wishes to be identified as a national company by the local population or where there are strong differences between countries as to product requirement and each subsidiary can cater for its own home market.

The third major organisational form is based on a group of countries rather than any single country and is suitable when there are regions covering similar and geographically close markets, such as North America or Western Europe. The intention is usually to encourage an interchange of ideas across national boundaries. Such an exchange can now occur *within* the organisation, which at the same time can gain the benefits of international economies of scale, especially in marketing.

Several writers have expressed the view that multinationals could eventually develop to the point where they have a global identity with no precedence given either to any national base or a parent company.[1] Such a situation has yet to occur since all multinationals, however large the scale of their overseas operations, still have a clearly recognisable national identity. A few multinationals have acquired a dual national identity, however, as in the case of the Anglo-Dutch multinationals Royal Dutch Shell and Unilever.

Some of the advantages of going multinational have already been mentioned, notably the opportunity this provides to evade tariff barriers or to avoid any hostility towards foreign firms. There are also international economies of scale to be achieved; the use of cheap labour, access to a supply of raw materials, marketing economies and so on. As well as these advantages, the multinational company can use its international structure to raise capital and to reduce its tax burden.

Capital movements

In raising capital, the multinational has access to several financial markets. It may reduce the borrowing costs for the whole corporation by borrowing where the cost is lowest and by transferring the funds to where they are most needed. In practice, government restrictions may prevent perfect cost minimisation through controls on capital movements, though these restrictions may be evaded to some extent through transfer pricing (see below). The other question which concerns the multinational in raising funds is the choice of currency. This decision will be based on the inter-relationship between current interest rates and expected movements in exchange rates. Accordingly, if the dollar is depreciating against sterling, it may be cheaper to borrow in dollars even if interest rates are lower in Britain than in the United States. This is because less pounds will be required to pay the interest on the dollar loan than would be required to finance an equivalent sterling loan. The desire of multinationals to hold assets in hard currencies and liabilities in weak ones leads them to be very active both in the foreign exchange and the eurocurrency markets. These operations can do great damage to particular currencies if, for example, they involve pulling all the company's funds out of an already weak currency.

Transfer pricing

When choosing between alternative locations, the multinational company will have due regard to the question of its likely tax burden in each country. A low rate of tax in one country may more than compensate for a lower rate of profitability, when compared with another offering high profits but a harsher rate of tax. Similarly, tax concessions and subsidies offered by a host country may make location there more attractive than in a lower-cost site without these incentives.

In attempting to minimise its tax liability, the multinational must also consider its *dual* tax liability, to that of its home country and that of the host country. It can reduce the total liability by transferring its profits to whichever of the two countries imposes a lower rate of tax. So if tax rates are lower in the host country there is an incentive to reinvest profits made there in the local economy and also to transfer profits made in high-tax countries to this subsidiary. The reverse will apply if tax rates are lower in the home country of the multinational. This movement of profits cannot be accomplished openly without provoking government action in one country or the other to raise the tax rate on exported profits. The result is that a system of transfer pricing is used.

Transfer pricing is the practice of selling goods between parent company and subsidiary (or between two subsidiaries) at artificial prices, i.e. prices higher or lower than would be the case if the two companies were separate concerns. Thus if tax rates are lower in the host country, the parent company will sell goods to its subsidiary at below cost, thereby reducing the profits of the parent company and raising those of its subsidiary. While attractive in principle, transfer pricing cannot be taken to its ultimate conclusion for fear of concerted action by all governments to clamp down on this form of tax avoidance. Apart from the exceptional case of the pharmaceuticals industry, transfer pricing is not used to the extent that might be expected.

The economic impact of multinationals

The size of the largest multinationals, in terms of their sales and assets, is such that they rival the national incomes of the smaller advanced countries like the Netherlands or Denmark and often completely overshadow those of the developing countries within which they operate. The effect of their activities on the world's capital, eurocurrency and foreign exchange markets has already been discussed. Of even greater significance is the impact they have on the economies of the countries within which they operate.

The parent country

Traditionally, overseas expansion by a major national company has been regarded as an encouraging development. For a prosperous country with full employment and a healthy balance of payments, foreign investment provides a means of utilising surplus funds to increase the company's productive capacity without harming the domestic economy. Such overseas investment also offers the prospect of increasing the flow of goods to the home market, especially supplies of raw materials. Despite the fact that such overseas investment represents a deficit item on the capital account of the balance of payments, this should be more than compensated for by the long-term flow of dividend and interest payments repatriated by the multinational's overseas subsidiaries. As the overseas activities of the company grow, however, there is a danger that the pursuit of higher profits may lead the company to neglect the interests of the country in which it originated. Of particular concern is the possibility that both capital investment and the creation of employment may take place abroad to the detriment of the home economy; British shipping lines using foreign registered ships or seamen, the closure of a factory in Britain as manufacture is shifted to a poor country, or a British retailer buying cheap clothing goods from Asian sweatshops are familiar examples.

The host country

We are concerned here not with the advanced countries, which can exert some control over the multinationals' activities within their borders, but with the impact of these large corporations on the economies of the developing countries. Even here, as Sanjaya Lall has pointed out[2], fashions change as to whether the multinationals should be welcomed or repudiated by developing countries. These changing attitudes reflect the fact that the developing country receives both benefits and costs from multinational penetration of its economy. It is the *net* effect which is difficult to determine.

Benefits

There are three main advantages to a country receiving foreign investment from a multinational company.

1. The contribution to the balance of payments. The establishment of a subsidiary by a foreign company assists both the current and the capital account of the balance of payments.

The precise impact on the **current account** depends upon the operations of the multinational and the type of economy within which it is operating. For *developing* countries in which the subsidiary produces raw materials for the parent company or finished goods for export to the parent company's markets, there is a gain through increased export earnings. Where the subsidiary is operating in an *advanced* country, the effect is a saving of foreign currency as imports are replaced by domestically-produced goods.

On the **capital account** there is an injection of foreign currency, in both instances, although this will entail future foreign currency payments as the multinational repatriates part of its profits.

2. The contribution to technology. A backward country with little or no advanced technology can be expected to welcome the establishment of a subsidiary by a multinational, resulting as it does in increased training and skills for the local workforce. There should also be spin-off effects for existing home-based industries or new industries which are now able to make use of the technological skills acquired. However, the benefits to be gained from the technology introduced by foreign companies are open to question, as a subsequent section will show.

3. The contribution to employment. Foreign investment can be expected to stimulate employment opportunities in various ways. Even if the multinational staffs its overseas subsidiaries exclusively with nationals of the parent company, these will stimulate local demand for goods and services through their own private expenditure. This extra demand will create employment in ancillary and service industries, leading to a situation similar to the growth in employment which follows the establishment of military bases in developing countries by the great powers. More commonly, the multinational will employ considerable numbers of local people in its factories and the host government can turn this fact to good use in carrying out its economic policies. The government can encourage the overseas company to go to those areas where unemployment is most acute, since foreign companies having no historical links with particular areas may be more receptive than local firms to the various incentives offered.

Costs
As well as benefits, a number of costs may arise from the international operations of a multinational.

1. Taxation. The measures taken by multinationals to reduce their tax liability may present difficulties to the host government in its attempts to determine the true profits of the company, especially as it receives no information direct from the parent company. On the other hand, it is not necessarily the object of the host government to maximise the tax burden of foreign companies operating within its borders and many developing countries actually offer tax concessions to attract foreign investment. Taxation presents problems for the parent country too, as it is also affected by transfer pricing (see above). One solution is to tax profits made by an overseas subsidiary when they are repatriated, even if they have already been taxed by the host country. Unfortunately this double taxation may result in the company reducing still further the extent to which it repatriates its profits. Another possibility would be to tax multinationals on a portion of their world-wide profits, irrespective of the profits made in particular countries.

2. Local technological development. The acquisition of new technology from multinationals is often regarded as relatively expensive for developing countries, especially as the multinational controls the dissemination of this new technology and may prevent its general use. Certainly where there are simple industries with stable technologies there is a strong case for licensing or copying foreign technologies, as the success of Hong Kong, Korea and Taiwan in this respect has shown. Where, however, the technology is highly complicated and still subject to rapid change, it is doubtful whether even the more advanced developing countries have the resources to develop their own technology. In these circumstances, reliance on the multinationals must continue. The difficulty then arises that the multinational may persist in using nationals from the parent country to direct research operations, with local workers being used only for unskilled tasks. Such a situation has detrimental consequences both for local career opportunities and for the development of local technological expertise. Nor is there any guarantee that the new technology will be suitable for the needs of the host country. Scarce resources may be devoted to uses in line with company strategy but contrary to national economic policy. Finally there is the question of whether such technology retards the development of local technological capabilities. Since multinationals do not usually transfer the potential to generate new technology to their subsidiaries in developing countries, such subsidiaries may depend entirely on the parent company for design, research and development. Indeed, if the multinational takes over an existing local company, it may even close down any rudimentary research and development capability.

3. Economic dependence. A common charge laid against multinationals is that they pose a threat to the host government's ability to conduct its own economic policy. Both company and government share a common interest in raising the standard of living, and thus the level of demand in the economy. However, the company is likely to be preoccupied with its own self-interest of increased sales, while the government may be trying to control demand in pursuit of wider economic objectives. When the policies of the two are in conflict, the government is likely to receive less sympathy from a large corporation with international interests and a foreign identity than it will from a local company whose loyalty and interests are more closely associated with national economic policy. At times the host government may be forced into moderating its policies to obtain the co-operation of the multinational for fear that the company will abandon planned new investment or even close down altogether, thereby damaging employment and national output. In Britain the threat of closure by Chrysler in the mid-1970s led to the government subsidising the company to avoid mass redundancies, though eventually Chrysler sold its British subsidiary anyway.

4. Competition with national companies. The advantages enjoyed by multinationals in competing with purely national companies are similar whether they are operating in a developing or an advanced country.

1. *International economies of scale.* By making use of cheap labour, internationally-based marketing strategies and financial and taxation economies, the multinational can maintain a competitive edge over its national rivals.

2. *Market leadership.* Because of the scale of its operations, the multinational can establish market dominance in a number of national markets, even to the extent of giving the lead in price and output policies. In Britain the price leader in the oil industry is Esso, the British subsidiary of the American multinational, Exxon. The multinational's impact on the industry may well be to reduce competition as weak firms are taken over or forced out of the market. Once dominant, the multinational may force up prices, reduce choice and standardise products to suit its international marketing strategy, without reference to local needs.

3. *Tax advantages.* Quite apart from the gains resulting from the use of transfer pricing, the multinational may be offered tax and other concessions not available to local companies in an attempt to secure investment by the company in the host country.

4. *Labour market dominance.* Because of its more efficient use of resources, the multinational may be able to offer higher rates of pay than its local rivals, so enabling it to attract the best qualified workers. Nor does this mean that workers will necessarily benefit from the advent of a multinational. The ability of the company to move its operations elsewhere may be used to coerce trade unions into acceptance of company policies. In their bargaining with the management of a multinational, trade unions are handicapped by their lack of co-ordination with similar groups in other parts of the company, while the multinational itself is able to bargain within the context of an overall group strategy. The movement of the multinational operations to developing countries where trade unionism is much weaker is an obvious attraction for a

company experiencing tough negotiations with labour in an advanced host or parent country. Even British multinationals like ICI have cut back their operations in Britain while expanding employment in other parts of the world.

Despite the potential costs or disadvantages outlined above, most developing countries extend a cautious welcome to investment from multinational companies. This is partly because the current recession and international debt problems have made alternative sources of foreign investment more difficult to obtain. In addition, the worst fears surrounding transfer pricing, the transfer of inappropriate technology and economic dependence have not been realised. It is also important to distinguish between the experiences of the poorer developing countries (LDCs) and the newly industrialising countries (NICs). While the former group may well feel intimidated by the activities of the multinationals, the NICs have grown in confidence in their dealings with multinationals and have used the increased investment and improved technology to establish their *own* multinationals. The problem of powerful competition for local firms from the activities of multinationals has been dealt with partly through government protection of local industry and partly through the growth of joint ventures between local firms and multinationals.

The control of multinationals

In order to maximise the benefits accruing from multinational operations within their border, host countries must exercise control over the multinational's ability to distort the local economy, notably through transfer pricing and capital movements. In other areas, such as co-operation with local firms, negotiation is more suitable than regulation, since the relationship between host government and multinational must involve some compromises. The multinational subjects itself to the laws and regulations of the state in which it is domiciled in exchange for the commercial benefits obtained, while the host government tolerates the greater freedom of the multinational in return for the advantages it receives in terms of investment, technology, employment and foreign exchange savings. If this compromise breaks down, both sides have recourse to extreme measures – the multinational can close down its operations and pull out, while the government can nationalise the company, with or without compensation. Ultimately the reprisals available to the state appear greater, since it can prevent the company from removing its funds and, short of economic or military sanctions by the parent government, little can be done. In fact the reality is more complex. A country which is perceived as hostile to overseas companies will be unable to attract foreign investment in future and most developing countries would arguably be infinitely worse off by taking such drastic action. Indeed, even the most suspicious Third World countries are now realising that control is best exercised through moderate regulation and general agreement on international codes of conduct.

National controls

The extent of national controls differs widely but all host countries regulate multinational activities to some extent. In the Third World there are often wide-ranging regulations to ensure that the interests of local companies and the national economy are protected. Among the most frequently found national controls are:

1. *Pricing.* Multinationals with strong monopoly power are frequently subjected to price controls in order to limit their profits. They are also required to adhere to the pricing policies laid down by some countries for all firms operating within their borders.

2. *Profit remittances.* Some South American countries have limits on the extent of profit repatriation; usually a percentage of the capital of the subsidiary. This type of control also helps reduce the abuses of transfer pricing.

3. *Taxation.* As well as standard tax rates, some countries subject foreign companies to supplementary taxes on profits, especially repatriated profits. There is also a constant battle of wits between taxation experts employed by these companies and the tax authorities. In Britain, for example, some international companies used a system known as double dip leasing whereby British tax allowances were used to offset the cost of overseas projects, with British-based 'front' companies leasing equipment abroad to foreign firms. This was stopped by the 1982 budget. Yet almost immediately a new loophole was found, companies with dual residence in the United States and Britain using double taxation agreements between the two countries to get full tax relief on projects undertaken outside the UK.

4. *Ownership.* In many of the developing countries there is an insistence on local participation between a local company and the multinational to restrict the level of foreign ownership.

Alternatively, there may be part ownership by the host government itself.

5. *Components and raw materials*. Where support industries are required to provide components or other back-up services, governments may insist on the use of local firms rather than permit imports from the multinational's other countries of operation. This may involve the company having to assist local firms financially in order to bring their operations up to standard.

6. *Personnel*. Increasingly, multinationals are being required to recruit key staff as well as manual labour from the local labour supply, rather than bring in their own nationals. Generally, multinationals are willing to comply with such requirements as they assist in the establishment of the company as a 'local firm' in the eyes of the host country's population.

International controls

In 1976 the Organisation for Economic Co-operation and Development drew up a voluntary code of conduct for multinational companies which to some extent reversed the trend of liberalising capital movements. The code is intended to ensure that multinationals behave with propriety in the movement of capital to and from countries, especially where conflict with national governments or with other interested parties (such as trade unions) might occur. In 1979 the EEC went further by legislating to ensure that trade unions are consulted by companies on any decision to move production or close plants. Similar regional controls over multinational companies exist throughout the world. In South America, for example, the Andean Pact countries co-ordinate industrial development and impose a number of controls on multinationals operating within the borders of these countries.

Globally, controls have not developed beyond the discussion stage. In 1974 a report commissioned by the United Nations recommended the establishment of centralised negotiating services to assist host countries in dealing with proposals for foreign investment. The report went on to argue that in their negotiations with multinationals, host countries should make provision for a periodic review of the terms of agreements made and that, in the case of LDCs, some provision should be made for an eventual reduction in the level of foreign ownership in the company. By the early 1980s no progress had been made in the institution of an international code of regulation. Since then demands for such regulations have faded as individual countries have grown more confident in their own dealings with multinationals. Indeed, there is a danger that further international controls could do more harm than good for the developing countries as future potential foreign investment might be frightened off.

Notes

1. See Howard V. Pedmulter and David A. Heenan, *Multinational Organisation Development*, Addison-Wesley, 1979.
2. 'Transnationals and the Third World: Changing Perceptions', *National Westminster Bank Quarterly Review*, May 1984.

Examination questions

The following questions are taken from the examination papers of various examining bodies which include the areas covered by this chapter in their syllabuses. Those marked with an asterisk (★) are representative of the main types of question asked and specimen answers for these will be found in Part II.

1.★ One of the advantages of a multinational form of operation is its ability to transfer goods between operating units of the organisation in different countries at virtually any price (internally) that it wishes. Under what circumstances would it be likely to charge
(a) a relatively high price
(b) a relatively low price
when invoicing goods to another country in this way?
(Dip. Marketing, June 1981)

2. The variety of tariff and other barriers may cause significant differences in the selling price of a given product in different countries. How may transfer pricing activities be used to counteract pricing situations which might otherwise be unfavourable to the operations of a multinational? (Dip. Marketing, June 1985)

3.★ Multinational firms have often contributed very considerably to the development of the infrastructure of a developing country, yet they are frequently viewed by the local population with dislike or distrust.
   Discuss why this situation should have arisen, and outline measures that could have been taken to improve the local attitudes. (Dip. Marketing, June 1984)

4. Discuss the part played by multinational organisations in the development of the infrastructure of a particular country. (Dip. Marketing, November 1982)

5.★ It is known that some large multinational companies have sales revenues as large as the GNPs of some countries.
   (a) How do you think that this state of affairs has come about? *(8 marks)*
   (b) What are the advantages and disadvantages to the world economy of multinational corporations? *(8 marks)*
   (c) How may governments control the activities of multinational corporations? *(4 marks)*
   (RSA Diploma for Personal Assistants, June 1980)

6. What are the distinguishing features of a 'multinational' company? How does multinational status contribute to profitable operation and does it have any disadvantages? (Dip. Marketing, June 1980)

7. Account for the increasing number of multinational companies, and discuss their effect on international economic stability. (ICMA Professional Stage I, November 1984)

Part two

Specimen answers to examination questions

Chapter One

3. Discuss the assertion that it is not possible for two countries to gain from international trade if one of them is more efficient at producing all goods than the other. (ICSA Part I, December 1980)

It is self-evident that countries benefit by specialising in the production of those goods in which they have an absolute cost advantage and trading these for other goods in which other countries enjoy the cost advantage. Less obvious is the principle of comparative advantage which is based on the premise that it is comparative, rather than absolute, costs which should determine trade between countries. Thus even if one country, because of its efficiency, is able to produce *all* goods more cheaply than another, there will still be differences in the extent of the absolute cost advantage from product to product. The efficient country is said to have a comparative advantage in those products in which its absolute advantage is greatest, whereas the inefficient country has a comparative advantage in those products in which its absolute *disadvantage* is least. Countries should specialise in the production of those goods in which they have a comparative advantage and leave to others the production of those in which they have a comparative disadvantage. This theory was developed by David Ricardo, who illustrated his argument with the example of England and Portugal and the production of wine and cloth.

In the table below, (a) shows a situation where both England and Portugal produce wine and yarn. Portugal has an absolute advantage in both products since she need expend less labour than England to produce either 1X units of wine or 1Y units of yarn. However, England's absolute *disadvantage* is less in the case of yarn because only 11 per cent more labour (100 units instead of 90) are

Table X

	Country	Unit of labour used	Barrels of wine	Yarns of cloth
(a) Before specialisation	England	100		1Y
		120	1X	
	Portugal	80	1X	
		90		1Y
	Total		2X	2Y
(b) After specialisation	England	220		2.2Y
	Portugal	170	2.125X	
	Total		2.125X	2.2Y
		Consumption of wine and yarn		
(c) After specialisation and trade – 1 unit of wine trading for 1 unit of cloth	England		1X	1.2Y
	Portugal		1.125X	1Y
	Total		2.125X	2.2Y

required to produce the same amount of yarn, whereas 50 per cent more labour (120 units instead of 80) are needed to produce the same amount of wine.

In section (b) of the table, England's comparative advantage in the production of yarn is exploited, with the labour previously employed in the production of wine diverted to cloth production. Portugal, meanwhile, concentrates on the production of wine, in which she has a comparative advantage. As a consequence of this specialisation, total production of both wine and yarn is increased.

In part (c), one possible rate of exchange after specialisation is shown. Here a rate of exchange of 1X for 1Y leaves both countries better off after trade. With the same expenditure of resources, England is able to consume more yarn and the same amount of wine, while Portugal enjoys more wine and the same amount of yarn. This is achieved by both countries specialising according to comparative advantages and trading the surplus production. Thus, provided that two countries do not have identical efficiencies in *all* products, it is possible for both countries to benefit by trade even if one country is more efficient in all industries than the other.

4. Is the principle of comparative costs an adequate explanation of the pattern of international trade in manufactured goods? (London, June 1984)

The principle of comparative costs, or comparative advantage, is based on the premise that it is comparative, rather than absolute, costs which should determine trade between countries. Thus even *if* one country, because of its efficiency, is able to produce *all* goods more cheaply than another, there will still be differences in the extent of the absolute advantage from product to product. The efficient country is said to have a comparative advantage in those products in which its absolute advantage is greatest, whereas the inefficient country has a comparative advantage in those products where its absolute disadvantage is least. Countries should specialise in the production of those goods in which they have a comparative advantage, and leave to others the production of those in which they have a comparative disadvantage.

It is possible to cite many examples of the principle of comparative costs in operation. In the nineteenth century, for example, Britain abandoned attempts to be self-sufficient in agricultural goods, despite being more efficient than most other countries, and concentrated on the production of manufactured goods in which she was even more efficient relative to other countries. In the present century, the advanced countries have tended to concentrate on the production of sophisticated manufactured goods, while leaving to the developing countries of the Far East the production of cheaper mass-produced goods. The obvious example of the 1980s is Japan. Since the Second World War, Japanese industry has proved to be more efficient than that of other countries in virtually every manufacturing industry. Nevertheless, Japan now specialises in high-technology manufacturing industries and leaves to the newly-industrialising countries, like Hong Kong and Taiwan, the production of cheaper goods. It is more profitable for Japan to concentrate on these industries in which she has a clear lead in efficiency rather than use scarce resources on the production of goods in which she has only a marginal advantage over the rest of the world.

Despite the part played by the principle of comparative costs in the pattern of international trade in manufactured goods, it is not the only determining factor. This is because the principle of comparative costs relies on a number of conditions unlikely to be met in the real world. Firstly, it assumes perfect mobility of factors of production within countries and total immobility of factors between countries. In practice, there is a limit to the process by which factors can be transferred from one use to another, and thus a limit on the extent of specialisation. Furthermore, factors of production such as capital and labour *are* mobile between countries. Secondly, the theory takes no account of economies or diseconomies of scale. While specialisation will yield the former, over-specialisation will result in the latter, so most countries are deterred from taking specialisation to the extent demanded by comparative cost theory. Thirdly, the theory is based on a presumption that there is free trade between countries. The existence of trade barriers and trade agreements distort or even cancel out comparative advantages. Fourthly, changed economic circumstances mean that countries may lose previously-held comparative advantages, though the industry will tend to struggle on, and even hold on to some long-established export markets. In other words, the trade in manufactured goods changes at a slower rate than do comparative advantages. Fifthly, countries are unlikely to abandon strategically important industries, such as steel or armaments, since political independence is regarded as being more important than comparative costs. Sixthly, demand patterns are assumed to respond to the increased volume of production resulting from increased specialisation. In fact there is no guarantee that world demand will rise when output is increased, so countries may have difficulty in selling their surplus output abroad. Finally, transport costs may well wipe out a theoretical advantage so that American manufacturers can export to Canada bulky goods in which Swedish firms have a comparative advantage but also higher transport costs.

5. What is meant by terms of trade? What causes changes in these terms and why may they be favourable or unfavourable to the economy? (ICMA Foundation, May 1982)

The terms of trade is the physical rate of exchange of the goods that a country exports for goods that it imports. In other words, the terms of trade relate the price of a country's exports to the price of its imports. The principal method of measuring the terms of trade is the 'barter terms of trade', which is the ratio of the export price index to the import price index over the same time period. This ratio is expressed as an index number, using the formula:

$$\text{Index of terms of trade} = \frac{\text{Export price index}}{\text{Import price index}} \times 100$$

Starting from a base of 100, a rise in the index to, say, 105 signifies an 'improvement' in the terms of trade: fewer exports need be sold in order to pay for a given quantity of imports. This improvement could have come about either through a rise in export prices or a fall in import prices. A fall in the index to, say, 95 indicates a 'deterioration' in the terms of trade, due either to a fall in export prices or a rise in import prices. The terms 'improvement' and 'deterioration' are somewhat misleading since the actual effect on the economy of a change in the terms of trade depends on the cause of that change.

If, for example, the relative rise in export prices were due to a rise in domestic costs of production, there may well be a fall in overseas demand for the country's goods and therefore in the volume of exports. If the fall in volume of exports is large enough, the value of goods actually sold abroad may fall. A similar situation could occur in the case of a country experiencing an inflation rate considerably higher than that of its trading competitors. In both these cases the effect of an improvement in the terms of trade depends on the price elasticity of demand for the country's exports, i.e. the responsiveness of world demand to changes in the prices of the country's exports. Only where demand is inelastic will higher export prices result in increased export revenue. Similarly an improvement due to a fall in the price of imports could result, where import elasticity of demand is high, in a rise in total expenditure on imports. If there is a relative rise in export prices in consequence of increased demand for the country's products, the rise in the terms of trade index represents a real improvement in the country's external position.

From the above discussion it is clear that changes in the terms of trade may be favourable or unfavourable to a country's economy. Where an improvement in the terms of trade leads to a rise in export revenue or fall in import revenue, the effect will be an improved balance of payments position, a net injection into the circular flow of national income and higher living standards. Where, however, the improvement in the terms of trade results in a fall in export revenue or a rise in import expenditure, there may well be a deterioration in the balance of payments, a net withdrawal from the circular flow of national income and deflationary pressures in the economy. In the same way a deterioration in the terms of trade index could have a positive effect on the economy if export demand is sufficiently elastic to increase total revenue, thereby improving the balance of payments and giving a boost to the economy. Such an outcome would depend, however, on the ability of domestic industries to respond to the increased demand for their goods, both at home and abroad.

8. 'A change in the level of export earnings will lead to a more than proportionate change in national income.' Discuss. (AEB, November 1983)

The national income consists of the total output of goods and services produced by the economy. In the absence of external intervention, all national income will flow between the firms who produce the goods and services and the households who buy this output with income generated by their contribution to the economic activities of firms. Any withdrawal of income from the circular flow, as savings, taxes or imports, will reduce the flow of income to domestic firms and ultimately reduce the level of national income. On the other hand, increased demand for the firm's output from outside the circular flow, from investment, government expenditure and exports, will raise the level of national income. For the national income to be in equilibrium, these withdrawals and injections must be equal. If withdrawals exceed injections there will be a downward pressure on national income, while if injections exceed withdrawals there will be an expansionary effect on national income. In such circumstances the national income must contract or expand until injections and withdrawals are brought once again into equilibrium. Thus an increase in export earnings will cause national income to rise until withdrawals have also risen by an amount equal to the initial increase in export earnings.

National income analysis predicts that, provided there are unused resources in the economy, an increase in export earnings will cause a rise in national income. The question remains as to how much national income will rise in response to a given injection of export earnings of, say, £10 m. The likelihood is that national income will rise by considerably more than £10 m because of the dynamic nature of national income changes. Suppose that the £10 m. is an order with a British engineering company for machinery. There will be an immediate increase in national income of £10 m. To this must be added, however, the further income created by the engineering company buying raw materials, installing capital equipment and paying extra workers. As long as the recipients of this income spend at least part of it in the domestic economy there will follow another wave of income creation. This process will be repeated until an amount equivalent to the original injection of export earnings has been withdrawn from the circular flow of national income in the form of savings, taxes and import expenditure, and total withdrawals once again equal total injections. This tendency for any injection to have a multiplied effect on national income is the 'multiplier effect' and, in the case of export earnings, is known as the foreign trade multiplier.

The size of the foreign trade multiplier is governed by the rate at which the original injection is dissipated by withdrawals at each successive wave of income creation. The greater the proportion of new income creation that is withdrawn from the circular flow, the smaller will be the multiplier effect, and vice versa. The proportion of income withdrawn at each stage of income creation is the marginal propensity to make withdrawals (MPW) and the multiplier is the reciprocal of the MPW. Thus if the MPW $= \frac{1}{2}$, the multiplier is 2. Applying these figures to the injection of the £10 m. referred to above, there will be a second round of income creation of £5 m., a third round of £2.5 m. and so on, a half of income being sliced off at each round. With a multiplier of 2 there will eventually be total new income creation of £20 m. Withdrawals will have risen to £10 m., so matching the initial injection. The size of the foreign trade multiplier varies with the nature of the export injection. Accordingly the multiplier is likely to be smaller where exports are made from imported raw materials than where the entire exported item is made from indigenous materials and using domestic labour and capital. The foreign trade multiplier is therefore higher in the case of earnings from tourism than in that of the export of goods manufactured at home but using foreign components. Finally, there will be no multiplier effect at all unless there are unused resources available to meet an export order. If not, the extra demand will have to compete with existing demand and may result in demand-pull inflationary pressures.

Chapter Two

2. Since the Second World War the pattern of UK overseas trade has changed drastically. What changes have taken place and why? (FCOT, May 1984)

The post-war period has witnessed a number of radical changes in the composition of Britain's overseas trade, both by area and by commodity. Comparisons with the early post-war period are limited in value since the era of reconstruction after 1945 and the Korean War of 1950–54 both had the effect of distorting trade patterns and temporarily boosting Britain's share of world trade. By the mid-1950s, however, a more stable pattern was emerging in which a third of Britain's trade was with Western Europe, a similar proportion to that with other developed countries, principally the United States and the older Commonwealth countries. The final third was with the developing countries, notably those of the new Commonwealth. With regard to the commodity composition of trade, Britain was essentially a manufacturing nation, exporting its goods to pay for essential raw materials from abroad, though a third of imports were manufactured goods.

Since the late 1950s a number of trends have become clear in the area composition of UK overseas trade. Firstly, Britain has become a European trading nation heavily dependent on trade with other EEC countries. Secondly, trade with most other industrialised countries, particularly those of the old Commonwealth, has declined, in relative terms at least. Thirdly, the share of Britain's exports going to the non-oil developing countries has declined sharply while that to OPEC members has risen. These developments reflect in part the tendency for the markets of Europe and those of the OPEC countries to grow at a faster rate than Britain's traditional markets of the Commonwealth and Latin America, a process reinforced by Britain's membership of the EEC and the loosening of Commonwealth ties. In addition, the industrialisation of some of the developing countries, the so-called newly industrialising countries (NICs), has led to a faster growth in the level of imports from these countries than from more traditional suppliers. More dramatic has been the change in the commodity composition of Britain's trade. Of most significance is the pronounced shift downward in the proportion of export earnings derived from manufactures while the manufactures share of total imports has risen steadily. The UK share of world exports of manufactures fell from 17 per cent in 1960 to 7 per cent in 1986, reflecting the slow growth of British manufactured exports over this period. Since 1979 this situation has deteriorated further with British manufactured export volume actually falling, while world markets were growing by 20 per cent. At the same time the continued growth of imports of manufactures meant that by 1983 Britain was importing more manufactured goods than she was exporting, in terms of value. This change around in Britain's trade in manufactures is the result of a failure to compete, effectively on price or any other major criterion, particularly in the face of growing competition from Japan and the NICs. Thus the UK has not only lost ground in her export markets, she has also found it increasingly more difficult to resist import penetration in a whole range of industries previously dominated by domestic producers. The other great area of change concerns the trade in oil. Since the mid-1970s, Britain has moved from being a country heavily dependent on oil imports to one which is a net oil exporter. This development has enabled oil revenues to supplement the export of manufactures to finance the import of essential raw materials. Also worthy of comment is the fact that improved farming techniques and slowed population growth have enabled Britain to reduce significantly the proportion of agricultural products imported and to increase her own exports of certain food products.

6.   Argue the case for and against import controls with respect to the United Kingdom economy. (London, June 1982)

In recent years, demands have grown for the imposition of import controls to assist in the resolution of Britain's economic problems. In large part these demands reflect the anxiety over Britain's trade performance and the serious doubts as to whether current trends can be reversed while free trade policies are in operation. The area of greatest concern is the trade in manufactures since there has been a marked rise in the level of import penetration in major manufacturing industries. In one industry after another, the value of export earnings has been overhauled by the expenditure on imports, from textiles in the 1950s, through motor vehicles in the 1970s to electrical engineering in the 1980s. The situation has deteriorated from that of the 1960s where Britain was unable to hold on to her export markets to that of today where she cannot even prevent the foreign domination of domestic markets. The reasons for this decline are several but can be summarised as Britain's failure to compete effectively with her trading rivals. The problems posed for the British economy in these circumstances are many. Firstly, increased import penetration represents a withdrawal from the circular flow of income and thus has a dampening effect on economic growth. Secondly, the decline of British manufacturing industries brings with it higher unemployment at a scale too great to be coped with by rising employment opportunities in other sectors of the economy. Thirdly, the effect on the balance of payments would have been disastrous were it not for the presence of a large surplus on trade in oil. When, eventually, North Sea oil runs out, Britain will be confronted by an enormous balance of trade deficit unless the manufacturing sector is able to resume its traditional role in the economy.

The arguments supporting import controls are based on the foregoing analysis of the state of the economy in general, and of the manufacturing sector in particular. Firstly, there may be a case for protecting some of our declining industries in the short term to enable them to be modernised, thereby restoring some of their competitiveness. Secondly, the very high unemployment rates might be used to justify protection on the grounds that high import penetration is effectively putting more and more British workers out of a job. Thirdly, import controls could be used to prevent 'dumping', i.e. the unloading of surplus output at below cost-price. The case for protection here is that such imports are subsidised by the foreign country's government so that the competition is unfair. Finally, it might be argued that Britain's future as a manufacturing nation will depend on the development of new industries, our old industries being a part of history. This is the 'infant industry' argument which points to protection being used mainly to help the new high-technology industries.

The case against import controls is also strong. In the first place the protection of old declining industries will merely perpetuate their existence without making them more competitive. If modernisation is the aim, assistance with investment is more appropriate than protection. While the argument that protection saves jobs is attractive, it ignores the fact that other countries are likely to retaliate. In such circumstances, world trade will decline and unemployment will be worse in *all* countries. This was the consequence of retaliatory protectionism in the 1930s. While the anti-dumping and infant industry arguments are more convincing, even they are likely to contribute to demands for retaliation by other trading nations. Finally, there is the question of international agreements. Our membership of the EEC, for instance, means that we could not put up trade barriers against goods from other EEC countries, these contributing some 40 per cent of our total imports. Similarly, we would be prone to sanctions if we reneged on our agreements under our membership of GATT (General Agreement on Tariffs and Trade).

On balance, a free trade policy appears more realistic, and less dangerous. However, should the decline of Britain's manufacturing base continue, import controls would become both potentially less damaging and more likely to be forced on a future government as a crisis measure.

8. Distinguish between tariff and non-tariff barriers to international trade. In view of the relative simplicity of operating the tariff system, why has the non-tariff approach become more prevalent? (Dip. Marketing, June 1984)

A tariff is a tax on imported goods. The effect of the tariff is to raise the price of the import, thereby reducing its price competitiveness against domestically-produced alternatives. The tariff uses the price mechanism, therefore, to reduce the level of demand for foreign goods. Non-tariff barriers, on the other hand, use legal controls to prevent or hinder the import of foreign goods. The simplest form of non-tariff barrier is the quota, a specific limit placed on the quantity of the good which may legally be imported. A second non-tariff barrier is exchange controls. Buyers of foreign goods need to be able to obtain foreign currency to pay for these goods and many countries control the level of imports by making it extremely difficult for their nationals to purchase foreign currency or hold foreign currency accounts. Other non-tariff barriers include all those regulations used by governments to reduce the flow of imports on technical or administrative grounds. Among the most important of these are import licensing, health and safety regulations, environmental controls, changes in technical specifications or standards and complex customs procedures. The range of non-tariff barriers has widened significantly over the past ten years as an alternative to traditional forms of import control.

While tariffs are relatively simple to operate, their use is limited both by practical considerations and by the international regulation of trade between countries. On practical grounds, the extent to which a tariff is successful in reducing demand for the imported product depends largely on the price elasticity of demand for that product. It is most likely to be successful where there are close substitutes available from domestic suppliers, or where price competition has kept profit margins too low to enable overseas suppliers to absorb the tariff themselves. Tariffs are relatively unsuccessful where demand is inelastic, as when there are no locally-produced substitutes or where the imported goods are so cheap that even with the tariff they are still much cheaper than the domestically-produced alternative. In recent years, tariffs have proved of little value in stemming the tide of cheap mass-produced goods from the newly industrialising countries (NICs) or the excess production of the Eastern bloc countries which is 'dumped' on western countries at giveaway prices. The other major limitation on the use of tariffs stems from the post-war growth in trade treaty obligations which restrict the use of trade barriers. The UK, for example, is bound by its obligations to the General Agreement on Tariffs and Trade (GATT) and by its membership of the European Economic Community (EEC), both of which restrict her freedom of action on the use of formal trade barriers. Finally, the use of tariffs is further limited by the existence of a floating exchange rate regime which greatly reduces the accuracy and effect of tariff measures.

While quotas are the obvious answer to some of the practical problems raised by the use of tariffs, they too are frowned upon by GATT so that many of the western industrialised countries have resorted to voluntary export restraints (VERs), i.e. agreements obtained from Japan and the NICs by which these countries voluntarily restrict their export of certain goods to the western countries, notably the EEC. At the same time the world recession has increased everywhere the tendency towards protectionism. Many countries, unable to use legitimately either tariffs or quotas for fear of retaliation, have resorted to the administrative and legal barriers outlined above. In addition, there has been a growth of bilateral trade, whereby countries buy from those countries which are willing to buy something in return.

9. When should a developing country adopt free trade policies and when should it not? (ICSA Part III, June 1984)

The arguments in favour of free trade are several. Firstly, free trade enables the development of international specialisation and economies of scale. This promotes the expansion of world output and greater efficiency in the use of the world's scarce resources. Secondly, the reduction in costs generated by greater efficiency raises living standards as goods are made available at lower prices. Thirdly, the world's population also benefits from a greater variety of goods and services and so a better quality of life. Fourthly, freer movement of goods between countries may be expected to stimulate cultural and technological interchange, and thus increase the rate of progress. Finally, trade encourages closer political understanding. All things being equal, therefore, all countries should support a free trade policy. None the less, political, strategic and economic considerations make it inevitable that all countries will seek to restrict trade where national interests are jeopardised.

Developing countries are in a particularly difficult situation since their economies are usually too weak to permit them to adopt economic policies without reference to the views of other countries. In general, the developing country should benefit by adopting a free trade policy since protectionism will be either irrelevant or dangerous. The country is unlikely to have powerful but declining industries demanding protection to save employment or to enable time for modernisation. The country's low living standards make it an unlikely candidate for the dumping of goods from other developing countries. In addition, the adoption of trade barriers may well provoke retaliation, with the developing country getting the worst of any trade war with the industrial nations. This is because its market is too small to damage the economies of the industrial countries while the developing country depends on the important markets of the advanced countries. Free trade, on the other hand, has much to commend it. Access to the markets of the advanced nations is likely to stimulate the developing country's economy, while it will not be flooded with the expensive exports of the industrial world. Furthermore, an open trading policy is more likely to attract the capital investment from overseas which all the developing countries need.

There are two strong arguments in favour of protection by developing countries. Firstly, there is the 'infant industry' argument. A number of developing countries are prevented from specialising in those industries in which they would have a comparative advantage because they cannot get these industries off the ground. When the infant industry is established, it cannot withstand the competition from those foreign industries which already have the benefit of economies of scale and it fails to survive. Protection gives the infant industry the breathing space to attain technical efficiency and scale production; the tariff or other barriers to trade can be removed once the industry has matured and can withstand foreign competition. The other argument in favour of protection is that it assists in the process of economic development. This might be called the 'infant economy' argument since it is closely related to that made on behalf of infant industries. Developing countries are justified in using short-term trade barriers in the early stages of industrialisation, according to this argument, because all their industries are weak and without protection economic development will not occur.

Chapter Three

1. What do you understand by the 'invisibles' section of a country's balance of payments account? Assess the importance of and recent influences on the invisible account of the United Kingdom or any other country with which you are familiar. (IOB 2A, September 1982)

The invisibles section of the balance of payments covers all those items on current account which do not arise out of the trade in exported and imported goods (the visible trade balance). The invisibles section is made up of several parts. Firstly, receipts and payments arising out of the supply and purchase of services such as banking, tourism, insurance and shipping. Secondly, the receipt of earnings by residents in the United Kingdom arising out of interest, dividend and rent payments on capital and property holdings overseas, and payments to overseas residents of income from similar holdings in Britain. Thirdly, the transfer of gifts, pensions and similar payments in currency between British and overseas residents. Fourthly, government transfers abroad in the form of overseas aid, the maintenance of military and diplomatic missions and the contribution made to the EEC.

Traditionally the United Kingdom has had a substantial surplus on invisibles, due both to her important role in world banking and other services and the large dividend and interest payments accruing from past overseas investment. While this surplus continues to hold today, there have been a number of important developments in recent years.

1. Tourism has become extremely important to the British economy in general, and the net deficit on tourism of the 1960s is now a substantial surplus. However, tourism is very much affected by the exchange rate, and fluctuations in the value of sterling in the 1980s have, at times, proved difficult for the tourist industry, as when sterling was relatively strong in the early 1980s.
2. North Sea oil development was largely financed by overseas oil companies and there has been a large growth in the payment of profits and dividends abroad as oil production has accelerated. Though important, these payments are dwarfed by the beneficial effects of North Sea oil on the visible trade balance.
3. The abolition of exchange control and the investment premium in 1979 made overseas investment both easier and more attractive. This has led to an increase in interest, profits and

dividends received by UK residents. Britain is still, for
example, the largest single foreign investor in the United
States.
4. The phasing out of British military bases overseas and other
government cuts in overseas expenditure have reduced the
level of government transfers. On the other hand, Britain's
membership of the EEC has resulted in a rise in government
transfers because of Britain's budget contribution.
5. There has been a shift in importance among the many service
industries contributing to Britain's invisible trade. The
growing contribution made by tourism has already been noted.
While banking and insurance continue to grow, shipping
services have declined as a net contributor due to the relative
decline in Britain's merchant marine.

4. What are the various parts which make up the balance of
payments? In what sense must a country's international receipts
and payments always balance? (Cert. Marketing, November 1983)

The balance of payments accounts record the economic transactions
of one country with all other countries. It is divided into three main
sections.

1. The current account. This records the receipts and payments of
the country arising from its trade and commercial transactions with
the rest of the world. It consists firstly of the balance of trade,
made up of the value of exported goods minus the value of
imported goods. There is also the balance of invisibles: this consists
of all those transactions involving the receipt and payment of
currency other than the trade in goods. Thus it includes the trade
in services such as banking and tourism, transfers of property
income in the form of interest, dividends etc., the transfer of
pensions and gifts, and certain aspects of overseas government
expenditure like the UK's contribution to the EEC budget. The
difference between the total income from invisible earnings and the
total of invisible payments is the balance of invisibles. The balance
on current account is obtained by adding together the balance of
trade and the balance of invisibles.

2. Investment and other capital flows. This section consists of
movements of capital into and out of the recording country. The
short-term capital account includes transfers of bank deposits and
currency dealings, changes in eurocurrency borrowing in London
and trade credit given on exports and imports. The long-term
capital account covers the purchase and sale of stocks and shares

by private investors. Foreign investment in the recording country is counted as an inflow while overseas investment by its residents is recorded as an outflow. The long-term account also includes long-term loans by one government to another. When added together, all these various items make up the balance on capital account.

When the current account and capital account balances are added together, they should yield a figure equal to the net receipt or loss of foreign currency over the year in question, i.e. the balance for official financing. This is the key indicator of how the recording country is faring in its external transactions.

3. Official financing. This section illustrates how a deficit is financed or a surplus is used. It consists of changes in the country's holdings of international liquidity, such as foreign currency or gold, and changes in the country's level of borrowing from international monetary institutions, notably the International Monetary Fund (IMF). A deficit could be financed either by a depletion of gold and foreign currency reserves or through borrowing from the IMF. A surplus will result in a rise in reserves or a reduction of the country's overseas debts. In practice, it is impossible to arrive at a totally accurate figure for the balance for official financing, so a balancing item is inserted to take account of errors and omissions and bring the total in line with that of the actual change in the country's official reserves and international indebtedness.

The balance of payments always balances in that disequilibrium on the current and capital accounts will be compensated by official financing. Thus if the total balance for official financing shows a deficit, this will be exactly matched by an equal figure in the official financing section. This will arise from either a depletion of reserves or borrowing from international monetary institutions, or a combination of the two. A surplus on the balance for official financing will be matched by an increase in reserves or a reduction in the country's international indebtedness. As an accounting identity the balance of payments will, in this sense, always balance.

7. Explain the various methods a government might employ to deal with an adverse balance of payments, commenting on the relative advantages and disadvantages of each method. (LCCI Higher, Autumn 1984)

An adverse balance of payments is a deficit on the balance for official financing. This deficit must be financed either by running down the country's official reserves or by borrowing, wheth from international monetary institutions or from the world' capital markets. If the deficit persists for several years, both re rves and international credit will be exhausted, so steps must þe taken to deal with a deficit. The measures available to the government in these circumstances are of three types. Firstly, direct controls. These consist of those policies involving the control of imports and the movement of foreign currency, notably tariffs, quotas, restrictions on overseas investment, exchange control and import deposits. The effectiveness of tariffs depends on the price elasticity of demand for imports, i.e. the extent to which import demand responds to higher import prices. The other measures are artificial barriers to the expenditure of currency abroad and are fairly crude instruments. All direct controls are dangerous because they invite retaliation. Furthermore, their use is very limited as they are often contrary to such international agreements as the General Agreement on Tariffs and Trade (GATT) and to membership of such organisations as the EEC. As an alternative to controlling imports, the government may seek to encourage exports through tax incentives, cheap export credit and subsidies to exporters. Such measures are at least less likely to provoke a trade war than a high-tariff policy.

Secondly, deflationary measures. By adopting measures to reduce aggregate demand in the economy, the government will hope to reduce the demand for imports and encourage home-based companies to export more in response to the drop in domestic demand. Monetary measures to control the availability of credit will also help the capital account, as higher interest rates attract capital flows into the country. Fiscal measures to cut government expenditure and raise taxes will also reduce demand, and thus the level of imports. The disadvantages of deflationary measures is that they are likely to reduce the level of economic activity, so raising unemployment and slowing the rate of economic growth. Such measures may also induce cost-push pressures which will raise prices and reduce export competitiveness. In such circumstances, direct control of prices and incomes may be needed in addition to the deflationary measures adopted.

Thirdly, devaluation. This is the deliberate, downward alteration of the value of the country's exchange rate. The effect is to make exports cheaper and imports dearer as the terms of trade deteriorate. If there were no change in the volume of trade, export earnings would fall and the national import bill rise. Devaluation will only reduce the balance of payments deficit provided that demand for the country's exports and domestic demand for imports are sufficiently responsive to the change in prices following devaluation. This means that the sum of the elasticity of domestic demand for imports and the elasticity of foreign demand for exports must be greater than unity. Even where demand elasticities are favourable to exporters, the supply of goods within the country must be sufficiently elastic to enable the country to capitalise on the increased competitiveness arising from devaluation. The disadvantage of devaluation is that the country must export more goods just to earn the same amount of foreign currency as before, while essential imports will now cost more in the local currency. Living standards must therefore drop until domestic income can be boosted via higher export demand.

There is the danger that pressure for higher incomes to offset the decline in living standards will cause cost-push inflation and erode the benefits of devaluation. More encouragingly, the higher demand for the country's exports will increase national output and stimulate economic growth. A formal devaluation is not possible for a country with a floating exchange rate but the same effects can be achieved by allowing the rate to float downwards under the pressure of market forces.

11. In what circumstances is a fall in the exchange rate most likely to be effective in reducing the deficit on current account? (ICMA Professional Stage, November 1981)

A fall in the exchange rate may occur in one of two ways. Under a fixed exchange rate regime the monetary authorities may devalue the currency so that the value of it is lowered in terms of other currencies. Alternatively, under a system of floating exchange rates, the authorities may permit, or even encourage, the exchange rate to depreciate. The effect in both cases is to make the country's exports cheaper and imports dearer and this might be expected to benefit the balance of payments. However, while devaluation or depreciation of the currency will make the country's goods more price competitive, the effect on the volume of trade and on the balance of payments is not immediately clear. Many potentially exportable goods will not fall in price by as much as the nominal devaluation, notably those produced domestically from imported raw materials. Even where devaluation has made the country's goods more competitive, exporters must have sufficient capacity to enable them to expand output and to take advantage of the lower prices. All that can confidently be predicted is that the terms of trade will deteriorate so that if there is no change in the volume of trade, export earnings will fall and the national import bill will rise. The success of devaluation depends, therefore, on the demand elasticity of exports and imports and the supply elasticity of exports.

Price elasticity of demand refers to the responsiveness of demand to a change in price. It is customarily measured mathematically by comparing the proportionate change in the quantity demanded to the proportionate change in price. Thus if the price of a commodity falls by 10 per cent and the quantity demanded rises in consequence by 20 per cent, the price elasticity of demand is 2. If, however, the quantity demanded had responded by rising only 5 per cent, price elasticity of demand would be $\frac{1}{2}$. Devaluation will have a favourable effect on the current account of the balance of payments if the sum of the elasticity of domestic demand for imports and the elasticity of foreign demand for exports is greater than unity. Suppose that the elasticity of demand for a country's exports is zero; a cut in prices has no effect on the overseas demand for that country's goods. The effect of devaluation or depreciation of the currency will be to leave export earnings, measured in local currency, unchanged. If the sum of elasticities is greater than unity, the elasticity of demand for imports must be also greater than unity so that devaluation, and higher import prices, leads to the value of imports measured in local currency falling. The balance of payments must therefore improve. The effect measured in foreign currency would be that, while foreign currency earnings fell by the same percentage as the devaluation, foreign currency payments for imports would fall by more than the percentage devaluation. The greater the sum of the demand elasticities for exports and imports, the greater will be the improvement in the current account.

The nature of a country's exports and imports will largely determine the demand elasticity for exports and imports. Generally the demand for services is more elastic than that for manufactures and the demand for manufactures is more elastic than the demand for raw materials and food stuffs. Even where demand elasticities are favourable for exporters, the supply of goods within the country must be sufficiently elastic to enable the economy to capitalise on the increased competitiveness arising from devaluation. There is normally a time lag between the devaluation and the full response by exporters to the new environment – the so-called 'J' curve effect. One other point concerns the transfer of interest, dividends, pensions etc., which are also included on current account. Such payments tend to be very inelastic and if the country is a net debtor nation, the fall in the value of the currency will place a greater burden on the rest of the current account.

Chapter Four

2. (a) By means of a diagram explain how an equilibrium rate of exchange is determined in a free market for foreign exchange. (*5 marks*)

(b) Explain how the equilibrium rate of exchange may be affected by:
  (i) the actions of speculators;
  (ii) changes in relative prices of imports and exports;
  (iii) changes in income levels;
  (iv) foreign investment;
  (v) government overseas expenditure. (*15 marks*)
(RSA Stage III, June 1984)

(a) In a free market, the equilibrium rate of exchange is determined by the intersection of the demand and supply curves for the currency in question on the foreign exchange markets. This can be illustrated by reference to the exchage rate of sterling against US dollars, as in Fig. X.

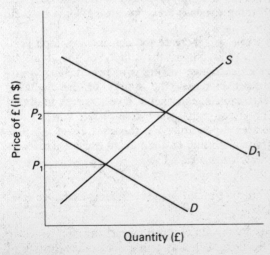

Fig. X

In Fig. X the equilibrium rate of exchange is at $P1$, where the demand for sterling from holders of dollars and the supply of sterling from those wishing to obtain dollars are in equilibrium. Any change in the demand or supply conditions operating in the market will result in a new equilibrium exchange rate. For instance, an increase in demand for sterling would lead to a rightward shift in the demand curve from D to $D1$ in Fig. X and a rise in the price of sterling from $P1$ to $P2$. In the same way, changes in supply conditions will also lead to a rise or fall in the exchange rate and a strengthening or weakening of the currency.

(b) (i) If speculators anticipate that sterling will fall on the foreign exchange market they will convert their pounds into other currencies. This would shift the supply of sterling to the right in Fig. X and lower the price of sterling, measured in dollars. If speculators expect the pound to strengthen they will increase their demand for sterling, so forcing up its price in dollars as demand shifts to the right.

(ii) This refers to a change in the terms of trade. All things being equal, an improvement in the terms of trade will mean that more foreign currency will be needed to buy Britain's exports while less will be needed by Britain to finance her own imports; so the exchange rate will rise. A deterioration in the terms of trade will have the opposite effect. In fact, a change in the terms of trade is more likely to affect the demand for exports and imports so that the exchange rate could *fall* if an improvement in the terms of trade led to the country's more expensive exports losing some of their world markets.

(iii) Higher income levels will increase the demand for imports so that the exchange rate will fall as the supply of the domestic currency on the foreign exchange market is increased.

(iv) Foreign investment increases the supply of the domestic currency on the foreign exchange market as investors seek to obtain other currencies. The effect is that the exchange rate falls.

(v) Government overseas expenditure has the same effect as a rise in imports. The supply of sterling on the foreign exchange markets is increased and the exchange rate falls.

3. Discuss the arguments for and against a floating exchange rate. (London, January 1980)

The main arguments in favour of floating exchange rates centre around the greater freedom such a system gives to the working of economic forces and to the operation of government policy.

1. They automatically restore equilibrium on the balance of payments. Where a freely floating exchange rate operates, the balance for official financing should, by implication, be zero. Any deficit on current account will push the exchange rate down and make investment in the country more attractive, thereby creating a surplus on capital account. A surplus will have the opposite effect so that in both cases the position on capital account should cancel out the current account balance. In addition, the current account will, to some extent, be self-adjusting; a deficit leads, through the lower exchange rate, to an increase in demand for the country's (cheaper) exports and a fall in demand for the country's (dearer) imports. For the current account to improve, however, it is necessary that the price elasticity of demand for exports plus the price elasticity of demand for imports together be greater than one.

2. Floating exchange rates eliminate the need for large holdings of official reserves. Because the balance of payments is self-adjusting, countries need not maintain reserves at a level so high that they can finance a series of deficits. At the same time the absence of permanent surpluses in some countries ensures a more even spread of world liquidity, rather than the accumulation of large unused reserve holdings by a small group of surplus countries. The need for reserves is further reduced by the fact that central banks are no longer required to support their currencies on the foreign exchange markets.

3. Floating exchange rates remove external constraints from government domestic economic policy. Since the exchange rate operates to maintain balance of payments equilibrium, the government has no need to adopt deflationary measures to correct a deficit. In consequence, fiscal and monetary policies can be suited to the requirements of the domestic situation with less fear of the external repercussions.

4. The exchange rate changes smoothly. Natural movements in the rate, either up or down, prevent it from getting out of line with its true market value. This helps avoid large devaluations or revaluations of the currency and the upheavals these bring, both internally and externally.

The arguments against floating exchange rates stem from the greater uncertainties attached to international trade by unstable rates of exchange.

1. They increase uncertainty. Because trade contracts often take a long time to complete, exporters and importers alike wish to

be able to predict future currency values. With floating rates, such predictability is lost and recourse must be made to the forward exchange market which, however, cannot eliminate entirely long-term uncertainty.

2. They hinder the attainment of price stability. If exchange rates are unstable, import prices and consequently domestic production costs are also prone to fluctuation. In particular, a downward floating exchange rate will make imports more expensive and increase any inflationary pressures already operating within the economy.

3. They may increase speculation. One advantage of floating exchange rates is that a massive overnight change in the exchange rate is highly unlikely. This might be expected to deter speculators from putting pressure on a currency since they have no hope of making the large, instant gains identified with devaluation or revaluation. In addition, it is more difficult for a speculator to predict in which direction the rate will move. On the other hand, the absence of a lower limit, below which the rate will not be permitted to fall, may allow a decline in the exchange rate to gain momentum as speculators and investors alike withdraw their funds. This may lead to a drain of confidence and result in the rate falling still further.

5. What factors are responsible for determining the rate of exchange of a country's currency? (*10 marks*)
What effects may a fall in the rate of exchange have on the economy? (*10 marks*) (RSA Diploma for Personal Assistants, June 1982)

In the absence of official intervention in the foreign exchange market, the exchange rate (the price of the domestic currency in terms of another) is found by the intersection of the demand and supply curves for the domestic currency on the foreign exchange market. The principal factors influencing the demand and supply of a currency are:

1. Relative inflation rates. Where one country has a higher inflation rate than others, its exports will become less competitive, so reducing demand for its currency and exerting downward pressure on the exchange rate.

2. Price elasticity of demand for a country's exports. Countries which export commodities with relatively inelastic demand enjoy strong economic bargaining power and are more likely

to have a balance of payments surplus and a strong exchange rate.

3. Interest rates. Short-term capital movements are highly responsive to changes in interest rates. Countries offering high interest rates can expect to attract foreign funds and so strengthen the exchange rate.

4. Economic factors within the country. Healthy economies are more likely to attract foreign investors and a strong exchange rate, while countries with a weakening economy will find capital leaving the country. The success or failure of the government's conduct of economic policy will also influence confidence.

5. Political factors. Political stability exerts a positive influence on the exchange rate, while uncertainty will have the opposite effect.

6. Expectations and speculation. The exchange markets seek to anticipate changes in such key economic indicators as the balance of payments and the level of interest rates. Thus unfavourable expectations will have a depressing effect on the exchange rate. Speculators, meanwhile, attempt to capitalise on the uncertainties of the future economic situation and may, by their own actions, cause the exchange rate to rise or fall.

A fall in the exchange rate may have several effects on the economy. Firstly, the terms of trade will weaken, with a greater volume of exports being necessary to finance a given volume of imports. Provided that the Marshall–Lerner elasticity condition holds, i.e. that the price elasticity of demand for exports plus the price elasticity of demand for imports together be greater than one, the balance of payments on current account will improve. If not, the current account will worsen. The capital account will, however, improve, as the country's assets can be obtained more cheaply by holders of foreign currency. Provided the overall balance of payments has improved, there will be a net injection into the circular flow of national income and this will lead to a growth in output and employment, provided there is not already full employment. If full employment does exist, there will be demand-pull inflationary pressures in the economy as demand for goods rises while the supply is unable to respond. Finally, the rise in the price of imported goods and services will result in higher prices of domestically-produced goods using imported raw materials and components. The effect is that cost-push pressures are introduced into the economy which, in turn, may reduce the competitiveness of the country's exports and exert further downward pressure on the exchage rate.

9.   For what reasons and in what ways might the monetary authorities seek to affect the level of a country's exchange rate? (IOB 2A, May 1984)

There are four main reasons for the monetary authorities seeking to influence the exchange rate.

1.   When a fixed exchange rate system is in operation, the central bank must be prepared to intervene in the foreign exchange market to defend the established parity from the full force of market pressures.
2.   The authorities may intervene even where there is a floating rate. This intervention would be to moderate the effect of sharp movements on the exchange market and is generally referred to as 'dirty' or 'managed' floating.
3.   The authorities may wish to devalue or depreciate the currency in order to improve the country's competitive position.
4.   The authorities may wish to revalue or appreciate the currency to reduce import costs and lower the domestic rate of inflation. This measure would also increase the value of a given volume of exports.

Measures available to influence the exchange rate may be divided into direct and indirect measures. When a country is operating a fixed exchange rate system it may adopt the direct policy of devaluation or revaluation of its currency. The Bretton Woods system of fixed exchange rates, for example, enabled countries to devalue or revalue their currencies against the US dollar (the dollar could only be devalued or revalued against gold). The most important fixed exchange rate regime currently in operation is the European Monetary System (EMS). The currency of each country in the EMS is linked to the others through an ECU-related central rate and devaluations or revaluations must be against this central rate. The other important direct measure available is intervention in the foreign exchange markets. In Britain the Bank of England uses its exchange equalisation account to buy sterling if it wishes to support the pound or sell sterling if it wishes to counter an upward movement of the exchange rate. In recent times, central banks have made increasing use of this intervention to influence the exchange rates of currencies other than their own, as when Japan and West Germany supported the US dollar in the early part of 1985.

The most obvious indirect method of influencing the exchange rate is the manipulation of interest rates. Since short-term capital movements are very responsive to changes in interest rates, a raising of interest rates will support the exchange rate by drawing in foreign funds and increasing the demand for the country's currency. In the same way, the monetary authorities can use all those measures which influence the demand and supply of the country's currency to affect the exchange rate. Thus monetary and fiscal measures to reduce inflation or to strengthen the balance of payments will increase confidence in the economy and give a boost to the exchange rate. The imposition of exchange controls or other barriers to the purchase of foreign currency will artificially reduce the country's demand for foreign currency and boost the exchange rate. Even the imposition of tariffs and other trade barriers, though potentially damaging to the world economy, will, ironically, boost the country's exchange rate.

Chapter Five

1. Assess the present role in the international monetary system of:
   (a) gold;
   (b) special drawing rights (SDRs);
   (c) the US dollar. (IOB 2A, May 1984)

(a) *Gold*. Despite being effectively demonetised at the 1976 Jamaica conference of the IMF, gold is still acceptable in settlement of international debts. Accordingly, gold holdings are maintained by most countries and serve both to bolster confidence and to finance trade in conditions of uncertain exchange rates, as in the case of the Soviet Union and other Eastern bloc states. In addition, gold is used for central bank transactions within the European Monetary System (EMS) and as collateral for trade credit arrangements.

(b) *Special drawing rights (SDRs)*. These were first issued in 1970 as non-repayable credits given to each member of the IMF in proportion to its IMF quota. When a country needs to finance a balance of payments deficit it may use its allocation of SDRs to obtain currencies from other countries, thereby providing a source of extra international liquidity. Despite the intention of the Second Amendment of the IMF in 1978 that the SDR should become the principal reserve asset, its importance remains relatively slight. This is partly because there has been resistance from some IMF members, mainly advanced western nations, to the creation of new SDRs for fear of provoking inflationary pressures. Thus after the original issues of $3 bn in each of the years 1970–72, the only subsequent allocations have been those of SDR 4 bn a year between 1979 and 1981. The delay in the expansion of SDRs is also due partly to the preference for gold and foreign currency among many of the world's trading nations. On the other hand, the SDR has established its position as the official unit of account of the IMF, while a number of countries now peg their exchange rate to the SDR. Commercial use of the SDR has also grown, to the extent that even issues of public bonds have been denominated in SDRs.

(c) *US dollar.* Since the early 1970s the ending of dollar convertibility and the decline of the dollar as a reserve currency have reduced its relative importance in the international monetary system. However, the dollar remains the most important reserve currency because of the key role played by the American economy in world trade; so the dollar retains its dominant position in international liquidity. Furthermore, the dollar is the most important unit of account for trading purposes with many commodities, such as oil, being priced in dollars and most multinational companies using it as their internal accounting currency. Finally, many currencies are pegged to the US dollar so that movements in the dollar exchange rate have a major impact both on the currencies and the economies of these countries.

2. (a) Outline the main changes that have occurred in the composition of international liquidity since 1971. (*15 marks*)
    (b) To what extent has the existence of floating exchange rates reduced the need for international liquidity? (*10 marks*)
(IOB 2A, April 1982)

(a) International liquidity may be defined as the total resources available to individual countries to finance balance of payments. Prior to the devaluation of the US dollar in 1971, international liquidity comprised US dollars; gold; reserve positions in the IMF; special drawing rights (SDRs), in that order of importance. Following the breakdown of the Smithsonian Agreement and the collapse of the Bretton Woods system of fixed exchange rates, there have been important changes in the relative importance of the various forms of international liquidity.

1. While the dollar remains the most important currency of all those held as foreign currency reserves, its decline as a reserve

currency is a notable feature of the post-1971 period. Holdings of other strong currencies, however, have grown rapidly. A further increase in currency holdings has occurred through leakages from the various eurocurrency markets into official reserve holdings.

2. Gold was officially demonetised at the 1976 IMF conference held in Jamaica. While this might be expected to have reduced the importance of gold as a source of international liquidity, the fact that gold holdings are now valued at market prices, rather than at the artificially low official price of 1971, means that their value has grown substantially over this period.

3. There has been some expansion of the role of SDRs, though not as great as might have been expected in 1971. Indeed, since the first issues of $3 bn in each of the years 1970–72, the only subsequent allocations have been those of SDR 4 bn a year between 1979 and 1981.

4. There have been increases in the reserve positions of the IMF by increases in the quotas of member countries. While this has served to increase international liquidity, the IMF has estimated that one-sixth of its currency holdings are of little value since they are not generally acceptable in settlement of trade transactions.

(b) In theory, floating exchange rates eliminate the need for large holdings of official reserves. This is because the balance of payments should be self-adjusting under a floating exchange rate regime, so that there is no need for reserves to finance a payments deficit. At the same time the absence of large balance of payments surpluses ensures a more even spread of world liquidity, rather than an accumulation of unused reserves by permanent surplus countries. The need for reserves is further reduced by the fact that central banks are no longer required to support their currencies on the foreign exchange markets, as they are with fixed exchange rates.

In practice, most countries operate a system of 'dirty' or 'managed' floating, whereby the central bank does intervene regularly in the foreign exchange market to influence movements in the exchange rate. In addition, balance of payments deficits and surpluses have not been eliminated. In particular, the large deficits incurred by many countries following the oil price rises of recent years have necessitated further increases in world liquidity. For both these reasons, most countries have had to maintain substantial levels of international liquidity.

3. Discuss both the desirability and the feasibility of a return to worldwide fixed exchange rates such as operated under the so-called Bretton Woods system. (IOB 2A, September 1982)

The principal claim made for fixed exchange rates is that they promote stability in the international financial system. This stability is manifested in a number of advantages.

1. Fixed rates enable traders to predict with greater certainty both prices and profits, thereby contributing to an atmosphere in which foreign trade is encouraged.
2. They promote stability in the international capital markets. Since capital may safely be left in overseas financial centres with reasonable confidence as to its future value, investors are more likely to consider making overseas loans. At the same time, speculators are able to make only limited gains from exchange dealings unless they are able, by concerted action, to engineer a major devaluation or revaluation.
3. They impose discipline on government economic policy. In order to avoid excessive strain on the exchange rate, governments must ensure that their economic policies do not lead to high rates of inflation or to severe balance of payments disequilibrium.

Unfortunately, the maintenance of a fixed exchange rate does impose severe restraints on the freedom of action of governments, with potentially harmful consequences for the domestic economy.

1. Large official reserves are required. The monetary authorities are required to intervene regularly to maintain the exchange rate at or near its official parity. When there is downward pressure on the exchange rate, the authorities will need large reserves to provide support over a long period. Large reserves are also required to finance balance of payments deficits, often a persistent feature of the economy under a fixed rate regime.
2. There is a tendency for exchange rates to move seriously out of alignment over a long period. The major devaluations and revaluations which follow can themselves tend to destabilise the international trading system.
3. Economic policy is subject to dictation by external pressures. Where the exchange rate is under pressure, the government is forced to adopt measures to restore confidence in the economy. Thus, instead of policies designed to promote economic growth and full employment, the government has to introduce defla-

tionary measures to assist the balance of payments and to support the exchange rate.

When discussing the desirability of a return to a system of fixed exchange rates, therefore, both the advantages and the disadvantages of the system must be considered. The international financial system would only benefit by a reversion to fixed exchange rates if there was sufficient evidence to show that the gains in stability and certainty outweighed the drawbacks of the system's rigidity. As to the feasibility of such a move, the factors which caused the Bretton Woods system to collapse in the first place are still very much present. Thus the widely varying inflation rates and large balance of payments imbalances which have been present since the early 1970s still make fixed exchange rates difficult to sustain over a reasonable time span. Indeed, the European Monetary System, which is based on a system of fixed exchange rates, is forced to make regular adjustments to cope with these problems.

4. Following the breakdown of the so-called Bretton Woods system in the 1970s most major currencies were allowed to float. To what extent have the theoretical advantages of floating exchange rates been borne out in practice? (IOB 2A, September 1984)

The main arguments in favour of floating exchange rates centre around the greater freedom such a system gives to the working of economic forces and to the operation of government policy.

1. They automatically restore equilibrium in the balance of payments. Any deficit on current account will push the exchange rate down and make investment in the country more attractive, thereby creating a surplus on capital account. A surplus will have the opposite effect so that in both cases the position on capital account should cancel out the current account balance, leaving the balance for official financing at zero. In addition, the current account will to some extent be self-adjusting; a deficit leading, through a lower exchange rate, to cheaper exports and dearer imports.
2. Floating exchange rates eliminate the need for large holdings of official reserves. Because the balance of payments is self-adjusting, countries need not maintain reserves at a level high enough to finance a series of deficits. The need for reserves is further reduced by the fact that central banks are no longer required to support their currencies on the foreign exchange markets.
3. Floating rates remove external constraints from government

domestic economic policy. Since the exchange rate maintains balance of payments equilibrium, the government has no need to adopt measures to cure a deficit, such as prolonged deflation of domestic demand. In consequence, fiscal and monetary policies can be suited to the requirements of the domestic economic situation with less fear of the external repercussions.

4. The exchange rate moves smoothly. Natural movements in the rate, either up or down, prevent it from getting out of line with its true market value. This helps avoid large devaluations or revaluations of the currency and the upheavals these bring, both internally and externally.

Taking these points in turn, the automatic adjustment of the balance of payments has not occurred in practice, at least as far as *current* accounts are concerned. This has been due partly to the failure of exchange rates to move in line with relative inflation rates, as predicted by the purchasing power parity theory. Equally important has been the impact of price elasticities of demand for exports and imports. Some strong trading nations have experienced an improvement in both their exchange rate *and* their current account under the floating rate regime. Automatic adjustment of current and capital accounts has occurred only through highly volatile short-term capital flows.

Because balance of payments positions have not been sufficiently self-adjusting, deficits have persisted for many countries and required them to maintain adequate official reserves. In addition, few countries have permitted free floating, even for a short period. Instead there has been a system of managed floating with official intervention as common as under a system of fixed rates and a consequent need for substantial reserves. In any case, the emergence of regional fixed exchange rate systems, such as the European Monetary System, has meant that many currencies are not truly floating.

Though there is no need to defend a particular parity under a system of floating exchange rates, the rate continues to be a constraint on domestic economic policies. Thus the strength of the dollar early in 1985 was a contributory factor to Britain's high interest rates at that time.

Finally, the events of 1985, in particular, show that exchange rates can move dramatically under a floating regime. Many of the major currencies experienced quite volatile changes in value over a very short period.

Chapter Six

3. For what reasons are rates of interest paid on deposits in the euromarkets usually higher than comparable rates paid on domestic deposits? How far does this factor explain the rapid growth in the euromarkets? (IOB 2A, April 1983)

The higher rate of interest offered on euromarket deposits arises out of the unregulated nature of these markets. In particular, the absence of reserve requirements means that virtually all deposits can be on-lent without a proportion being lodged with central banks. This lowers the effective cost of these deposits to the banks operating in the markets who can therefore offer a higher return. Sometimes the higher rates offered in the euromarkets are the result of a shortage of deposits due to exchange controls preventing the flow of deposits from the domestic markets to the euromarkets. Finally, the ability to offer higher rates is bolstered by the economies of scale obtained in the euromarkets through a concentration on wholesale transactions.

While higher deposit rates have been an important cause of the growth of the euromarkets, so too have been the *lower* rates charged to borrowers. These lower rates are also the consequence of the lack of reserve requirements which allows the banks operating in the euromarkets to offer finer rates of interest than the domestic markets. These lower rates are also the consequence of the euromarkets' concentration on wholesale transactions.

In addition to the important contributions to the growth of the markets made by competitive interest rates, several other factors have been important.

1. The general acceptability of dollars in the finance of international trade made many companies wish to hold a dollar balance for financial and commercial use. Many of these multinational companies have since used the markets as temporary havens for surplus funds and as a way of hedging against fluctuations on the foreign exchange markets.
2. The gradual easing of exchange controls in Europe has resulted in many European residents taking advantage of the competitive lending rates offered by the euromarkets. Convertibility also encouraged the development of euromarkets in other currencies, notably sterling, Swiss francs and deutschemarks.
3. The euromarkets grew rapidly after the oil price rise of 1973 when much of the combined balance of payments surplus of

the oil-producing countries was deposited with them. The euromarkets were chosen because they appeared a more attractive proposition for short-term funds than the more uncertain eurobond market. The surpluses of the oil-producing countries were matched by corresponding deficits in other countries, notably the non-oil-producing developing countries, who were forced to borrow from the commercial banks to supplement their liquidity.

Yet despite the importance of these factors in stimulating growth of the markets, the most important contribution has been that of the more competitive interest rates available. This is evidenced by the fact that the eurosterling market has grown much more slowly than most of the other euromarkets because the very low reserve requirements imposed in Britain result in the eurosterling market having only a minute competitive edge over the domestic sterling money markets.

4. What factors have contributed to the rapid growth of the eurocurrency markets in recent years? To what extent has this growth been a cause of concern to the world's monetary authorities? (IOB 2A, April 1984)

In recent years the growth of the eurocurrency markets has reflected those factors which have promoted the expansion of world banking activity generally. Firstly, the continued expansion of world trade, despite the recent slowing of this process, has assisted the internationalisation of the world economy. This in turn has led to an increasing number of multinational companies using the eurocurrency markets as temporary havens for surplus funds and as a hedge against exchange rate changes. Secondly, the large balance of payments surpluses received by the oil-producing countries have been recycled to deficit countries via the banking system, in particular through the eurocurrency markets. Thirdly, the non-oil-developing countries have sought to solve their shortages of international liquidity by borrowing from the eurocurrency markets. Such borrowing has been preferred to an approach to the International Monetary Fund (IMF) for assistance because of the IMF's practice of making its loans conditional on the borrowing nation adopting economic measures acceptable to the IMF. Finally, the unregulated nature of the markets has assisted in their growth since the resultant absence of reserve requirements has enabled the banks to on-lend all such funds received. In addition, the ability to lend all funds received, rather than keep low-profit reserves, has enabled the bank to quote higher interest rates to depositors and lower interest rates to borrowers. Despite the continued growth of the eurocurrency markets, the level of new lending has fallen since 1982. This development has followed the world recession, the reduction in balance of payments deficits and the growing concern among both central and commercial banks about the level of indebtedness of some of the heavier borrowers in the markets.

The growth of the eurocurrency markets has given cause for concern in a number of areas. Firstly, there is the growth in international indebtedness of the developing countries referred to above. Should these countries be unable to meet their international financial obligations, excessive strain would be placed on the international banking system. In 1984 the Midland Bank, in Britain, was under some pressure due to the failure of an American subsidiary, partly as the result of such lending. An international banking crisis would undoubtedly pose threats to the stability of world trade. The second major concern is the lack of regulation of the eurocurrency markets. The international monetary authorities have raised their fears that such unregulation has led to excessive use of the markets by deficit countries to finance their balance of payments. Furthermore, some banks seem to have over-reached themselves when free of the normal restraints imposed on their domestic activities. Despite the monitoring of borrowing by developing countries undertaken by the World Bank, no international agreement for the control of the markets by the world's central banks has so far been secured.

The third concern relates to the growth of international liquidity. The growth of the eurocurrency markets has created extra world liquidity over which the international monetary authorities have no direct control. Such liquidity could, under conditions of expanding world trade, result in inflationary pressures in the world economy. Finally, the eurocurrency markets provide a large pool of highly mobile short-term funds. The rapid movement of these funds between the various major international financial centres could prove highly destabilising to the foreign exchange markets. In time, such a situation could seriously affect the ability of countries to pursue their chosen domestic monetary policies because of the relationship between the eurocurrency and other money markets.

5.   What is a eurodollar? Why are changes in eurodollar interest rates of importance to the foreign exchange markets? (IOB 2A, September 1984)

A eurodollar is a dollar deposit held in a bank outside the United States. The primary distinguishing feature of eurodollars compared to domestic dollars is that transactions in eurodollars are conducted exclusively by banks operating outside the United States and using a different interest rate structure from that in America, since eurodollar deposits do not come under the influence of the monetary policies of the Federal Reserve Bank of the United States. The largest eurodollar market operates in London but there are others throughout the world, with the exception of Africa and Latin America.

Changes in eurodollar interest rates are of importance to the foreign exchange market for two reasons. Firstly, other things being equal, an increase in eurodollar interest rates will put upward pressure on the spot dollar exchange rate. This is because interest rates are a key determinant of exchange rate movements so the demand for dollars on the exchange markets will rise as investors seek to obtain dollars for investment in the eurodollar markets. On the other hand, a fall in eurodollar interest rates will reduce the attractiveness of eurodollar deposits and thus of dollars generally, resulting in a downward pressure on the spot dollar exchange rate.

The second impact of eurodollar interest rates on foreign exchange markets occurs in the forward market. Forward exchange rates are determined by those factors influencing spot rates plus expectations as to how the spot rate will move in the short term. If the dollar is expected to strengthen, the forward rate will be quoted at a premium; while if it is expected to weaken, the forward rate will attract a discount. If interest rates rise today, the likelihood grows that the next movement will be downwards. Thus while the spot rate for the dollar rises, the rate on the forward market is weakened, thereby narrowing the forward premium or widening the forward discount. When interest rates fall today, the reverse will apply and the forward discount narrow or premium widen.

6. Your customers, European Consortium Limited, wish to establish a manufacturing and trading enterprise in Holland to service their EEC and Scandinavian needs. During a visit to their office you discuss with the finance director various methods of raising short-, medium- and long-term finance for their operations in Holland.

Required:

Brief notes explaining the various methods of obtaining finance, other than sterling, which will satisfy your customer's needs. (IOB 2B, September 1982)

Funds can be obtained either locally in Holland or through the eurocurrency market raised in other centres.

Short-term:
Currency borrowing in either Dutch guilders or eurocurrency can be raised in the UK from British banks in three ways:
  (i) Overdraft facilities in foreign currency with interest rates based on the average eurocurrency LIBOR, plus a margin.
 (ii) Short-term eurocurrency loans on a fixed basis with the rate based on eurocurrency LIBOR plus margin.
(iii) Overdraft facilities arranged at a Dutch bank, either in Dutch guilders or in a eurocurrency and secured by a guarantee from a British bank.

Medium-term:
For terms of one to five years, facilities can be arranged in eurocurrency.
  (i) Fixed-rate loans with interest rates based on the appropriate LIBOR plus margin. The rate is fixed for the entire period agreed and the total loan is repayable on the final date. Such loans are difficult to arrange because market conditions are usually too unpredictable to enable fixed-rate contracts of more than one or two years.
 (ii) Roll-over syndicated loans. These are suitable for large loans of periods of two to five years or more. A eurocurrency loan can be arranged either direct through a UK bank or, in the case of very large loans, through a syndicate of banks. While the loan is fixed for a long period, the interest rates charged are linked to LIBOR plus a margin and would be subject to variation at each roll-over date. Roll-over may be at three-, six-, or twelve- month periods, with the bank effectively relending the funds for each new period at the interest rate prevailing at the time of roll-over. This facility is normally available only to first-class customers.

Long-term:
  (i) Foreign securities issued in the traditional manner. These would be denominated in the country of issue, underwritten by a national syndicate, and would be sold mainly in the country of the underwriting syndicate.

(ii) Eurobonds. These are usually for substantial sums of money and have the following characteristics:

(a) They are raised and issued by international syndicates and are underwritten by international banks or financial institutions for first-class names.

(b) They are usually sold on international capital markets, and normally in a country other than of the currency of the bond.

(c) Funds raised in this way are not liable for withholding tax and there is usually a secondary market in operation.

(d) It is usually possible to raise longer term funds by bond issues than by euroloans.

(e) Eurobond issues may be either at fixed or floating rates of interest.

Chapter Seven

1. Over the past year, several countries have revealed figures of international indebtedness which have cast serious doubts on their national solvency, and the willingness of lending countries to extend further credit. What is likely to be the effect on world trade in general, and for such countries in particular? (Dip. Marketing, June 1983).

Since 1979 a succession of countries, probably as many as forty, have fallen into arrears in repaying their borrowing and in meeting scheduled interest payments. This development was largely unforeseen, since the rapid growth in international indebtedness after the oil price rise of 1973–74 had been absorbed fairly comfortably by the international financial system. The causes of the crisis of the 1980s stem from several inter-related factors. Firstly, the unregulated growth of commercial bank lending led to the banks overstretching themselves and then attempting to cut back their lending when the threat of default became apparent. Secondly, the high level of real interest rates in the 1980s caused an escalation of debt service costs, especially as existing debts came up for renewal. Thirdly, the world recession has hit the developing countries hardest. They have suffered both a fall in demand for their exports and a slump in their export prices so that export earnings have fallen, and with them the prospects of an early reduction in their overseas debts. By 1981, debt service payments by developing countries equalled approximately half their current account receipts, compared to less than a third in 1977. This difficulty was aggravated by the fact that much of this international lending was accounted for by a dozen or so countries.

The growth of the international indebtedness of the non-oil-producing developing countries posed, by 1982, two major threats. First, there was the possibility that some of the largest debtors might default on their debts and send a shock-wave through the international banking system. Second, there was the risk of a banking collapse brought on by banks straining their liquidity in an attempt to shore up the debt structure of countries threatening to default. Since a number of banks were anxious to reduce their level of lending to the developing countries for fear of default, the biggest danger at this time was that the banks might precipitate the very thing they feared most by attempting to stop new lending. The immediate crisis has been averted largely by the intervention of the IMF and the rescheduling of debts. However, this rescheduling programme has brought its own problems. The IMF has taken a hard line in demanding fierce austerity measures as the price of its support for a restructuring agreement. These austerity programmes have brought hardship to the peoples of the debtor countries, retarded the growth necessary to enable these countries to solve their problems and, coupled with the prevailing high interest rates, meant that the debtor countries were paying for the economic policies of the advanced nations.

In the absence of a more liberal attitude being taken by the industrialised countries to the debtor problem, future prospects for world trade and for the debtor countries are not encouraging. In its 1984 annual report, the World Bank argued that the advanced countries should be encouraging industrial and export growth in the debtor countries through greater provision of aid, instead of erecting protectionist trade barriers against the exports of developing countries. The alternative may well be default by the debtor nations. Such a move has become more attractive as the debt crisis has led to many of the developing countries becoming more self-sufficient in raw materials and less dependent on trade with other countries. Default might also follow as the result of the slow growth of the developing countries since their export earnings are unlikely to expand sufficiently to enable a reduction of the debt burden.

2. Distinguish between the roles of the IMF (International Monetary Fund) and the World Bank (International Bank for Reconstruction and Development). Why may they both be seen as of increasing importance? (ICMA Foundation, November 1983)

Both the IMF and the World Bank were set up under the Bretton Woods Charter, which came into force in December 1945. The IMF was established with the primary objective of promoting a freer system of world trade and payments through the encouragement of stable exchange rates and the elimination of exchange controls. It was also expected to provide assistance to member countries to enable them to deal with balance of payments problems and so reduce the threat of protectionism in international trade. Two roles were therefore required of the IMF. Firstly, it had to provide its members with a code of international behaviour and ensure that this was followed. Secondly, it was responsible for the provision of additional international liquidity for countries with payments difficulties. For the first twenty years of its existence, the IMF fulfilled its first role through the operation of a system of fixed exchange rates. Member countries were expected to make every effort to maintain the chosen rate against the US dollar, and to consult with the IMF before making any change. Assistance could be given to members with payments problems from the reserves available to the IMF through the subscriptions, or quotas, of member countries. Here again the supervisory role of the IMF was evident since assistance was generally linked to conditions aimed at rectifying the borrowing country's underlying economic weaknesses.

Since the late 1960s the role of the IMF has developed in line with the changing demands of the international monetary system. The most notable features of this development have been:

1. The recognition that a system of fixed exchange rates was no longer sustainable in the period after 1971 and the subsequent support given to the present floating regime.
2. The greater contribution made to the supply of international liquidity through the various increases in quotas, together with the issues of special drawing rights (SDRs).
3. The growing awareness of the needs of the developing countries, as evidenced by the demonetisation of gold and the sale of the IMF's gold holdings to assist these less prosperous IMF members.

The World Bank was established to help finance the reconstruction of areas devastated during the Second World War, and to aid the development of the poorer nations of the world. Since the late 1940s its activities have been exclusively devoted to the problems of the developing countries, which it assists by providing loans to governments or to government-backed organisations to cover the foreign exchange costs of capital projects. The funds of the World Bank are raised through the subscriptions of the wealthier member countries and from loan issues floated on the world's capital markets.

The importance of both the IMF and the World Bank has increased dramatically since the onset of the international debt crisis of the 1980s. The IMF has played a leading role in co-ordinating rescheduling operations. By insisting on borrowing countries adopting economic policies aimed at tackling their economic problems, the IMF has made it easier for commercial banks to participate in the rescheduling of the debts. The IMF's own ability to assist borrowing countries was increased by the 50 per cent increase in quotas agreed at the end of 1982 and the further increase in 1984. Yet, despite this assistance, the IMF has been criticised both by the borrowing nations and by the World Bank for the hard line it has taken in demanding fierce austerity measures as the price of its support for a restructuring agreement. The World Bank, meanwhile, has taken on the role of champion of the developing countries by demanding greater development assistance from the advanced nations.

4. What problems have been posed for international liquidity requirements by the large balance of payments surpluses accruing to oil-producing countries in recent years? To what extent have the eurocurrency markets helped in overcoming these problems? (IOB 2A, September 1982)

International liquidity may be described as the total resources available to individual countries to finance balance of payments deficits. The large balance of payments surpluses of the oil-producing countries have led to equally large deficits for other countries and it is these continuing large deficits which have posed problems for international liquidity. This is because the surpluses of oil-producing countries have resulted in a reduction of the level of reserves of some deficit countries to the point where traditional sources of liquidity (gold, foreign currency, special drawing rights and IMF quotas) are no longer adequate to finance further deficits. Thus a shortage of international liquidity has followed from the accumulation of large reserves by oil-producing countries.

The eurocurrency markets have enabled the international liquidity shortage to be at least partially solved. Many of the non-oil-developing countries have borrowed from the international banking system to supplement their liquidity and most of this borrowing has occurred via the eurocurrency markets because of the lower rates of interest offered to borrowers in these markets. The banks, in turn, have obtained their funds from the surpluses of the oil-producing countries, these being largely deposited in the eurocurrency markets. In effect, the eurocurrency markets have recycled the oil producers' surpluses to finance the deficits of the developing countries.

Despite the success of the eurocurrency markets in solving the liquidity shortage in the short term, the use of the markets in this way poses a number of problems in the long term. Firstly, the increased international indebtedness of many of the deficit countries has reached alarming proportions and raised doubts about their ability to honour their commitments, with potentially serious consequences for the international banking system. Secondly, there is the tendency for recycled funds obtained by deficit countries to find their way back to the eurocurrency markets via the central banks of surplus countries. These funds can then be re-lent and contribute to a cycle of excessive and uncontrolled creation of liquidity, giving rise to inflationary pressures. Thirdly, a future oil price rise would raise the difficulties of international liquidity shortages again for countries apparently unable to redeem existing debts. The eurocurrency markets cannot provide a long-term solution to the problems of international liquidity shortages. These require concerted action, both by the major international monetary authorities and by the major trading nations, to ensure that international liquidity grows in line with the demands made upon it.

8. Explain why international trade tends to operate to the detriment of less developed countries and suggest actions which might improve their trading position. (AEB, June 1985)

The theory of international trade predicts that the most advanced countries will benefit by specialising in those industries in which they have the greatest relative efficiency, whilst leaving to other countries the production of those goods in which the relative efficiency is smaller. Inevitably this results in the advanced countries concentrating on the production of sophisticated industrial goods, while the less developed countries are left to produce basic raw materials and other cheap labour-intensive products. The developing countries are disadvantaged by this trading relationship in several ways. Firstly, the fact that they are producing and exporting cheap raw materials and semi-manufactures while importing essential manufactured goods and capital equipment results in a poor terms of trade. This leads to a substantial volume of exports being required to finance the import of a small volume of expensive items from the industrialised countries. Secondly, the world market prices of raw materials fluctuate more dramatically than those of manufactured goods so that export earnings are more difficult to predict for the developing countries. Thirdly, the world demand for raw materials is dominated by the industrialised nations and a recession in these countries substantially reduces the demand for the products of the developing countries. Fourthly, the income elasticity of demand for the products of the developing countries is much lower than that for manufactured goods. Thus even during periods of trade expansion, the developing countries benefit less than the industrialised countries. Finally, the developing countries both buy from and sell to large multinational companies who can dictate terms when dealing with small national companies or state bodies anxious to sell to the industrialised world.

In the situation outlined above, the aim of the less developed countries must be to improve their bargaining position in trade with the advanced countries. One solution is for countries producing similar raw materials to form a cartel and negotiate jointly with buyers of their products, rather than negotiate as individuals. The most successful example of this type of organisation is the Organisation of Petroleum Exporting Countries (OPEC). Oil prices *fell* between 1950 and 1970 by over 20 per cent, but this trend was reversed after the formation of OPEC. The oil-producing countries now ceased being picked off individually by the great multinational oil companies and in 1973 agreed restrictive quotas, thereby succeeding in quadrupling oil prices. A similar exercise led to a further doubling of oil prices in 1979–80.

The oil-producing countries were able to improve their trading position by joint action. They were assisted in this by the dependence of the industrial world for oil as its primary energy source. Such an option is not available to most developing countries. Their best hope lies in using their advantages of a cheap labour supply and lack of hidebound industrial practices to establish their own industries, perhaps through joint-participation schemes with multinationals to obtain the necessary capital. The production of competitively-priced mass-produced goods will enable the developing countries both to diversify their trading patterns and to improve their terms of trade with the industrial countries. Already the so-called newly industrialising countries (NICs) such as Korea, Hong Kong and Taiwan have proved successful in penetrating the domestic markets of the industrialised countries and in establishing their own multinational operations. The major problem facing many of the less developed countries is that they lack both the domestic capital and the attractiveness to potential overseas investors to break out of the poverty cycle and a dependence on traditional economic patterns.

Chapter Eight

2. What advantages have accrued to the UK in terms of international trade as a result of EEC membership? (*10 marks*)
Is our continuing membership economically desirable, in view of a trend towards increasing trade barriers in recent years of recession? (*10 marks*)
(RSA Diploma for Personal Assistants, June 1984)

The aim of all customs unions and free trade areas is the promotion of greater prosperity for each member state. This is to be achieved primarily through the reduction of trade barriers between members and a consequent enlargement of each member's 'home' market. The EEC goes much further, however, since it seeks to increase the efficiency of the productive system of the Community. This involves the adoption of policies which will enable the development of international economies of scale through the free movement of labour, capital and enterprise. The establishment of free trade between members and the encouragement of intra-Community trade is thus a first step in the establishment of one unified economic super-state.

The general principle of free trade within the EEC is that goods should be able to move freely throughout the territory of the Community. Quotas for industrial products were abolished in 1961 and customs duties in 1968. The UK came into line in 1977. The effect on the structure of UK international trade of EEC membership has been dramatic. Whereas in 1958 only 20 per cent of British exports had gone to EEC countries, this figure had doubled to 41 per cent by 1982. This growth in trade with other EEC members has been extremely advantageous to the UK for several reasons. Firstly the markets of Europe have grown much faster than those of Britain's traditional trading partners of the Commonwealth and South America. Thus Britain's exports have grown faster than they would have done had her old trading patterns persisted. Secondly, Britain has gained access not only to the European markets, but also to other established markets of France, Holland and the other European nations. Thirdly, the economies of scale achieved by the expansion of 'home' markets have led to British multinational companies being able to develop their potential for growth. Fourthly, the relaxation of barriers to trade has enabled British consumers to benefit from a wider variety of goods and at a lower price than would have been the case in the absence of free trade.

Unfortunately, barriers to trade have not entirely disappeared within the Community. In the first place the member countries retain their different tax structures which distort competitive conditions. Secondly, obstacles to trade are posed by the complex customs formalities maintained by each country. While these had their origins in bureaucratic regulations, their survival may well be due to a residual resistance to free trade. Thirdly, the Community has attempted to outlaw technical barriers to trade, except where legitimate concerns over safety or health are involved. Yet such barriers persist, and have grown, as a way preventing the entry of goods from other Community countries.

While the world recession has contributed to the greater willingness to use trade barriers to protect domestic industries, Britain would be unlikely to benefit, on trade grounds, in leaving the EEC. In the first place the British economy is now far more sensitive to developments in the Community as a whole and 'going it alone' would be a far more difficult task than it would have been if we had never joined. Secondly, the raising of trade barriers to British goods would harm British industry far more than any similar barriers raised by Britain against the products of EEC countries. Finally, on a broader issue, Britain's economy is much weaker, comparatively, than it was when we joined and we would lose the various benefits enjoyed in terms of regional development, industrial assistance and technological co-operation available to EEC members.

6. Discuss the economic arguments for and against British withdrawal from membership of the European Community. (London, June 1983)

The principal economic argument in favour of Britain's withdrawal from the European Community (EEC) is that the present structure and objectives of the Community do not reflect the best interests of the British economy. More specifically, the EEC is primarily an agricultural community geared to the needs of the large farming interests of the member states, while Britain's interests lie mainly in industry, trade and commerce. This results in a number of problems for Britain. Firstly, the heavy subsidisation of agriculture by consumers raises food prices in Britain to a level above what they would be had supplies continued to come from traditional sources. Thus withdrawal would enable British governments to revert to a 'cheap food' policy, to the benefit of the poorer sections of the population. Secondly, the large proportion of the total EEC budget spent on agriculture results in Britain receiving far less from it than she contributes. While it would be self-defeating for the Community if each member expected to take out exactly what it put in, Britain has frequently made by far the largest contribution, despite being the fourth poorest of the ten members in 1984. Despite some improvements to the system of EEC finance following the ministerial summits of the 1980s, Britain remains a net contributor to the budget. Apart from the direct effects of the budget contribution on the balance of payments, problems are also posed for the conduct of government policy. Efforts to cut government expenditure in 1980, for example, were frustrated by the extra £1,200 m. the government had to find for the Community. Thus the other major argument for withdrawal is that the government would have greater control over the conduct of economic policy – the more so since the country would be free of EEC regulations on trade, industry, competition policy and so on. Finally the government could once again more strongly support domestic industry at the expense of outside goods.

The economic arguments against withdrawal are based on the benefits the British economy receives through our membership of the EEC. Britain has gained from easier access to European markets and these markets would be more difficult to penetrate if we were outside the Community. Furthermore, the economies of scale achieved by the expansion of 'home' markets to Europe has enabled British multinational companies to achieve their potential for growth. At the same time the relaxation of trade barriers has permitted British consumers to benefit from a wider variety of goods and services, and at a lower price, than would have been the case in the absence of free trade. Britain has also gained directly from the various industrial grants from EEC funds and this has undoubtedly stimulated both domestic and overseas investment in the UK's depressed areas. All these gains would be in jeopardy were Britain to leave the Community. Instead of being an integral part of this very large market, Britain would be reduced to a small, not very wealthy, island whose industries would face trade barriers from their traditional markets. At the same time any prospects of benefiting from a long-term development of the Community's industrial policy would be lost forever. While there may have been some alternative to joining in the first place, disentanglement from the Community would certainly leave Britain economically weaker than when she first became a member.

8. Outline the main features of the European Monetary System (EMS). What do you consider to have been the successes and failures of the system? (IOB 2A, September 1983)

The European Monetary System (EMS) is a semi-fixed exchange rate system which was established in 1979. Its membership comprises the six original members of the European Economic Community together with Denmark and Ireland. The key features of the EMS are:

1. The creation of a European Currency Unit (ECU), the value and composition of which are defined in terms of a basket of currencies. The function of the ECU is to serve as the *numeraire* for the exchange rate mechanism, thereby providing a basis for measuring divergence between currencies and acting as a means of settlement between Community monetary authorities.

2. The provision of an exchange rate and intervention mechanism. Each currency has an ECU-related central rate, and fluctuations of exchange rates between currencies are limited to $2\frac{1}{4}$ per cent either side of the central rate, except in the case of countries with floating currencies which are allowed margins of up to 6 per cent. There are also divergence thresholds fixed at 75 per cent of the maximum spread of divergence. When a currency crosses this threshold, the authorities of the member state concerned are required to take appropriate measures to correct the divergence, or to adjust central rates.

3. The co-ordination of exchange rate policies vis-à-vis the rest of the world.

4. The European Monetary Cooperation Fund (EMCF) exists as a stablilisation fund to which all the member states have deposited 20 per cent of their dollar and gold reserves in return for ECU credits.

Since its establishment, the EMS has had some successes. The intervention mechanism has the advantage that stabilisation is the responsibility of both the country with the strong currency and the country with the depreciating currency. Thus if intervention becomes necessary, the central bank of the strong currency buys the weak currency and the central bank of the weak currency buys the strong currency. If it does not possess sufficient reserves, it borrows the currency required from the other central bank. These credit facilities are arranged through the EMCF and are expressed in ECUs.

Yet despite the success of the EMS in providing relative exchange rate stability, it has failed to develop fully into European Monetary Union, as envisaged at the time of its formation. Divergent economic policies among the member states coupled with consequent differences in inflation rates and other key economic indicators have led to the need for regular realignments of the central rates. Originally it was envisaged that the ECU could be used to settle all debts between member central banks but as yet progress has failed to get beyond the point where 50 per cent may be settled in ECUs. Nor has the EMCF developed into a European Monetary Fund with central bank powers, a development originally intended for March 1981, but now postponed indefinitely. Even the depositing of reserves with the EMCF is illusory since there is no physical transfer of reserves, the deposits being in the form of three-month revolving swaps. Even the ECU has been more successful in its role as a widely-used unit of account than as a reserve asset for EEC members.

9.   Your customers, Europe Forever Limited, call to see you to discuss the renewal of their existing facilities for the coming twelve months. As a large import/export organisation, they are always interested in movements of foreign currency. Among the subjects they raised during your discussions is the rise in the use of European Currency Units (ECU). They are interested in this type of currency and want to discuss the use of currency certificates of deposit and eurobond issues, both of which they think might be expressed in ECUs.

Required: A brief explanation for your customers of the salient features of:

- (a) an ECU and the reasons for its rise in popularity over recent years   (*6 marks*)
- (b) a currency certificate of deposit; and   (*7 marks*)
- (c) a eurobond   (*7 marks*)

(IOB 2B, April 1984)

(a) The ECU was created with the establishment of the European Monetary System (EMS) in 1979. The value and composition of the ECU are defined in terms of a basket of all thee currencies of the European Community, apart from those of Greece, Portugal and Spain. It includes sterling even though the United Kingdom has remained outside the EMS. The weight of each currency in the basket is allocated on the basis of EMS central rates so that when they are adjusted the weighting of each currency changes. The original and primary function of the ECU is to serve as the *numeraire* for the exchange rate mechanism of the EMS, thereby providing a basis for measuring divergence between currencies and acting as a means of settlement between Community monetary authorities.

The ECU is attractive to residents of countries with weak currencies since buyers who denominate deals in ECUs protect themselves against the depreciation of their own national currency. This is because the spread of the basket over a number of stronger currencies means that the large changes which may occur between two currencies are spread out over all the currencies in the basket. Countries with strong currencies, such as West Germany, do not have the same interest in ECU investment. Because of the growth in use of the ECU, many banks are willing to open deposit and savings accounts in ECU as well as current accounts which were made available as early as 1979. The ECU is also increasingly used as a denomination for loans and in 1984 an ECU clearing system was established, based on the Bank for International Settlements.

(b) Currency certificates of deposit are negotiable bearer instruments issued by a bank and certifying that a stated sum has been deposited with that bank. They are issued for periods of up to five years by banks to increase their deposits in the currency of the certificate, and they are also issued in ECUs. Interest is paid annually on the anniversary of the data of issue and at maturity at a rate slightly below that of the ordinary fixed-term deposit.

(c) Eurobonds are issued in European capital markets in a currency or currencies other than that of the issuer. They are underwritten by an international syndicate and are not subject to the rules of the issuing body of any country. Accordingly, their coupon rates may be quite different from those on domestic issues in the same currency. They are used by governments, multinational companies and other large institutions to obtain funds for long-term capital borrowing of five years or more. Eurobonds are normally issued by placement with an issuing syndicate arranging for purchasers to take up the offer. The interest rate may be either fixed or variable and a market is made for subsequent dealings in these issues.

Chapter 9

1. One of the advantages of a multinational form of operation is its ability to transfer goods between operating units of the organisation in different countries at virtually any price (internally) that it wishes. Under what circumstances would it be likely to charge
   (a) a relatively high price
   (b) a relatively low price
when invoicing goods to another country in this way? (Dip. Marketing, June 1981)

Multinational companies frequently have the choice of a number of locations in which to base their operations. The final location decision will have due regard to the question of tax rates in each country under consideration. A low rate of tax in one country may more than compensate for a lower rate of profitability when compared with another country offering high profitability but with a harsher tax regime. Similarly, tax concessions and subsidies offered by a host country may make location in that country more attractive than in a low-cost site without the incentives. In attempting to minimise its tax liability, the multinational must also consider its dual tax liability; to both the host country in which it operates and the parent country to which profits are likely to be sent. The company can reduce its tax liability by transferring its profits to whichever of the two countries imposes the lower tax rate. So if tax rates are lower in the host country, there is an incentive to reinvest profits made there in the local economy, and also to transfer profits made in the parent country to this subsidiary. The reverse will apply if tax rates are lower in the parent country.

   This transfer of profits cannot be accomplished openly without provoking government action in one country or the other to raise the tax rate on exported profits, so a system of transfer pricing is used. Transfer pricing is the practice of selling goods between parent company and subsidiary (or between two subsidiaries) at prices artificially lower or higher than would be the case if the two companies were separate concerns. The aim in each case is to ensure that profits are maximised where tax rates are low and minimised where tax rates are high. Thus if tax rates are lower in the host country, the parent company will sell goods to its subsidiary at below-cost prices, thereby reducing its own profits and raising those of the subsidiary. The reverse would apply if tax rates were high in the host country.

(a) Tax rates are higher in the country receiving the goods. The multinational charges high prices to its company operating in this country to enable profits to be concentrated in the low-tax selling country.

(b) Tax rates are lower in the country receiving the goods. The multinational charges low prices to its company operating in this country to enable profits to be concentrated there rather than in the high-tax selling country.

While transfer pricing is attractive, it cannot be taken to extremes for fear of concerted action by all governments to clamp down on this form of tax avoidance. Thus no multinational would go to the extent of lowering profits to zero in high-tax countries.

3. Multinational firms have often contributed very considerably to the development of the infrastructure of a developing country, yet they are frequently viewed by the local population with dislike or distrust.

Discuss why this situation should have arisen, and outline measures that could have been taken to improve the local attitudes. (Dip. Marketing, June 1984)

Developing countries receive three main benefits from the operations of multinational companies within their borders. Firstly, there is a contribution to the balance of payments. Whether the company is producing raw materials for the parent company's operation or finished goods for export to the multinational's markets, the result is increased export earnings and an improved current account. The capital account also benefits through an injection of foreign currency when the multinational establishes its operations, though this will entail future foreign currency payments as the multinational repatriates part of its profits. The second benefit is a contribution to the nation's technology. Not only will the company add to the national stock of capital, it will also increase the level of skills and training in the local workforce and stimulate the growth of local industries able to make use of the newly-acquired technology and to provide support for the multinational's operations. Thirdly, the contribution to employment. Apart from the direct creation of jobs in the multinational's factories, employment will also be created in service and ancillary industries necessary to the company's functioning.

Despite these benefits to developing countries, the activities of multinational companies do give cause for concern to host countries. In the first place, measures taken by multinationals to reduce their tax liability leads the local population to the conclusion that the multinational is contributing less to the local national budget than might reasonably be expected from a country of its size. Secondly, the acquisition of technology from multinationals is often regarded as relatively expensive, especially as the multinational controls the dissemination of this new technology and may prevent its being used generally. In addition, the multinational may persist in using nationals from the parent company to direct research operations, with local workers being used only for unskilled tasks. Such a situation has detrimental consequences, both for local career opportunities and the development of technical expertise in the local population. Nor is there any guarantee that the new technology will be suitable for the needs of the host country, especially if scarce resources are devoted to uses in line with company strategy but contrary to the host country's national economic policy. A third problem is the threat of economic dependence on the multinational. At times the host government may be forced to moderate its policies to obtain the co-operation of the multinational for fear that the company will abandon planned new investment or even close down altogether, thereby damaging employment and national output. Finally, there is the question of competition with national companies. Because of its economies of scale and market domination, the multinational may well inhibit the development of local firms in the industry. The multinational may also intimidate trade unions by its ability to close down in that location. Thus, both local companies and local workers will feel threatened by the power of multinational companies.

There are several measures available to the multinational to allay the fears of the people of the developing country. Firstly, it may ensure that a substantial proportion of the profits made in the host country are reinvested in the local economy and keep transfer pricing to a minimum. Secondly, the company may engage in joint participation and joint ownership schemes to encourage the support of local industry. Thirdly, it may encourage local workers to achieve managerial positions within the company and generally adopt an image to make it appear a local, rather than a foreign, company.

5.   It is known that some large multinational companies have sales revenues as large as the GNPs of some countries.

(a) How do you think that this state of affairs has come about?   (*8 marks*)

(b) What are the advantages and disadvantages to the world economy of multinational corporations?   (*8 marks*)

(c) How may governments control the activities of multinational corporations?   (*4 marks*)

(RSA Diploma for Personal Assistants, June 1980)

(a) The twentieth century has seen the growth of many large multinational corporations of American and European origin and, since the 1970s, of Asian origin too. Many of these multinational companies have grown to a size where their sales revenues rival the GNPs of even advanced European countries like the Netherlands or Denmark. This growth has occurred because, once established, such companies can exploit the various advantages they enjoy over purely national companies. Firstly, they obtain international economies of scale such as marketing economies, access to their own supplies of cheap raw materials or labour. Secondly, they have access to several capital markets and may reduce the borrowing costs for the corporation as a whole, by borrowing where the cost is lowest and transferring the funds where they are needed. Thirdly, they can reduce their tax liability through the practice of transfer pricing, whereby profits are transferred artificially to the subsidiary in the country of operation with lowest tax rates. Fourthly, the scale of its operations enables the company to establish market dominance in a number of countries and to dominate the markets for factors of production, particularly labour.

(b) The advantages to the world economy of multinational corporations arise mainly out of the economies of scale referred to above. These enable a more efficient use of resources in the organisation of production and distribution, thereby increasing the rate at which wealth is created and living standards are raised in the countries within which they operate. In addition, the multinationals give a number of direct benefits to the economies of their countries of operation. Firstly, they contribute to the balance of payments, through the repatriation of profits and savings on import expenditure on current account. In addition, developing countries benefit on capital account by injections of capital investment. Secondly, they introduce new skills and new technology to developing countries and so speed the process of economic development. Thirdly, they contribute employment opportunites in countries in which they choose to operate. Finally, they promote the expansion of international trade by stimulating the movement of goods between countries. In turn, this increases the supply and range of goods available to consumers.

The disadvantages to the world economy of the operations of the multinationals occur because of the strong economic power enjoyed by such companies. They can avoid taxation through transfer pricing. They can seriously disrupt the capital and foreign exchange markets by their movement of funds from one country to another. They may inhibit the development of indigenous industries in the developing countries by their market domination and control of technology. In some cases these companies may be so powerful that they can control the economic policies of the weaker developing countries, especially those which are heavily dependent on the multinationals for investment funds and new employment.

(c) Governments can control the activities of multinational companies in several ways. Firstly, host governments may limit the extent to which profits can be removed from the country, or possibly impose a tax on repatriated profits. Secondly, host governments can insist on part-local ownership to ensure that the company identifies, to some extent, with the local interest. Thirdly, they can ensure that there are direct benefits to the local economy by insisting on supplies or components or local labour being used by the multinational in its operations. Where, in the most serious cases, the multinational is too powerful to control by these methods, nationalisation may be the only answer.

Bibliography

The theory of international trade

Kindleberger C P 1973, *International Economics*. Irwin.
Milner C & Greenaway D 1979, *An Introduction to International Economics*. Longman.
Robson P 1984, *The Economics of International Integration*. Allen & Unwin.
Sodersten B 1981, *International Economics*. Macmillan.
Williamson J 1984, *The Open Economy and the World Economy*. Harper & Row.

International trade in practice

Cable V 1983, *Protectionism and Industrial Decline*. Hodder & Stoughton.
Dawkins S 1985, The new protectionism, *British Economic Survey*. Spring.
Greenaway D 1983, *International Trade Policy: From Tariffs to the New Protectionism*. Macmillan.
Greenaway D 1984, Multilateral trade policy in the 1980s, *Lloyds Bank Review*. Jan.
Henderson P D 1983, Trade policies: trends, issues and influences, *Midland Bank Review*. Winter.

The balance of payments

Stern R 1973, *The Balance of Payments: Theory and Economic Policy*. Macmillan.

Thirlwall A P 1980, *Balance of Payments: Theory and the UK Experience*. Macmillan.

Thirlwall A P 1978, The UK's economic problems: a balance of payments constraint?, *National Westminster Bank Review*. Feb.

Zis G 1978, *The Balance of Payments*. Philip Allan.

Exchange rates

Brittan S 1970, *The Price of Economic Freedom – A Guide to Flexible Rates*. Macmillan.

Tew B 1977, *The Evolution of the International Monetary System, 1945–77*. Hutchinson.

The IMF and international liquidity

Ainsley E 1979, *The IMF – Past, Present and Future*. University of Wales Press.

A return to Bretton Woods?, *Midland Bank Review*. Autumn/Winter 1981.

Solomon R 1977, *The International Monetary System 1945–76: An Insider's View*. Harper & Row.

Tew B 1977, *The Evolution of the International Monetary System, 1945–77*. Hutchinson.

Wright C 1982, A long look at the dollar, *Barclays Review*. Nov.

Capital movements and the eurocurrency markets

Davies A & Ball A 1984, International banking markets, *Barclays Review*. May.

International bond markets, *Midland Bank Review*. Spring 1980.

McKenzie G 1976, *The Economics of the Eurocurrency System*. Macmillan.

Scott Quinn B 1975, *The New Euromarkets*. Macmillan.

The international debt problem

Bevan Sir T 1984, International indebtedness, *Barclays Review*. May.

Crawford M 1985, Third World debt is here to stay, *Lloyds Bank Review*, Jan.

Gorman D & Morales J 1985, Economic adjustment in Latin America, *Barclays Review. Feb.*

Gorman D & Radford P 1984, The World Bank – its role in financing development, *Barclays Review.* Aug.

International lenders and world debt, *Midland Bank Review.* Winter 1984.

The European Economic Community

Beesley M & Hague D 1974, *Britain in the Common Market; a New Business Opportunity.* Longman.

Britain and the European Monetary System, *Midland Bank Review.* Winter 1979.

The Common Agricultural Policy, *Midland Bank Review.* Winter 1984.

Drew J 1979, *Doing Business in the European Community.* Butterworth.

European Monetary Union?, *Midland Bank Review.* Winter 1977.

The EEC budget and the UK, *Midland Bank Review.* Summer 1980.

Lomax D 1983, Prospects for the European Monetary System, *National Westminster Bank Quarterly Review.* May.

The multinational companies

Dunning J 1981, *International Production and the Multinational Enterprise.* George Allen and Unwin.

Hood N & Young S 1979, *The Economics of Multinational Enterprise.* Longman.

Lall S 1980, *The Multinational Corporation.* Macmillan.

Lall S 1984, Transnationals and the Third World: changing perceptions, *National Westminster Bank Quarterly Review.* May.

Solomon L 1978, *Multinational Corporations and the Emerging World Order.* National University Publications, New York.

A guide to sources

The following list, and associated discussion, is intended to high-light some of the more useful sources for statistical data and information on the various areas of international economics.

Statistical sources

The following contain important statistical series and, in some cases, articles commenting on those series or on related issues. The addresses given are those for enquiries about *orders* and *subscriptions*.

Annual Abstract of Statistics. Central Statistical Office, PO Box 569, London SE1 9NH
This gives annual figures for the previous ten years on a wide range of subjects. Of relevance here are the figures on UK trade and the UK balance of payments.

Bank of England Quarterly Bulletin. Economics Division, Bank of England, London EC2R 8AH
This provides data for official reserves and foreign exchange rates.

British Business. British Business FREEPOST, London SW1P 4BR
This is published weekly and gives detailed statistics on UK foreign trade and balance of payments transactions, often highlighting particular industries. It contains articles on EEC and other overseas trade news.

Economic Trends. Central Statistical Office, PO Box 569, London SE1 9NH
This is published monthly and contains tables and charts illus-

trating trends in the UK economy, including balance of payments figures.

UK Balance of Payments. Central Statistical Office, PO Box 569, London SE1 9NH

The *Pink Book* is the most comprehensive source available for balance of payments statistics. Published annually, it breaks down the official statistics of the balance of payments into their various components. Comparisons with previous years are also provided.

European Economy. HMSO, PO Box 569, London SE1 9NH
This publication appears in March, July and November of each year. It is published by the Commission of the European Communities and presents the main economic indicators, for the Community as a whole and for individual member states.

Eurostat. HMSO, PO Box 569, London SE1 9NH
This is the publishing title of the Statistical Offices of the European Communities and gives the main indices of economic activity within the EEC.

International Monetary Fund Publications. HMSO, PO Box 569, London SE1 9NH
There are several important sources of statistics available from the IMF.
World Economic Outlook. This is published annually and presents and analyses economic projections for individual countries. The industrial countries, oil-exporting countries and LDCs are examined as separate groups.
International Financial Statistics. This annual publication gives detailed figures of official reserves, IMF reserve positions and IMF borrowing of IMF members. World trade figures are also included.
Annual Report. This is primarily the document containing the IMF's views on the state of the international financial system. However, it also contains figures on international liquidity, international debts and so on.

United Nations Publications. HMSO, Box 569, London SE1 9NH
UN Statistical Yearbook. This annual publication covers a wide variety of indices of economic activity for industrial and developing nations.
World Economic Survey. This is published every other year and examines fluctuations in the world economy, by individual coun-

tries and by groups of countries, for a variety of economic indicators. Problems and prospects for these various groups are examined, as is the outlook for world trade.

Other sources

The annual reports of the Bank for International Settlements and of the World Bank relate mainly to the activities of those organisations. However, they do contain useful statistics on international banking and international indebtedness. They are available from HMSO, at the address quoted for the IMF.

Information sources

The following publications are useful in updating and elaborating on current international economic issues. They also frequently contain some statistical information.

Publications of the European Communities. HMSO Publications Centre, 51 Nine Elms Lane, London SW8 5DR
European Documentation. This is a regular series of periodicals which examine various aspects of the economy of the EEC. New editions are constantly being made available.
European File. This takes the form of a series of pamphlets on the work of the Community and includes areas of economic interest.

HMSO International Organisations Publications. PO Box 569, London SE1 9NH
This annual catalogue lists all items available from HMSO in that year for the various international organisations referred to in the section on statistical sources.

Economic Progress Report. Publications Division, Central Office of Information, Hercules Road, London SE1 7DU
Published monthly by the Treasury, these reports carry articles and statistics on various aspects of the UK economy including comparisons with other countries.

British Economic Survey. Oxford University Press, Walton Street, Oxford OX2 6DP
A twice-yearly update on the current state of the British economy. Among its main sections are ones on the balance of payments and the world economy.

Bank reviews

These are often available free, on application. All carry articles on current international economic issues, though the emphasis varies. Thus *Barclays Review* frequently contains articles on international banking, the *Midland Review* is good on the EEC, and so on. All are published quarterly.

Barclays Review. Group Economics Department, 54 Lombard Street, London EC3P 3AH

Lloyds Bank Review. The Editor, Lloyds Bank Review, 71 Lombard Street, London EC3P 3BS

Midland Bank Review. The Manager, Public Relations Department, Midland Bank plc, PO Box 2, Griffin House, Silver Street Head, Sheffield S1 3GG

National Westminster Bank Quarterly Review. The Editor, National Westminster Bank plc, 41 Lothbury, London EC2P 2BP

The Three Banks Review. The Royal Bank of Scotland plc, Edinburgh EH2 0DG

Index